The Royal Breadshow

Published by
Axle Contemporary
P.O. 22095
Santa Fe NM 87502
www.axlepress.com

ISBN 978-0-9858116-6-2
0985811668

Designed by Jerry Wellman and Matthew Chase-Daniel.
Front cover loaf of bread by Susanna Carlisle.
Back cover sculptures by Maxine Chelini.

We want to thank Avra Leodas and the staff at Santa Fe Clay; bakers Willem Malten, Dharam Khalsa, Cesar Araiza, and Amy Quirke; Irene Hoffman, Janet Dees, David Merrill, Sage Sommer, and the staff at SITE Santa Fe.

Most importantly we wish to thank the community of artists, writers, ceramicists, bakers, and art enthusiasts that made this project possible.

The Royal Breadshow is supported in part through individual donations, and grants from the City of Santa Fe's 1% Lodgers' Tax, The McCune Charitable Foundation, New Mexico Arts, a division of the Department of Cultural Affairs, the National Endowment for the Arts, and SITE Santa Fe's *Spread* crowdsourced microfunding.

The Royal Breadshow

an

Axle Contemporary project

Santa Fe, New Mexico

2013-2014

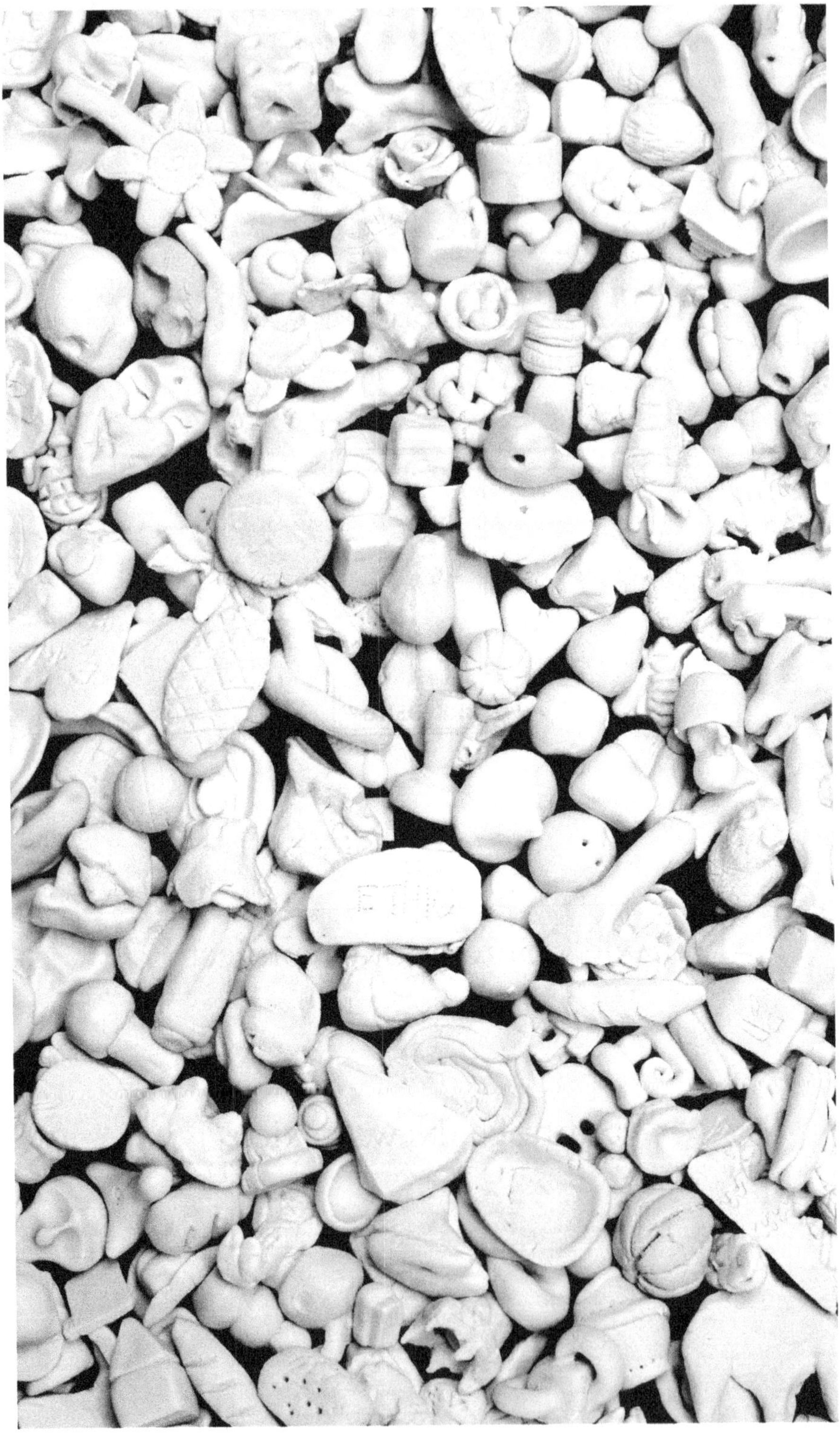

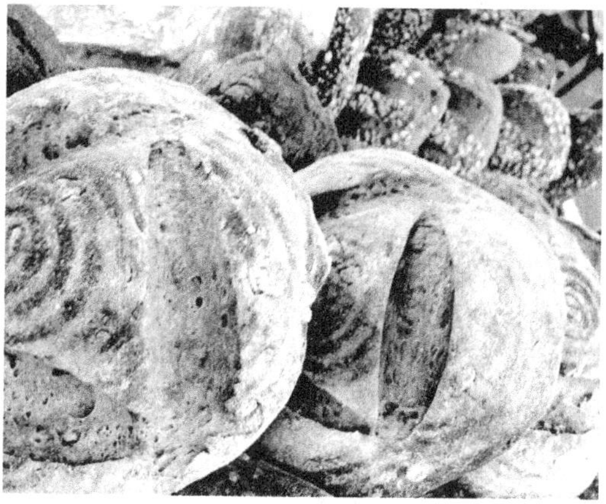

For over two millennia, in many parts of the world, special breads have been used as an important part of seasonal celebrations. In many cultures, hidden inside these special loaves, variously called Kings' Cakes, Galettes des Rois, or Roscas de Reyes, is a small object of symbolic value. When the bread is sliced, one lucky person gains certain rights and responsibilities associated with the hidden prize. The recognition of royalty is extended to everybody: The farmer, baker, artist, teacher, writer, child, grandmother: All of us.

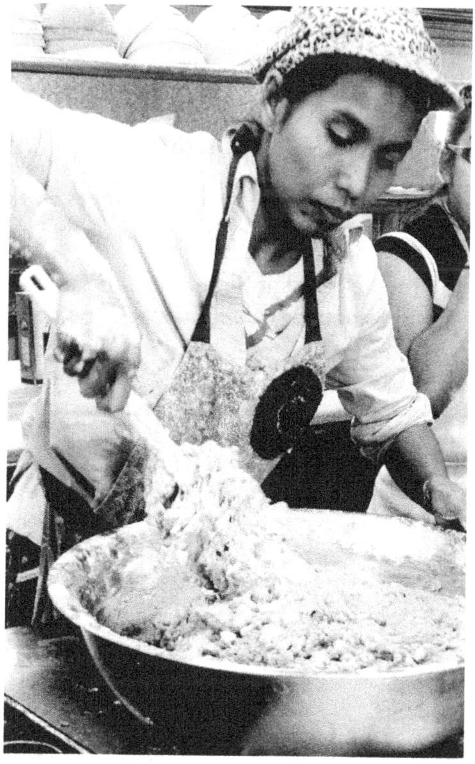

This book documents activities, sculptures, and writings from Axle Contemporary's *Royal Breadshow*. Inspired by these traditions that traverse cultures across the globe, we created a community project with hundreds of participants in Santa Fe, New Mexico. Over the course of six months, over 200 artists, students, elders and others made miniature porcelain sculptures to be used as the prize baked into our breads. In the following pages you will discover photographs of the sculptures as well as a selection of writing submitted by poets and writers to express and celebrate many aspects, attributes, and thoughts that spring forth from our relationships to bread.

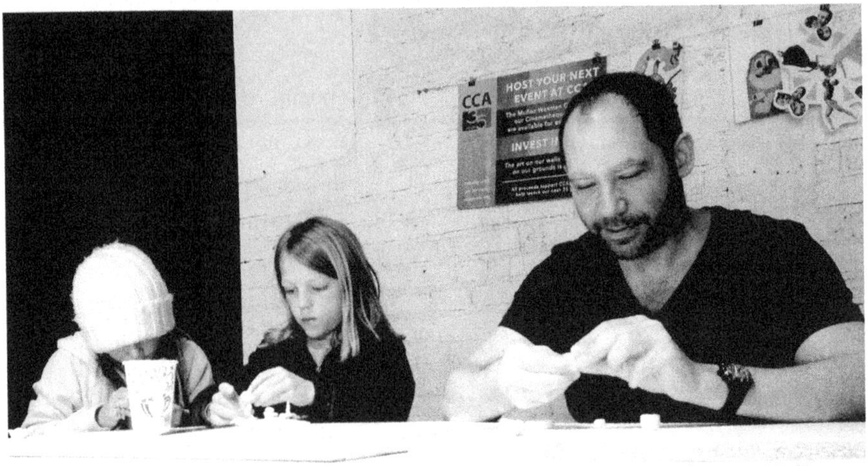

Axle Contemporary collaborators Matthew Chase-Daniel and Jerry Wellman ran a series of free clay sculpture-making workshops at The Center for Contemporary Arts, Warehouse 21, Zona del Sol, Rainbow Vision, and El Castillo. Christy Hengst worked with elementary school students at Fayette Street Academy. Paula Castillo and Maia Sampson-Michael worked with their students at Santa Prep. Tom Miller, with his sculpture students at The Santa Fe University of Art and Design, also contributed work. Staff from SITE Santa Fe brought clay to work with students at the Santa Fe Youth Development Project. Many others worked in their homes and studios and dropped their work for us at Santa Fe Clay (who donated all of the clay for the project) and at SITE Santa Fe.

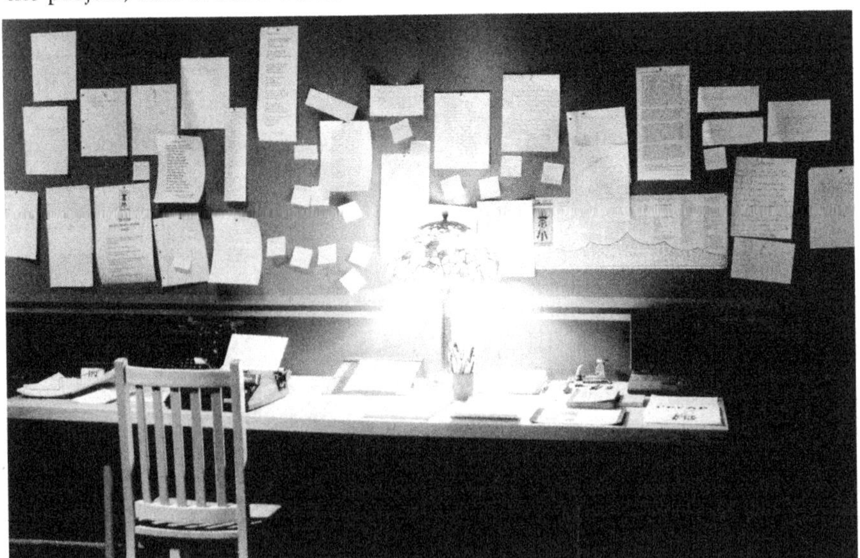

We celebrate the act of making in *The Royal Breadshow*. Ceramics, like bread, utilizes heat to transform raw material into a new and remarkable state of being. Ceramics range from simple utilitarian objects to artistic exaltations of the human creative spirit. Both baking and ceramics rely heavily on the hands of the maker. As we work with our hands we engage

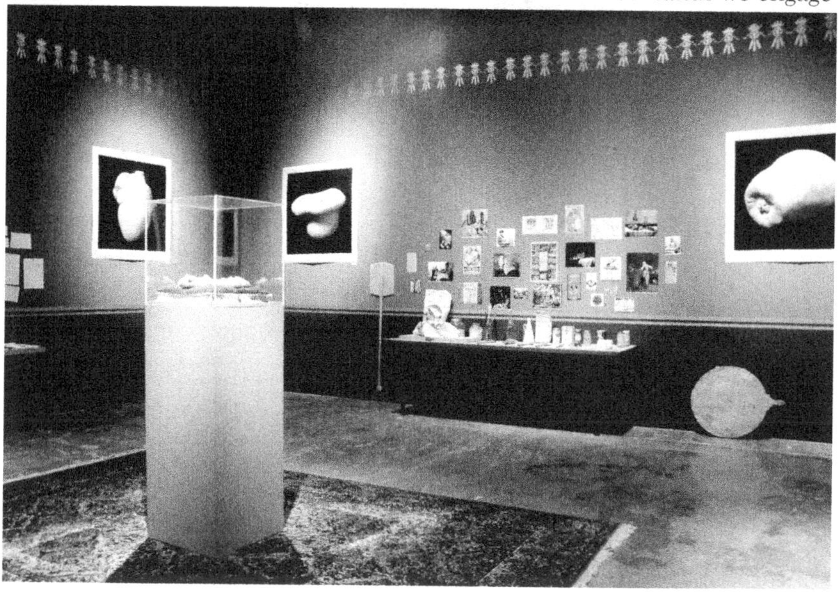

our minds. We find meaning in work, celebration, ritual, and the joy of making. Our actions in the world, our work with our hands, a great gift, engage our most profound thought and support expanding exchanges and possibilities. Like bread and ceramics, our roots are humble and our potentials are endless.

In its early phase, this project received support from a proposal that was presented at SITE Santa Fe's micro crowdsourced funding initiative: *Spread*. Receiving the grant from SITE came with an invitation to create an installation in the their exhibition, *Feast:Radical Hospitality in Contemporary Art*. We created a 900 square foot room-sized installation. In the room we set three tables with tools and ingredients representing the three major components of the exhibition, baking, writing, and ceramics. On these tables were invitations for public paricipation in creating work for the project. Behind each table hung images and objects. In the center of the room was a pedestal with a specially made velvet pillow holding a rotating weekly display of freshly baked bread.

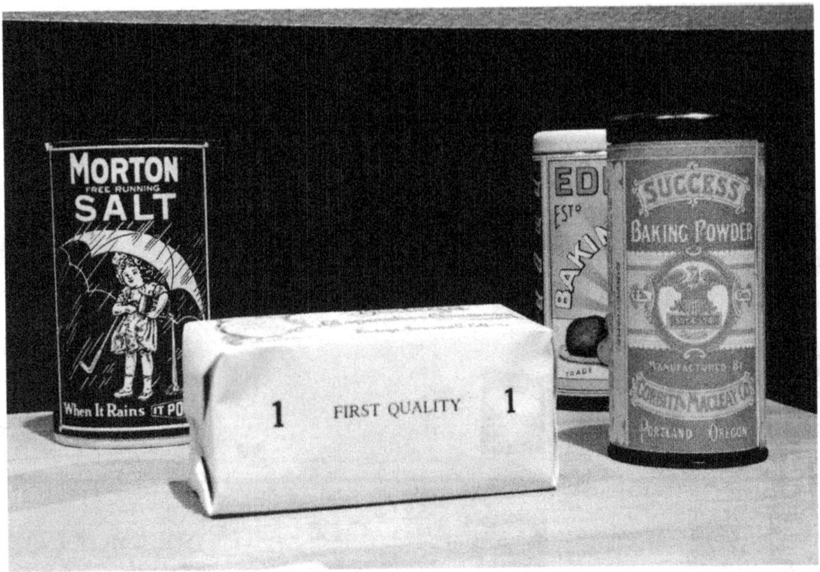

In May 2014, Axle Contemporary presented an exhibition in our mobile gallery of the many miniature porcelain sculptures. The sculptures were then distributed to four local bakeries, Intergalactic Baking Company, Chocolate Maven, Cloud Cliff Bakery, and Panaderia Sani. Each bakery incorporated the sculptures into special loaves of their own design. Each loaf sold was accompanied by a paper crown with a special laudatory word and selections from the writings about bread. The bread was sold by the bakeries, at the Santa Fe Farmers Market, and in the Axle Contemporary gallery. Proceeds from the sales of loaves were donated to local organizations that feed the hungry.

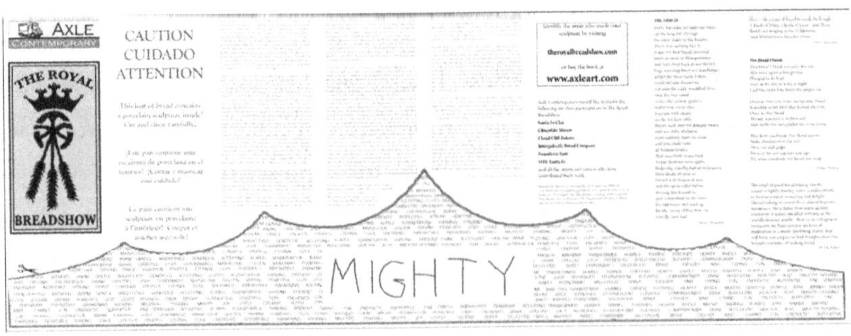

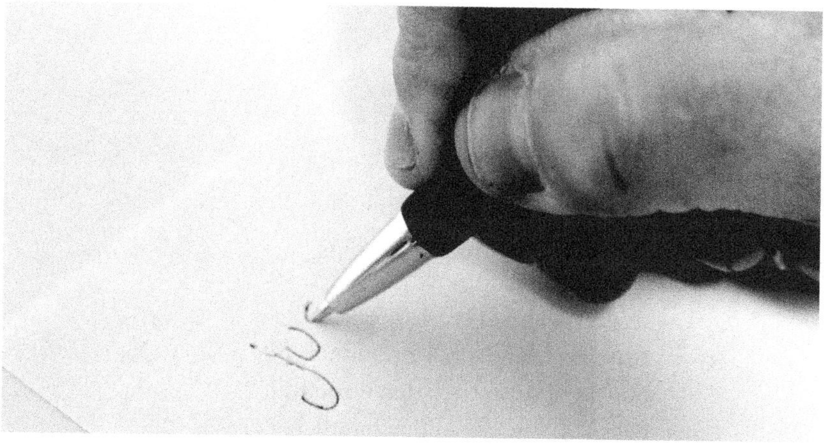

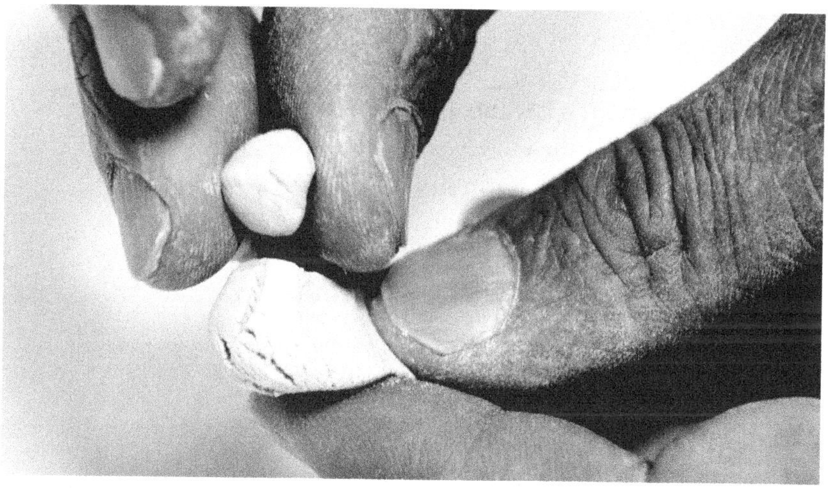

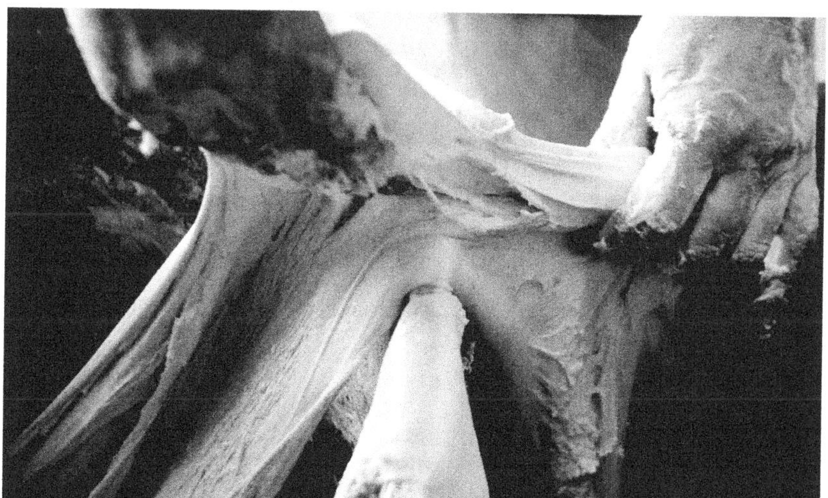

THE LOAVES

Every Saturday we rode our bikes
up the long hill through
the early shade to the bakery.
There was nothing like it:
it was the first bread shoveled
from an oven in Mesopotamia,
and we'd drop back down the hill,
bags whirring from our handlebars
under the trees made before
mankind was dreamt of,
out over the eddy-muddled river,
over the lazy canal,
under the railway girders,
to the first warm slice
fragrant with steam
on the kitchen table.
Butter sank into the dough's weave
and our slabs of cheese
went rubbery from the heat,
and you could taste
all human history.
That was thirty years back.
Today there we were again,
flickering into the hall of sycamores,
their shade all over us
barred with beams of sun,
and the open valley below
shining like it used to,
and somewhere in the trees
the old house still waiting
for the steam of that first cut
into the new loaf.

-Henry Shukman

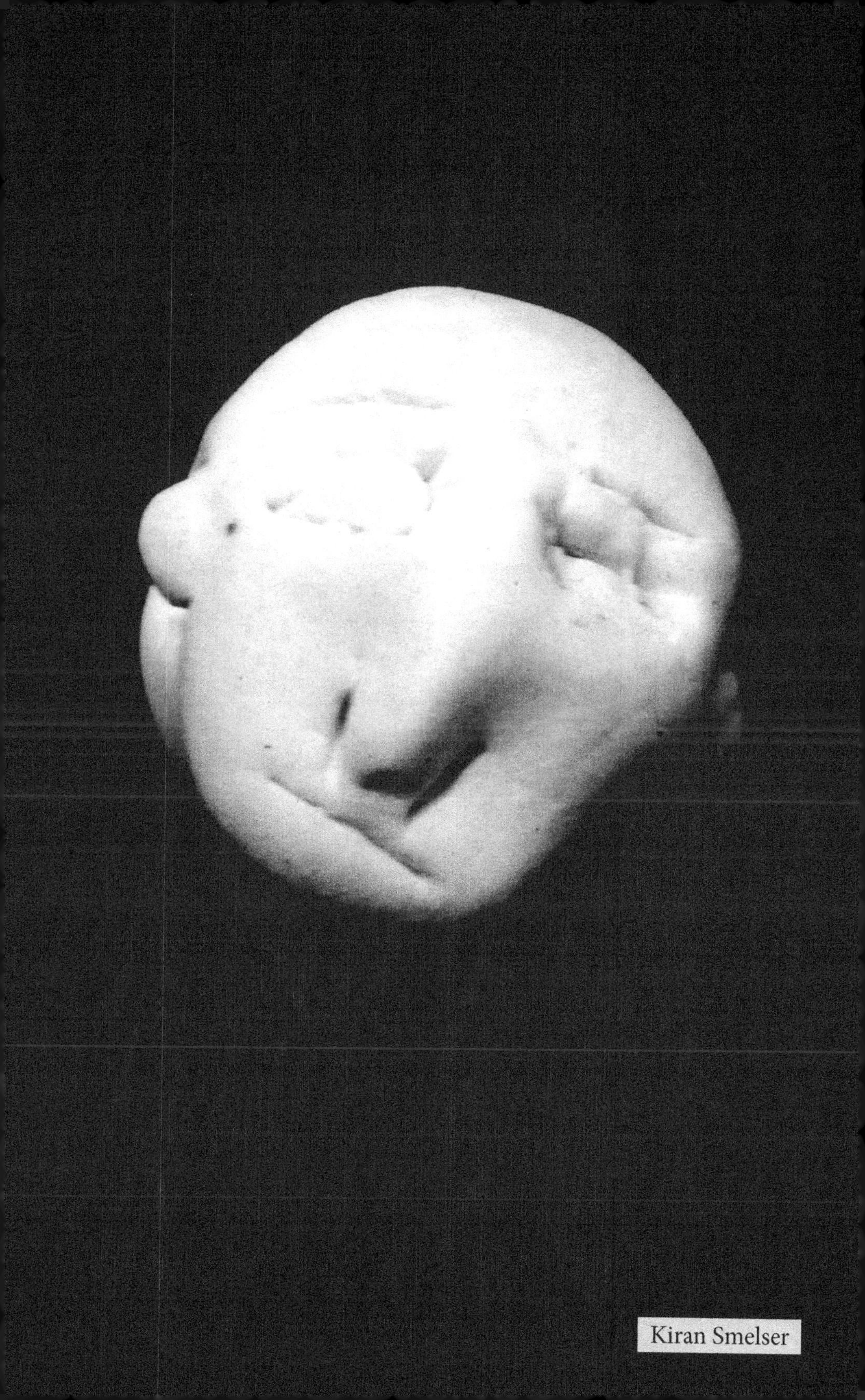

Kiran Smelser

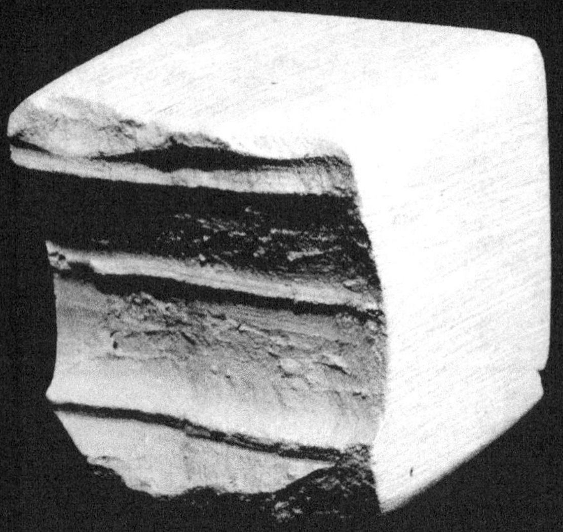

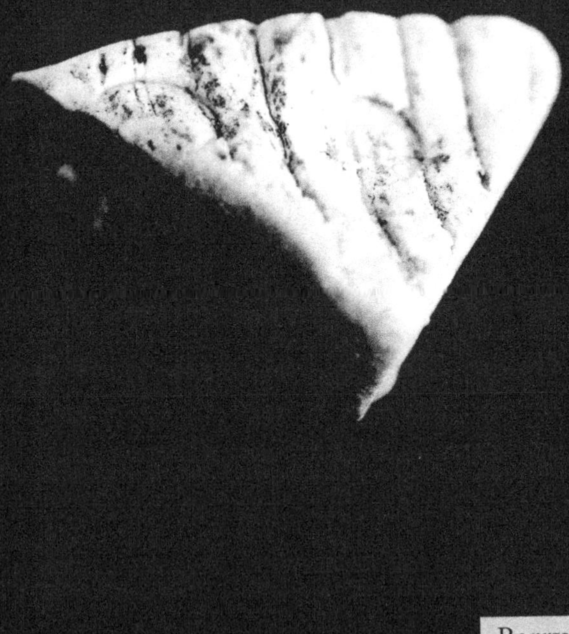

Barry Freedland

Leslie Holland

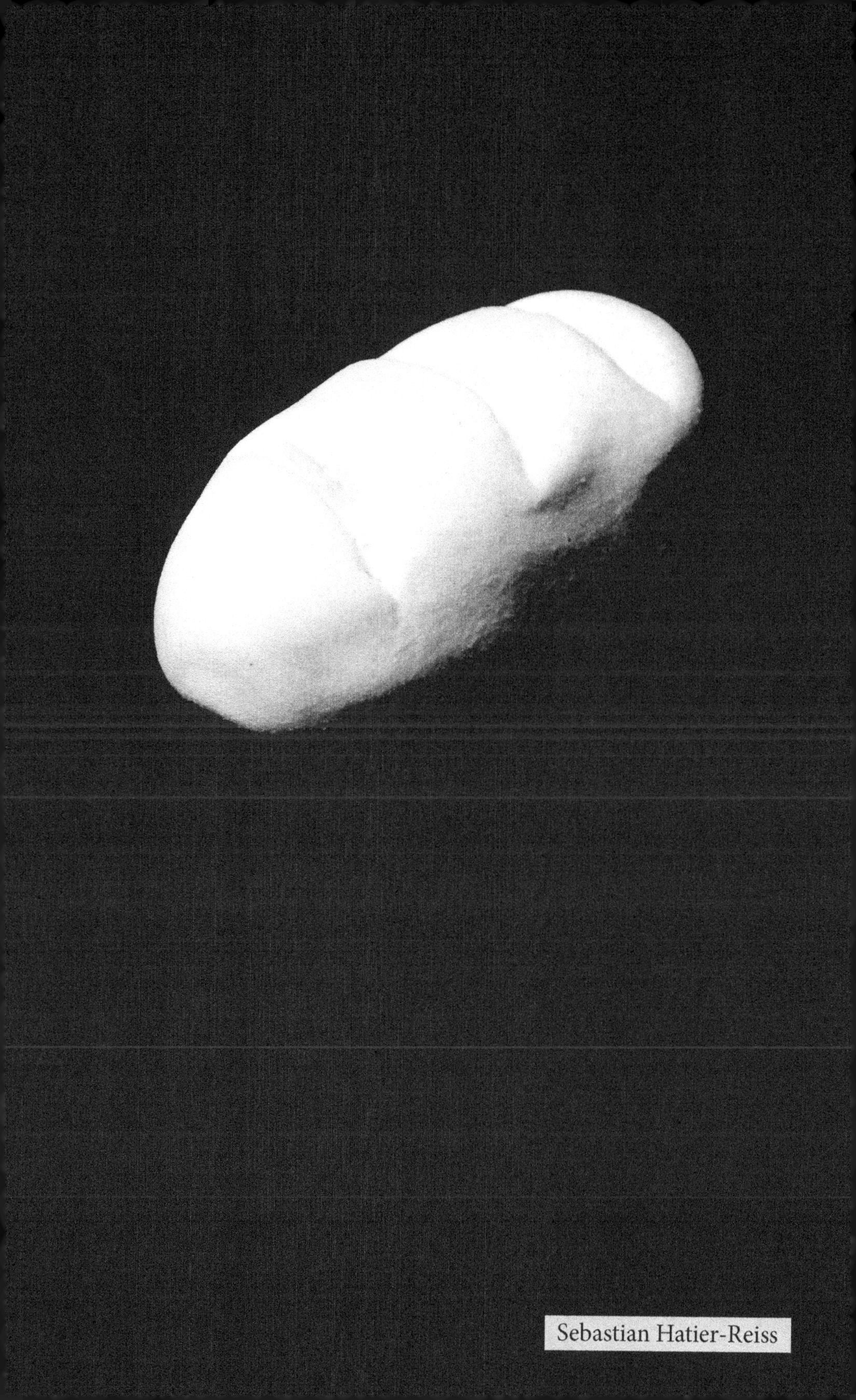

Sebastian Hatier-Reiss

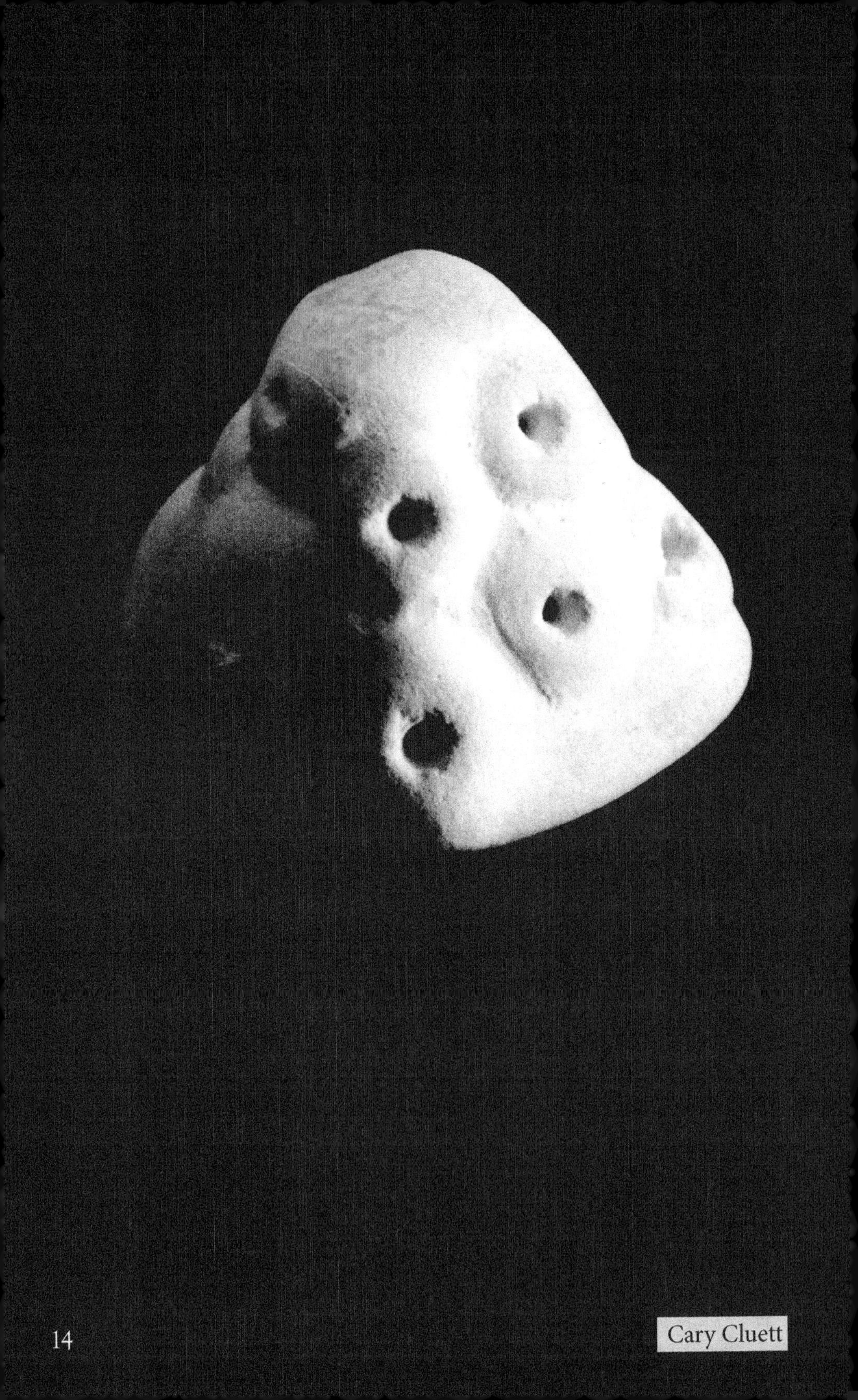

Cary Cluett

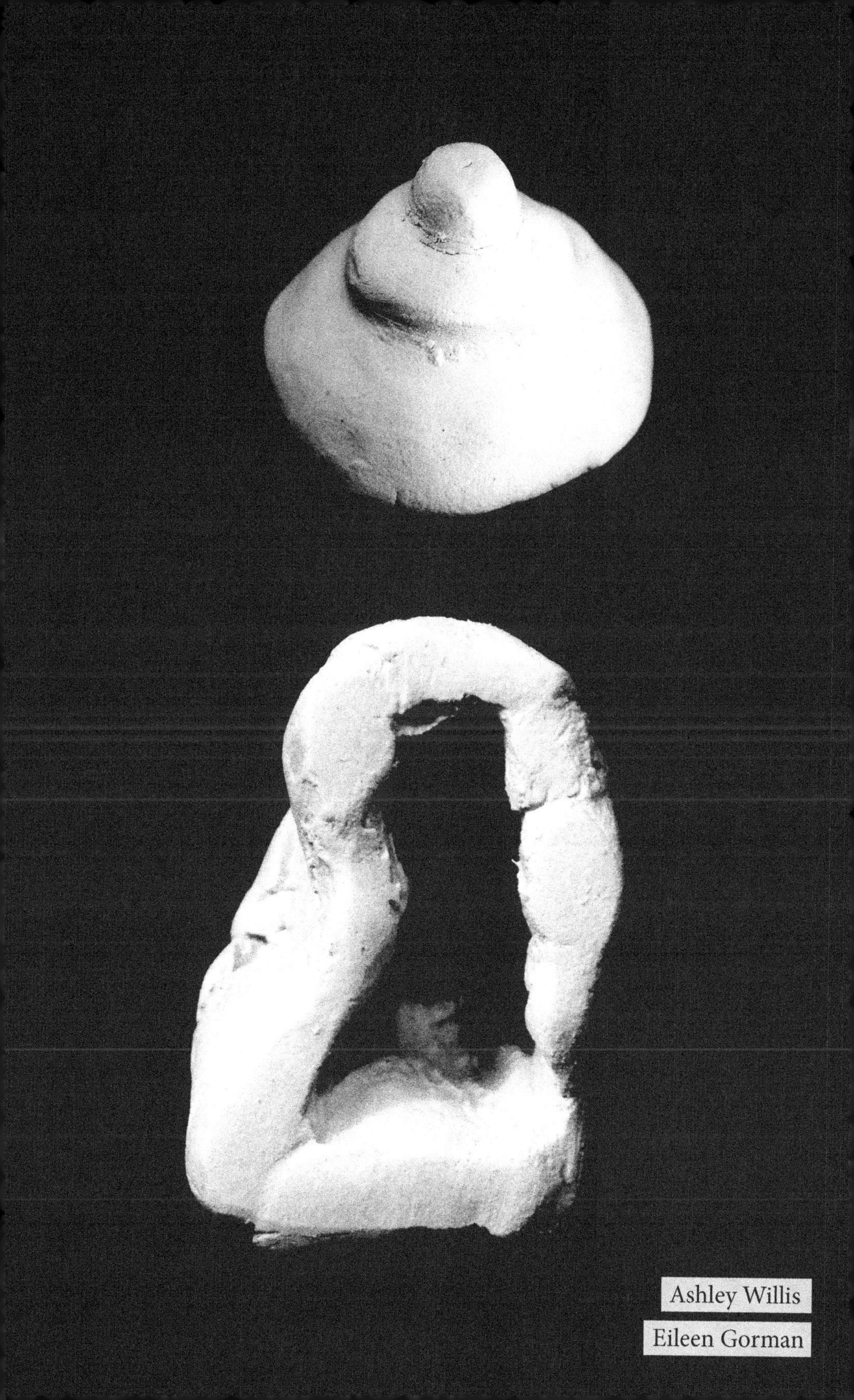

Ashley Willis

Eileen Gorman

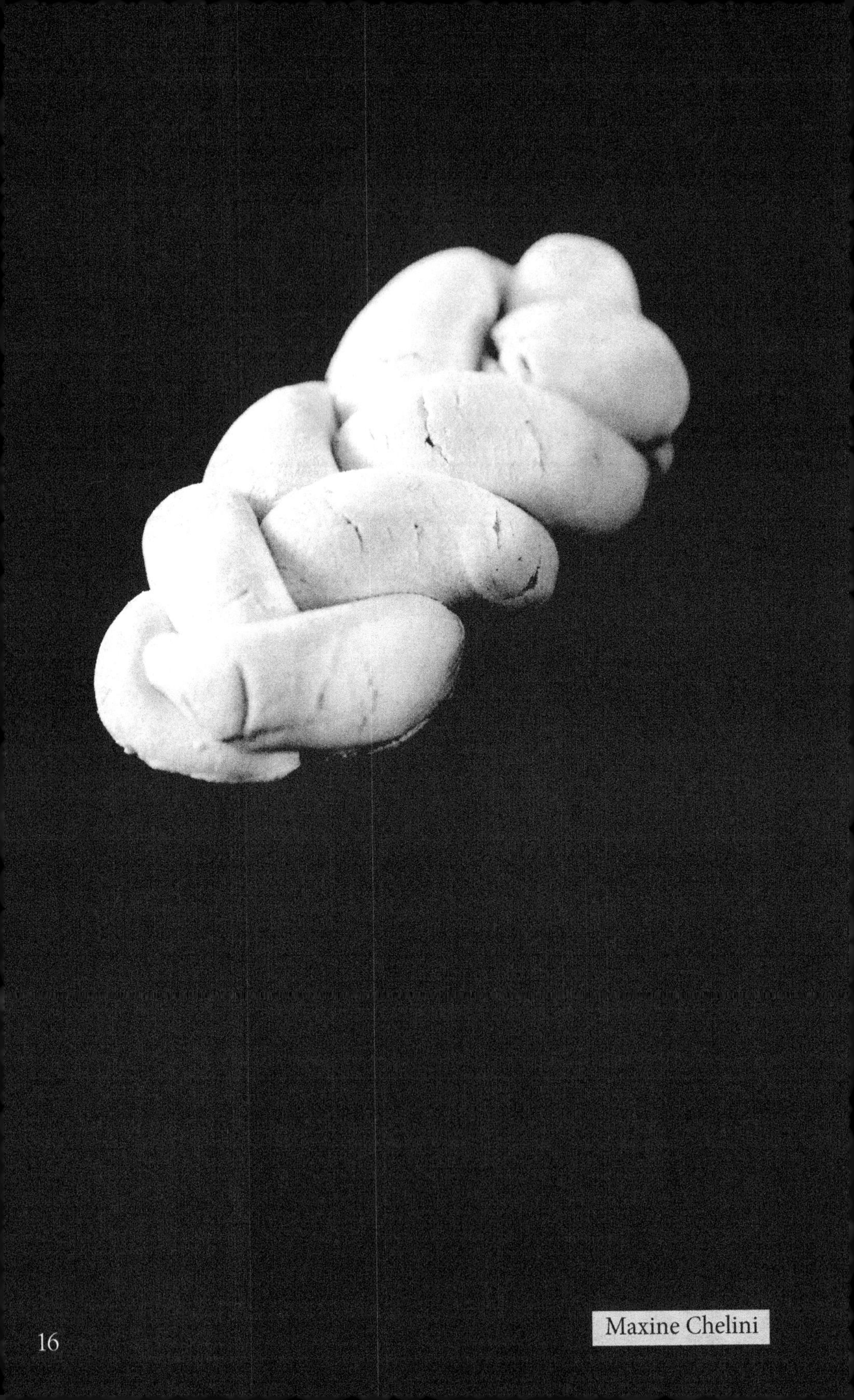

Maxine Chelini

Challah At The Columbia County Fair

Under glass, its deflation, a defection.
Yet one Mary O'Malley, Austerlitz, NY,
had entered and dreamt Best Of Show,
challah that barely rose, that no observer
would be tempted to unbraid, to salivate its airy lift, its eggy chew,
to raise its sweet crusted cloud to God. No silver candlesticks to light its rise, no
goblet of wine to toast Shabbat. True, it was August, humidity that forced
fried dough to slip from fingers and greased a hundred upstate lips and cheeks.

What was it doing under glass and who was Mary of the pummel and heavy palm?
Its ID hung like a lost holiday tag from one unseeded hump. Though too short,
too thin, kneaded by *goyisha* hands, baked in a too hot oven, this loaf
was draped with a gleaming red ribbon, silver etched: Second Place.

Had the judges of preserves and squash, pies and pickles, tried to pronounce,
in announcing winners, the requisite *kh*, that scraped gutteral, backward snore
part laugh, part *inshallah*?

I might have declared
Manna arrives in multiple forms or
Sabbath in the unexpected

but sweating in that hall among drivers of tractors and breeders of pigs
I thought, how foreign my braided history;
how happily powdered the fried familiar handed down
from a dozen shocking pink trailers.

-Barbara Rockman

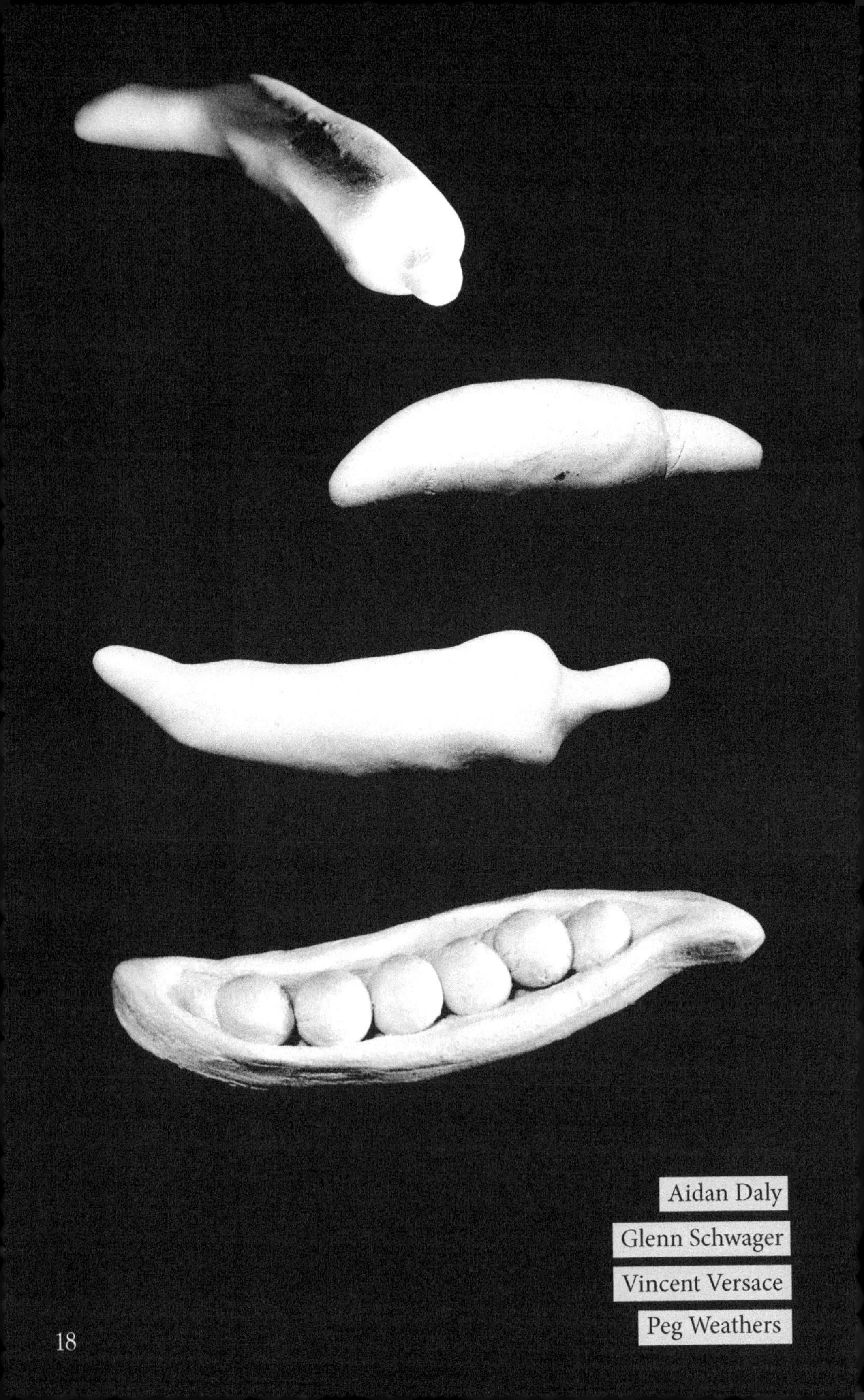

Aidan Daly

Glenn Schwager

Vincent Versace

Peg Weathers

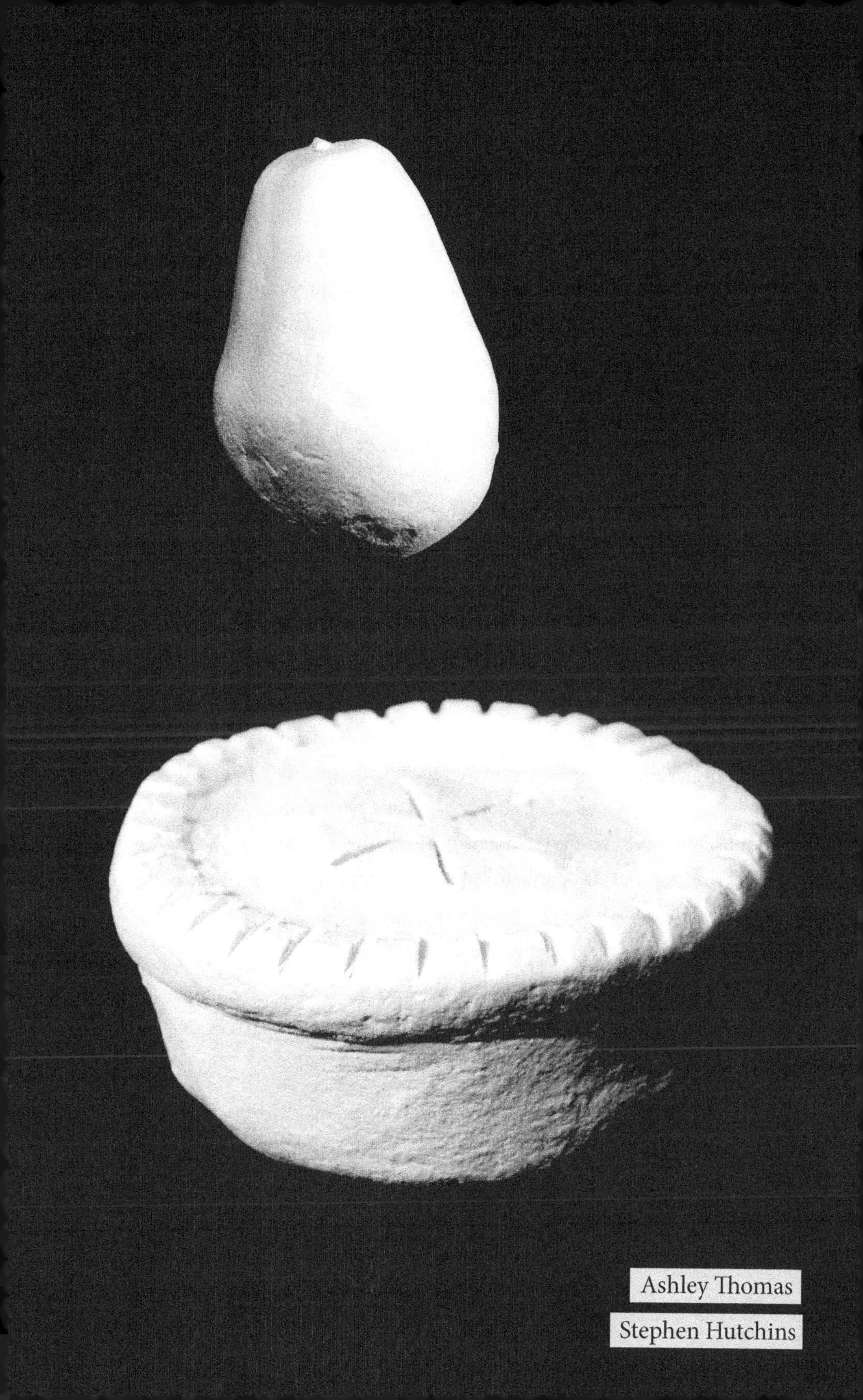

Ashley Thomas

Stephen Hutchins

When my first child was small, she was such a picky eater. Though she'd grab and eat handfuls of wild spinach, very few things appealed. The one thing she liked was bread. I was a young hippie-esque mother who each week made yogurt, granola, and bread. I followed a recipe in Joy of Cooking for Health Bread. I still have the book and the stained archival recipe. It called for oats, milk, wheat germ, whole wheat or rye. I would add eggs from our chickens, molasses, and soy flour. It made a meal in itself and toasted with butter and home made apricot jam from the giant trees outside our three room adobe. We lived there three years and the ritual of canning, baking, and yogurt brewing continued. We grew a plump, rosy cheeked child, healthy as the day was gone.

That child is still lovely, a beautifully grown woman and particular about her diet. She rarely eats a slice of bread now that gluten has become arch enemy #1. I mourn the passing of gluten, that magical substance and texture we kneaded into being. I have, of late, been making granola and made rolls for Thanksgiving, gluten free. I am feeling the bread maker rise up in me.

-Joan Logghe

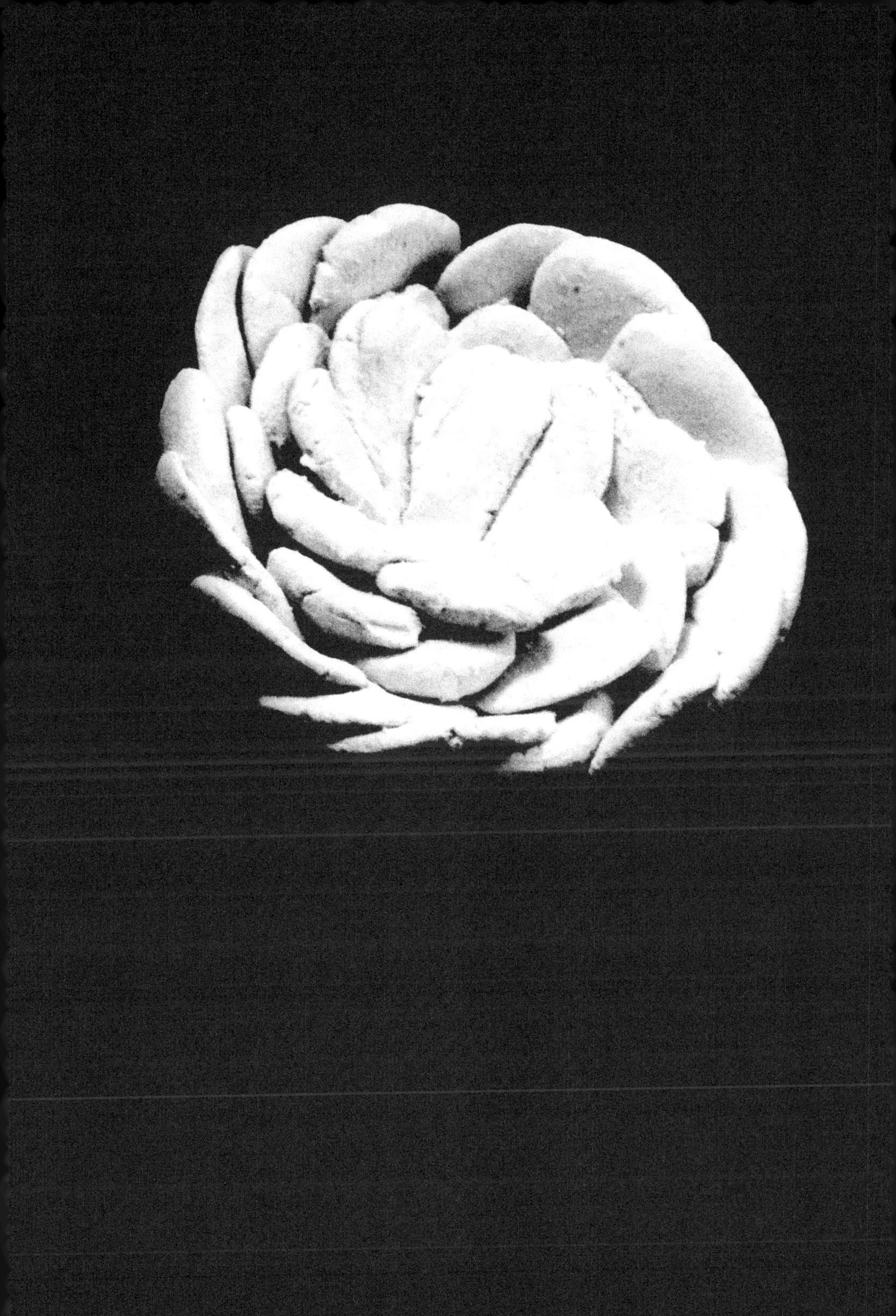

Tyler Bertram

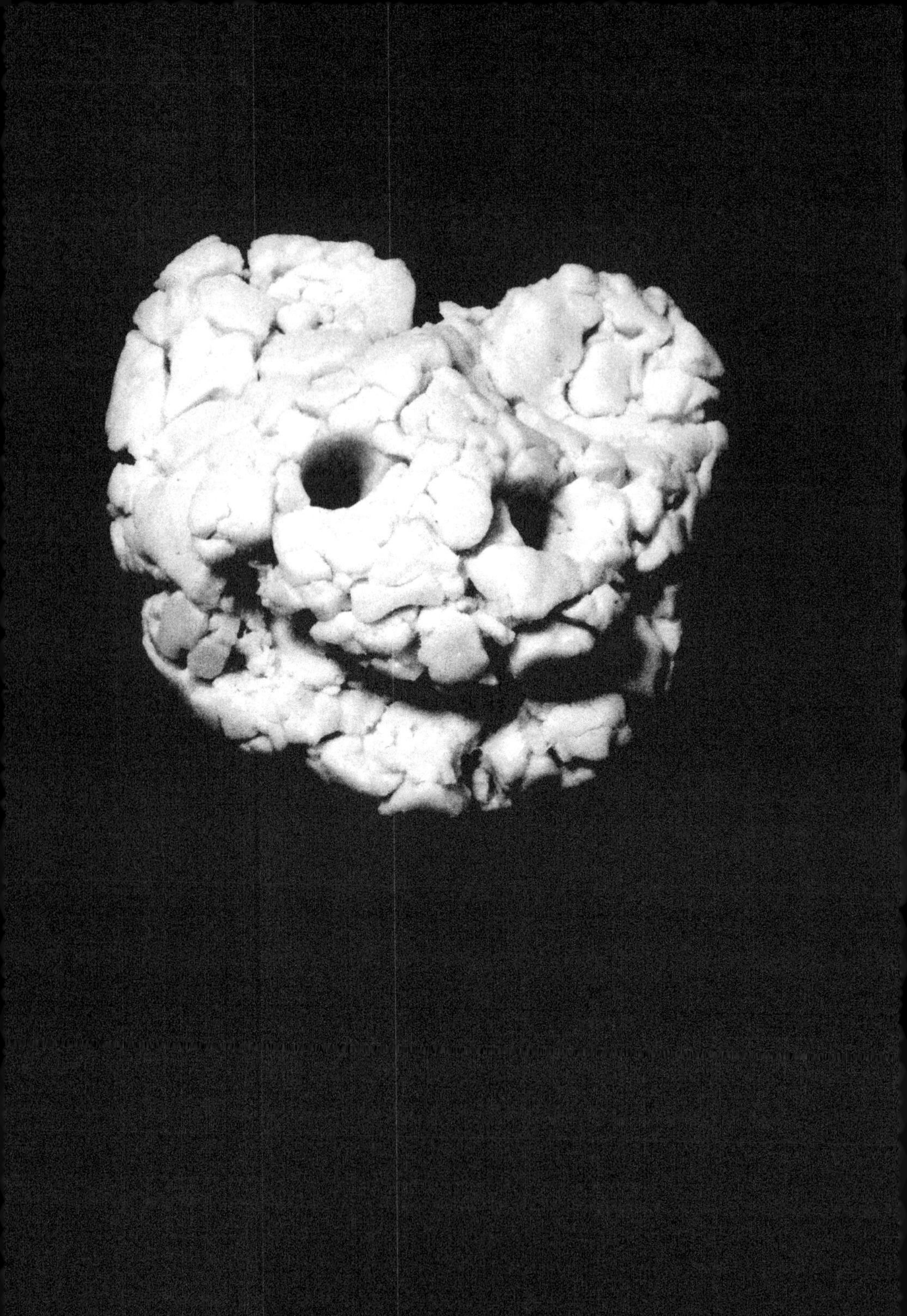

Emmanuel Asprodites

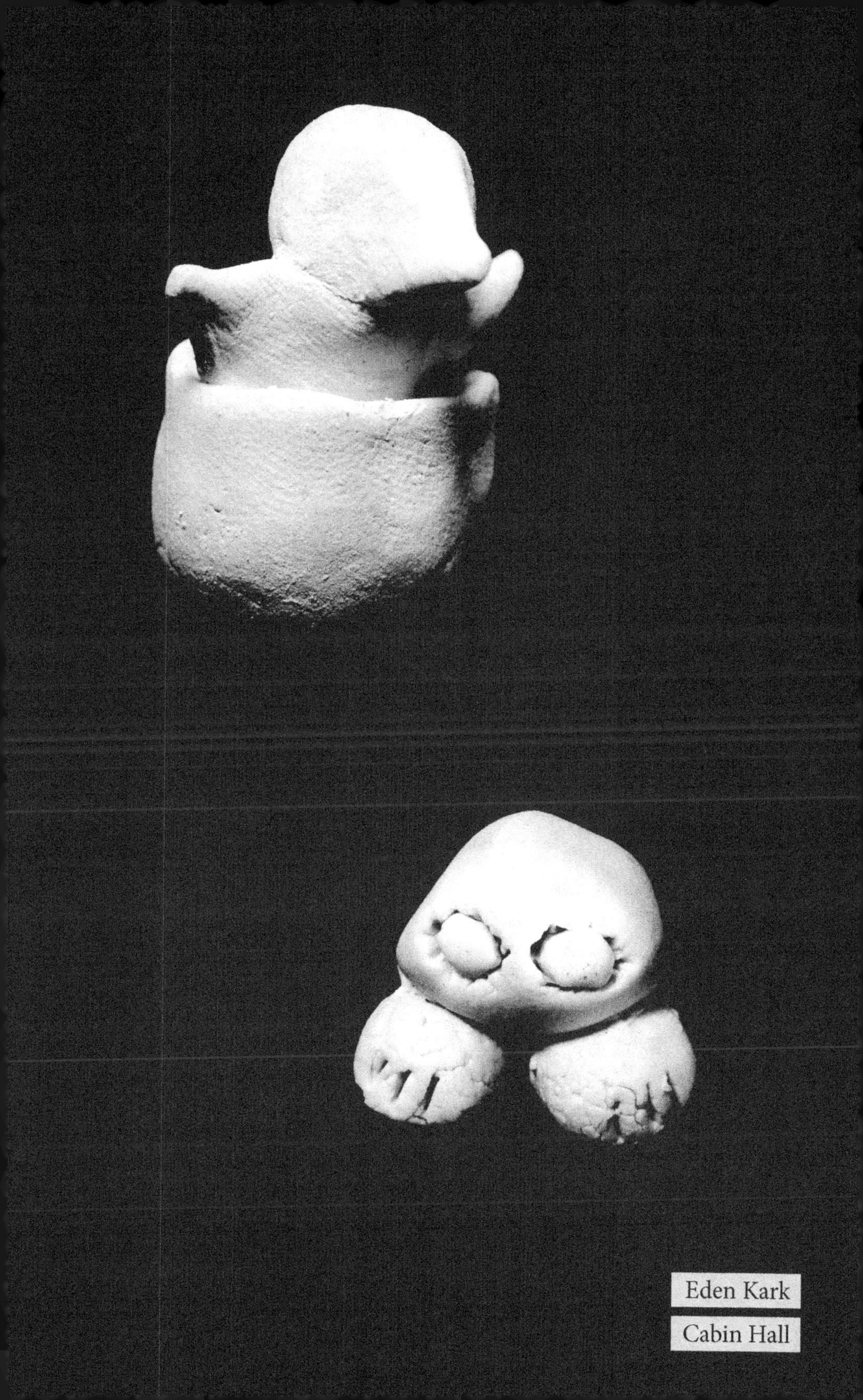

Eden Kark

Cabin Hall

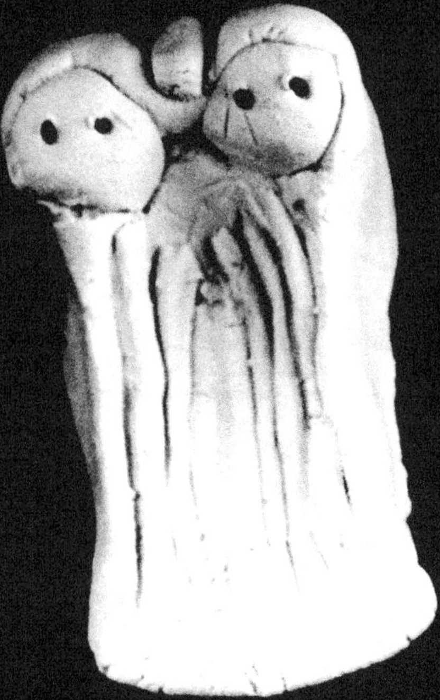

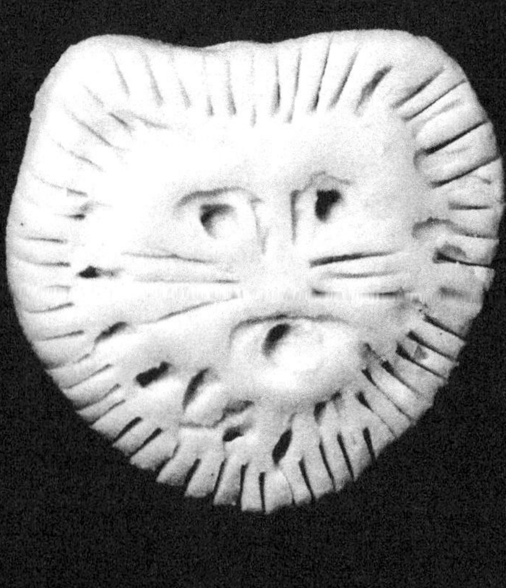

Naomi Gibbons

Urszula Bolimowski

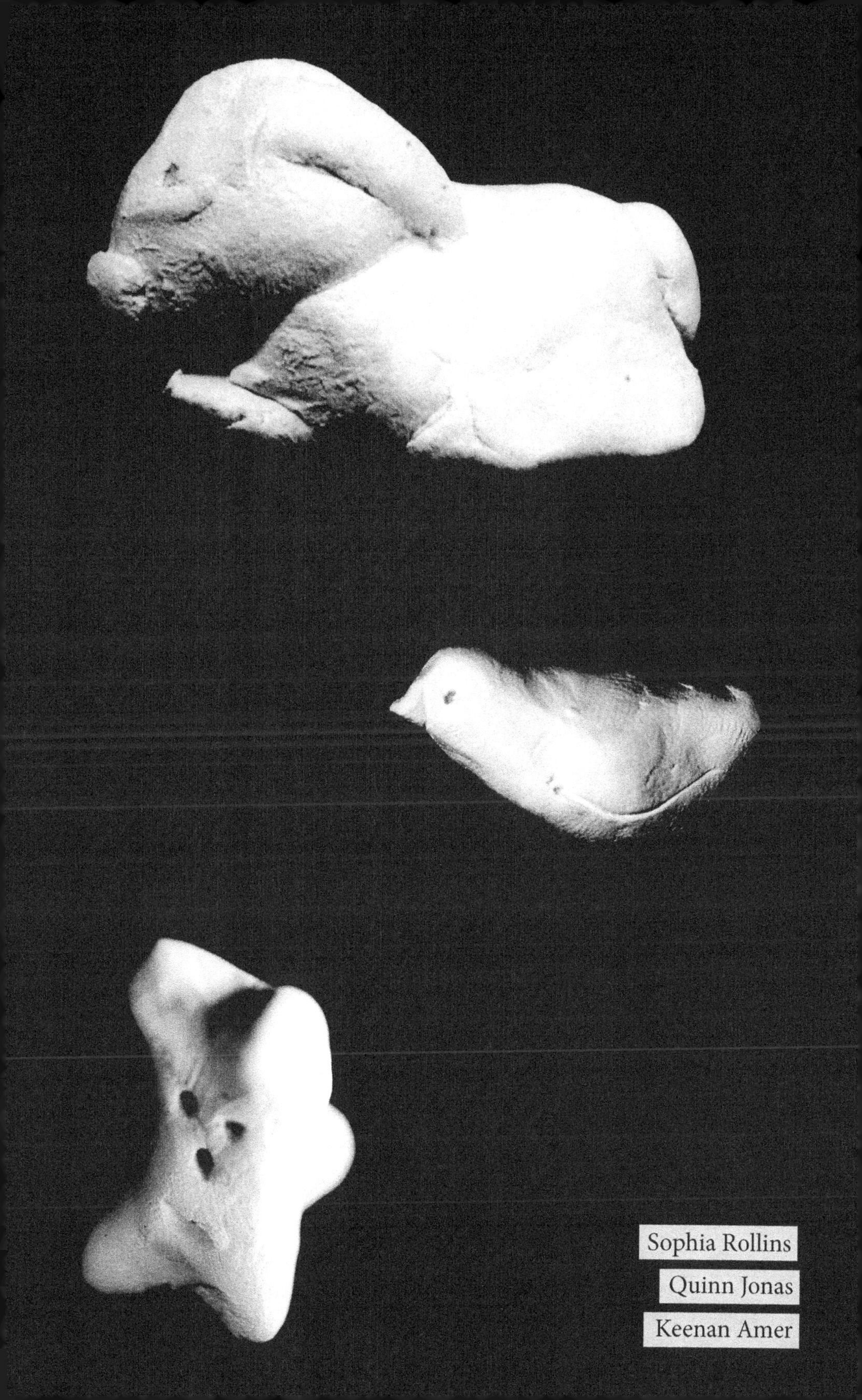
Sophia Rollins
Quinn Jonas
Keenan Amer

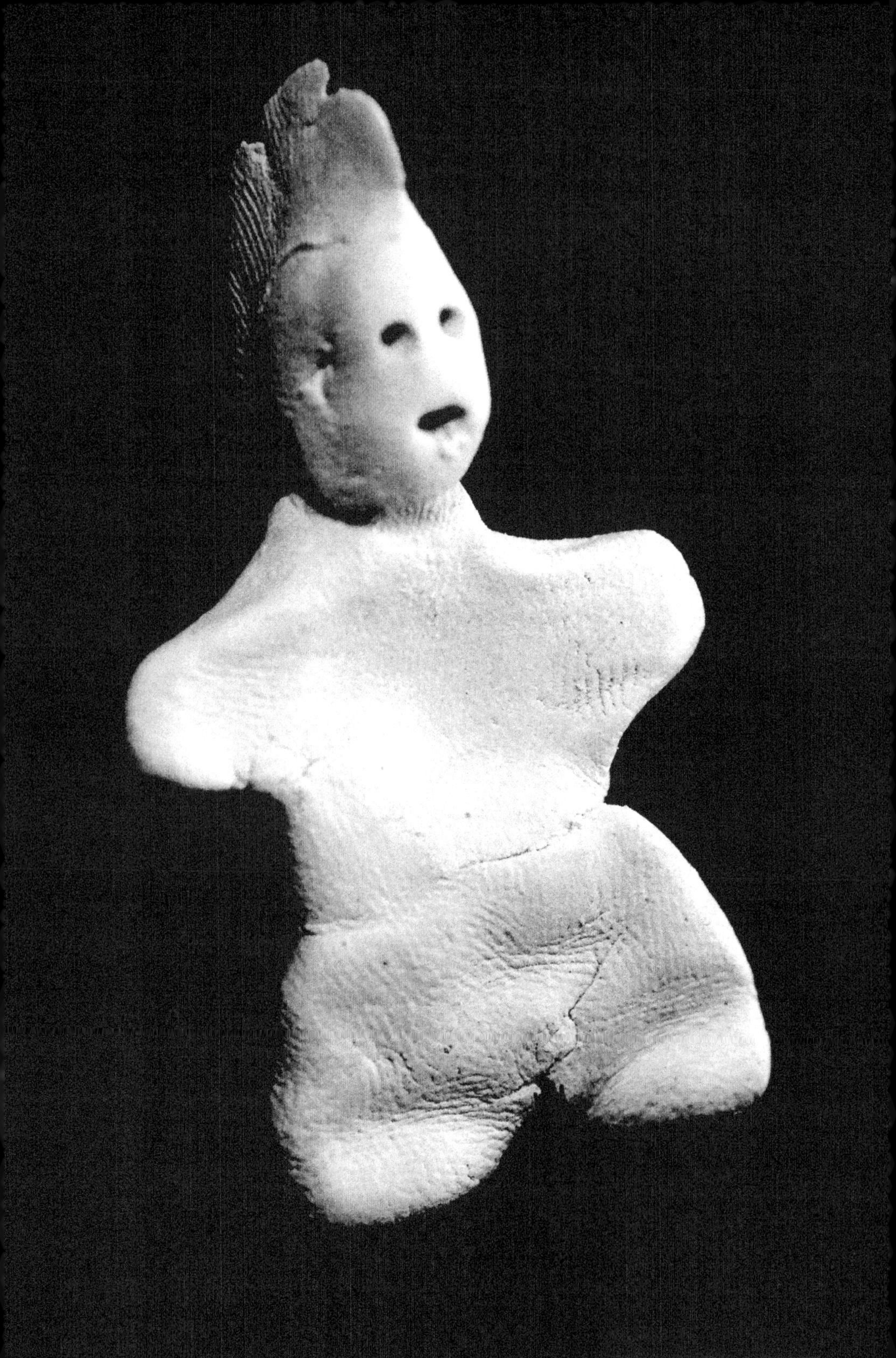

Adam Weyhrauch

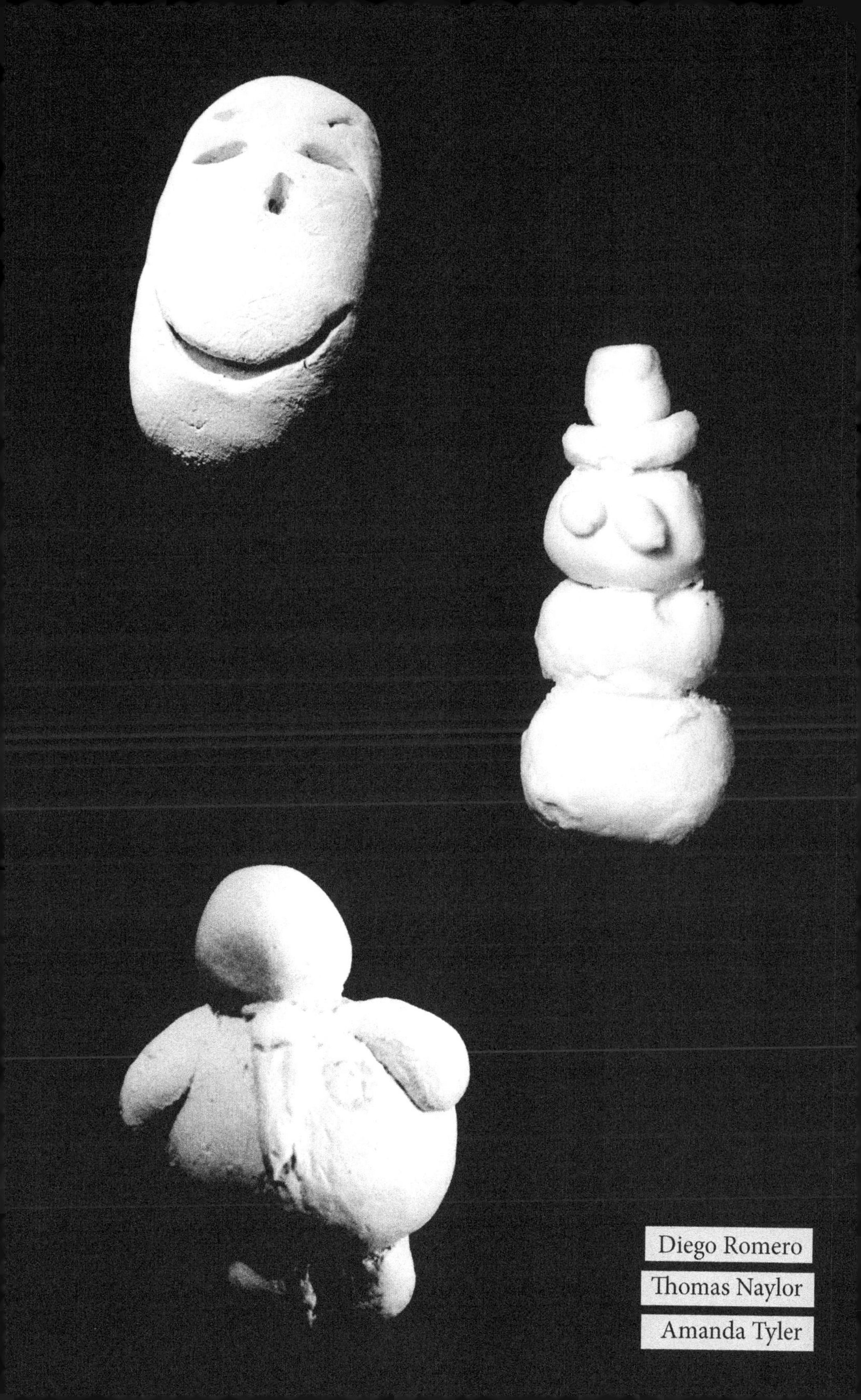

Diego Romero
Thomas Naylor
Amanda Tyler

Up The Street

When I lived in Istanbul for 3 years, my family used to send me up the street to get bread. I remember the tiring walk up the hill, walking past familiar faces and signs even though I couldn't read any of it. When I walked into the shop I was rewarded with the smell of fresh bread as I looked at the cookies. I think it was one Turkish lira to buy one baguette. As I walked back down the hill I remember not being able to wait and I would start picking at the fresh warm bread.

–Anonymous

My father always said that bread, makes a meal, and is the thing that united us all in the end of all things. My grandmother said the bread is the most important part of the meal itself. It is the platform of our prayer. Without bread it seems that a meal cannot be a full meal. It is VITAL.

–Anonymous

The best bread ever made was by my great-grandma. The best tortillas are now made by my grandma Annie and the best frybread is made by my grandma Alice and the best biscuits by my mom. How did my grandma make the best bread and it took only one person to do that which now take 3 people to do. They sure don't make them like they used to. I miss you Great-Grandma and love you very much. I will do my best when it is my turn to make the bread.

-XOXO your "aweii" (baby)s

–Anonymous

Recently I had to give up eating all bread for health reasons. I am left my four senses: I smell its freshness at the bakery as I walk by and my nose feels drawn towards the warm yeasty scent. I see the fresh inviting loaves lined up in all their color, shape and variety of delightful savor, but do not let myself touch any of them. There is nothing I hear except the active growling in my stomach as I smell the forbidden loaves. The stomach knows. The nose invites. The eyes veer towards the breads. I quicken my steps to escape what my ancestors have told me to eat. Darn doctors.

–Anonymous

I gave up gluten for a month. Then I was obsessed with TOAST.

–Anonymous

One of my first jobs after college was cleaning a bakery, 10 pm to 2 am every morning. By that time, the dough, which had been soft and pliable and full of possibility 20 hours before, had become as hard as concrete, seemingly permanent on the concrete floor and sturdy wooden tables and on the walls, even.

I'd scrape it with a big chisel and broomstick until my forearms ached. The bread had been sold, the detiritus hardened and then scraped and put in the trash. But the smell remained, that glorious fresh bread smell.

Here was a lesson in the cycles of life, perhaps my first training, years before I could recognize it, in what would become a spiritual practice: Remaining here, now, while experiencing the vagaries of the passage of time.

–Anonymous

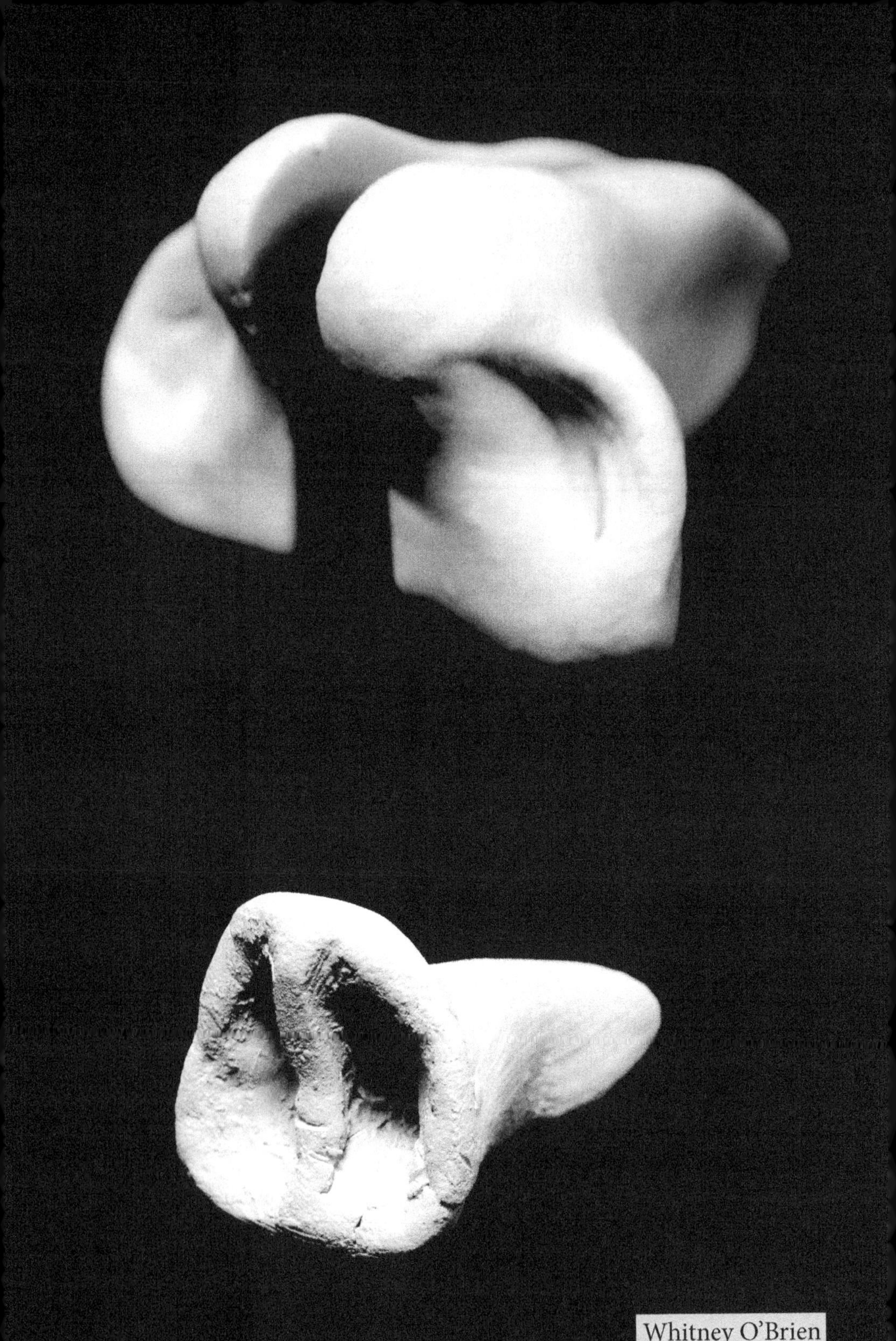

Whitney O'Brien

Thomas Lehn

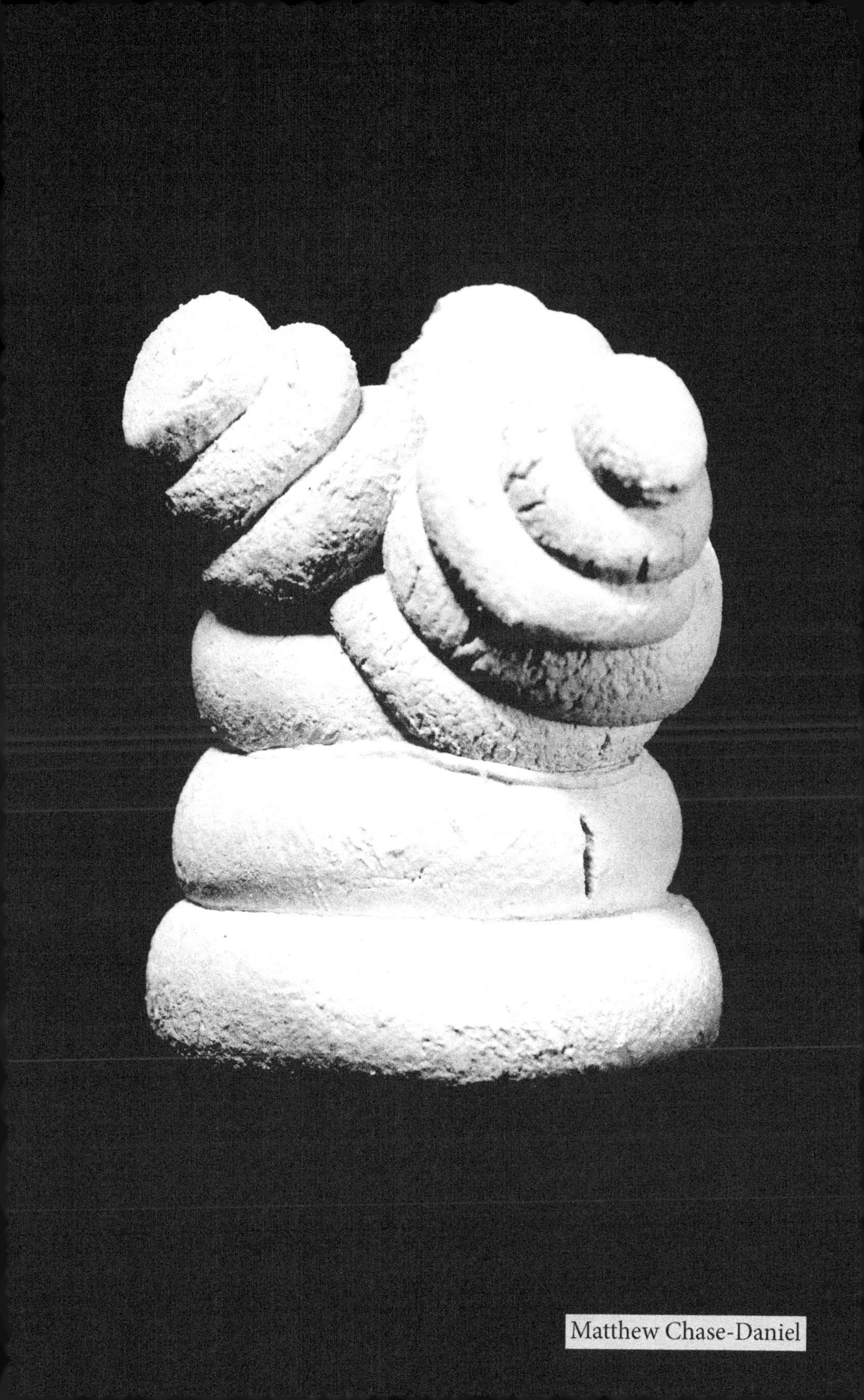

Matthew Chase-Daniel

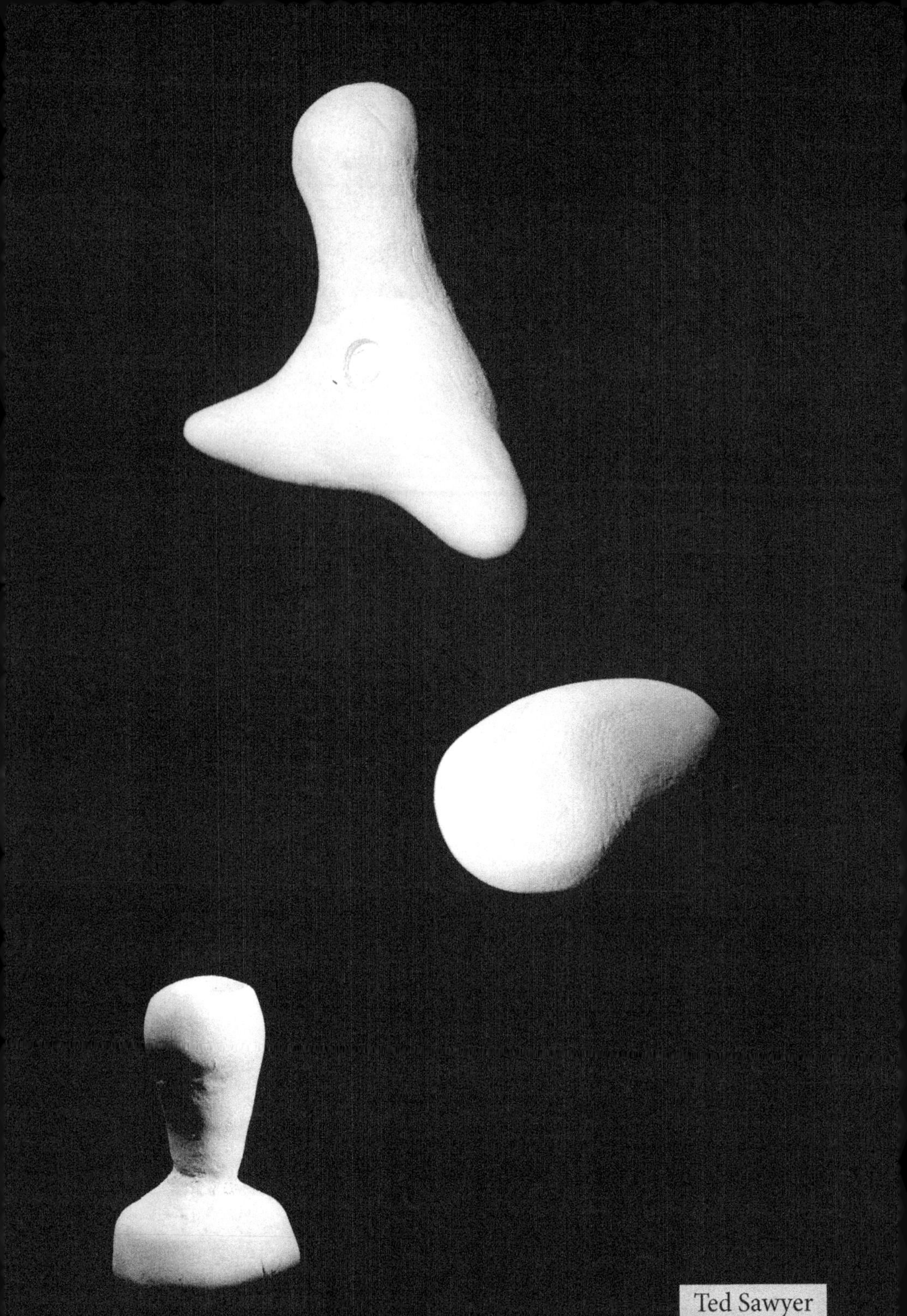

Ted Sawyer

Santa Fe Youth Development Program

Santa Fe Youth Development Program

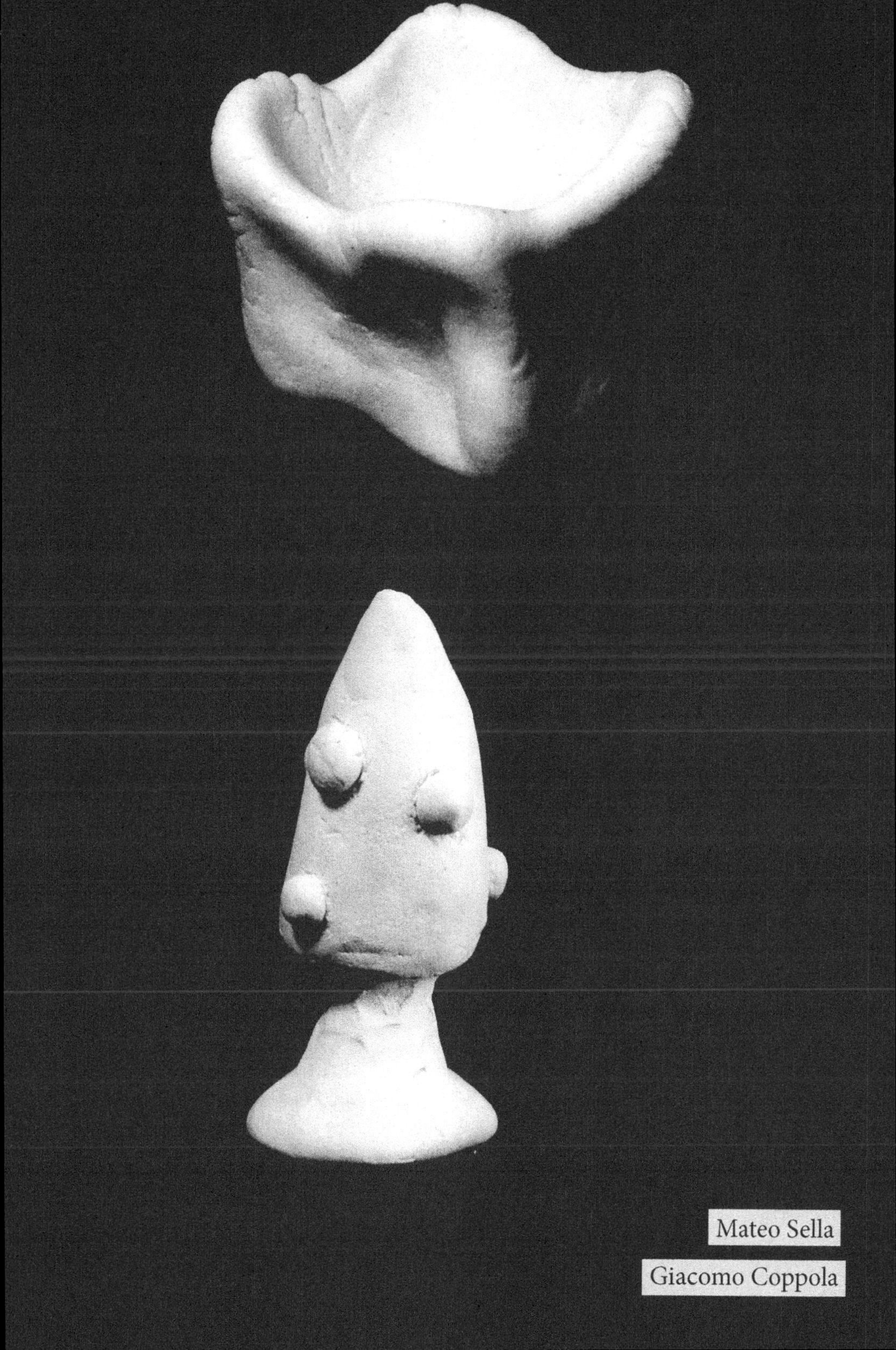

Mateo Sella

Giacomo Coppola

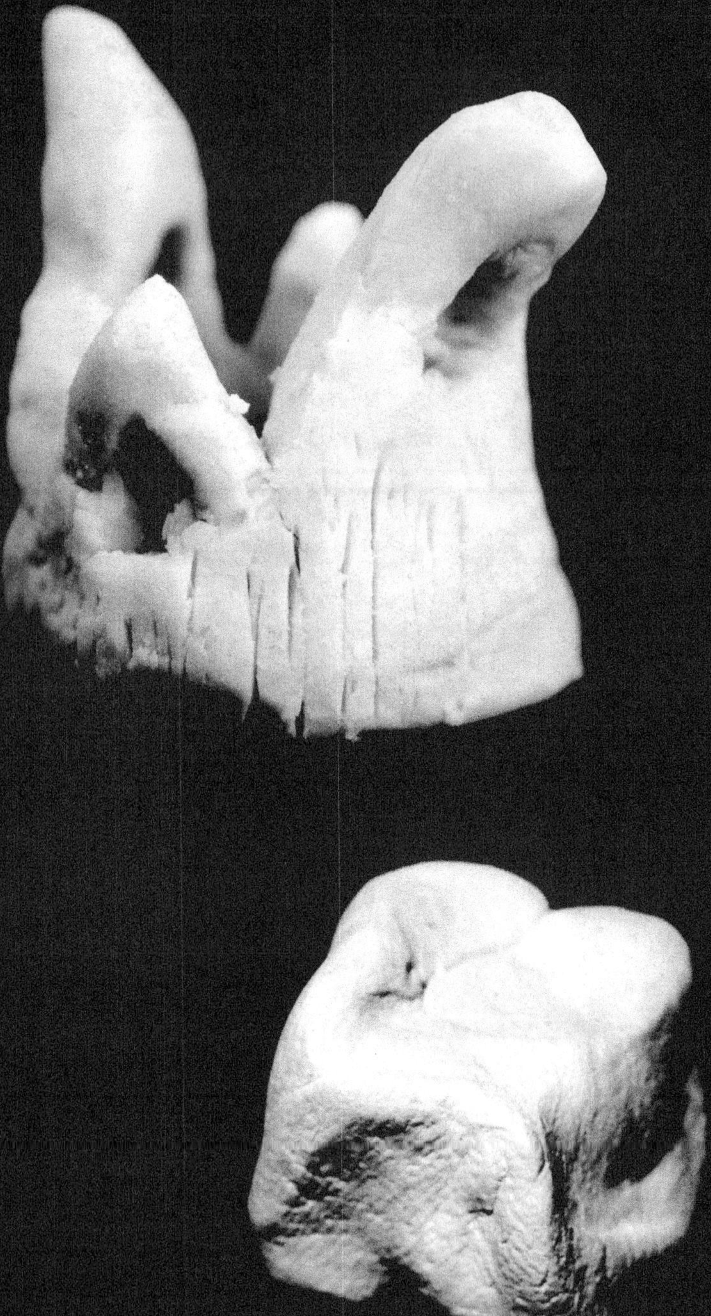

Rima Miller

Ruth Belinsky

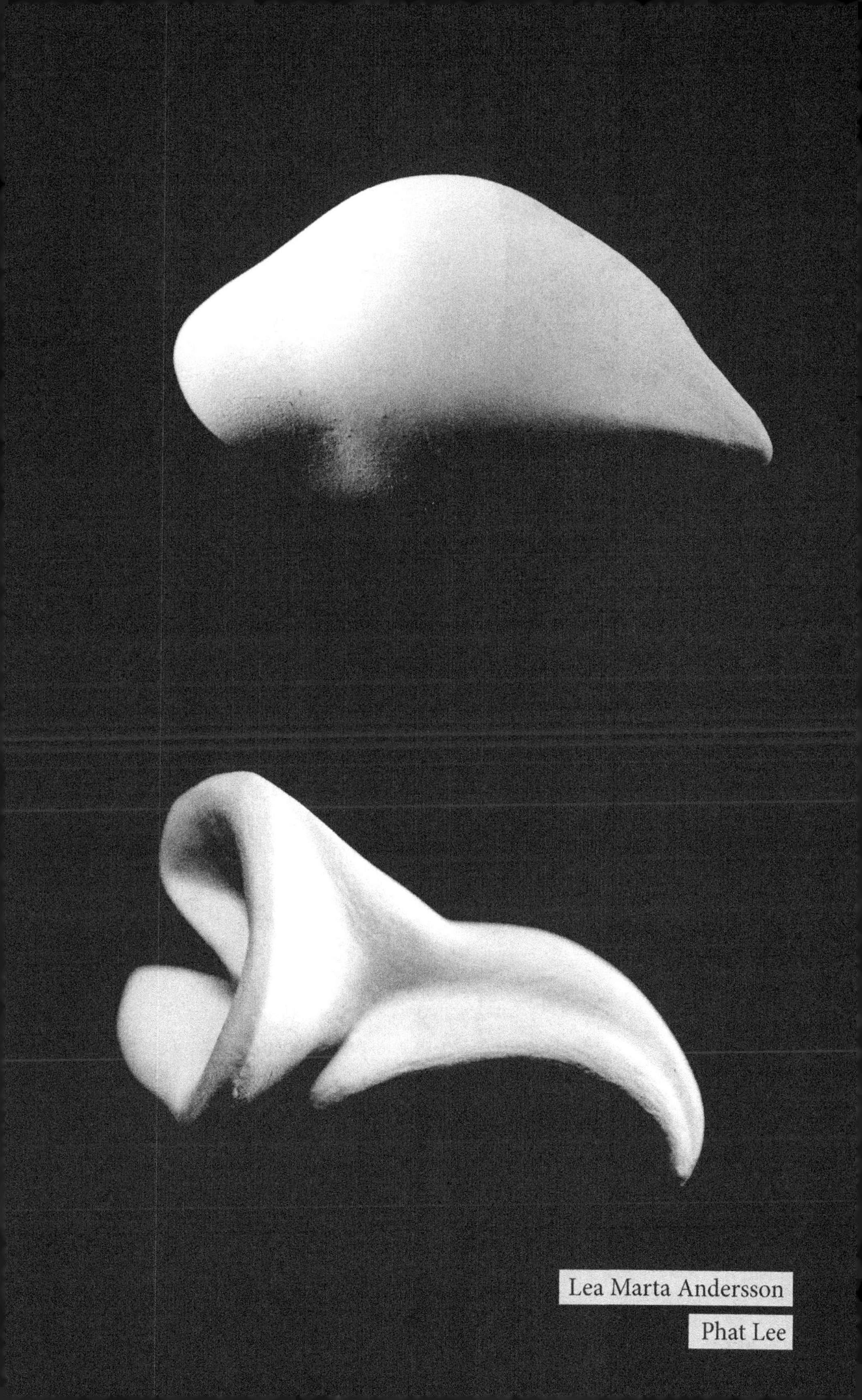

Lea Marta Andersson

Phat Lee

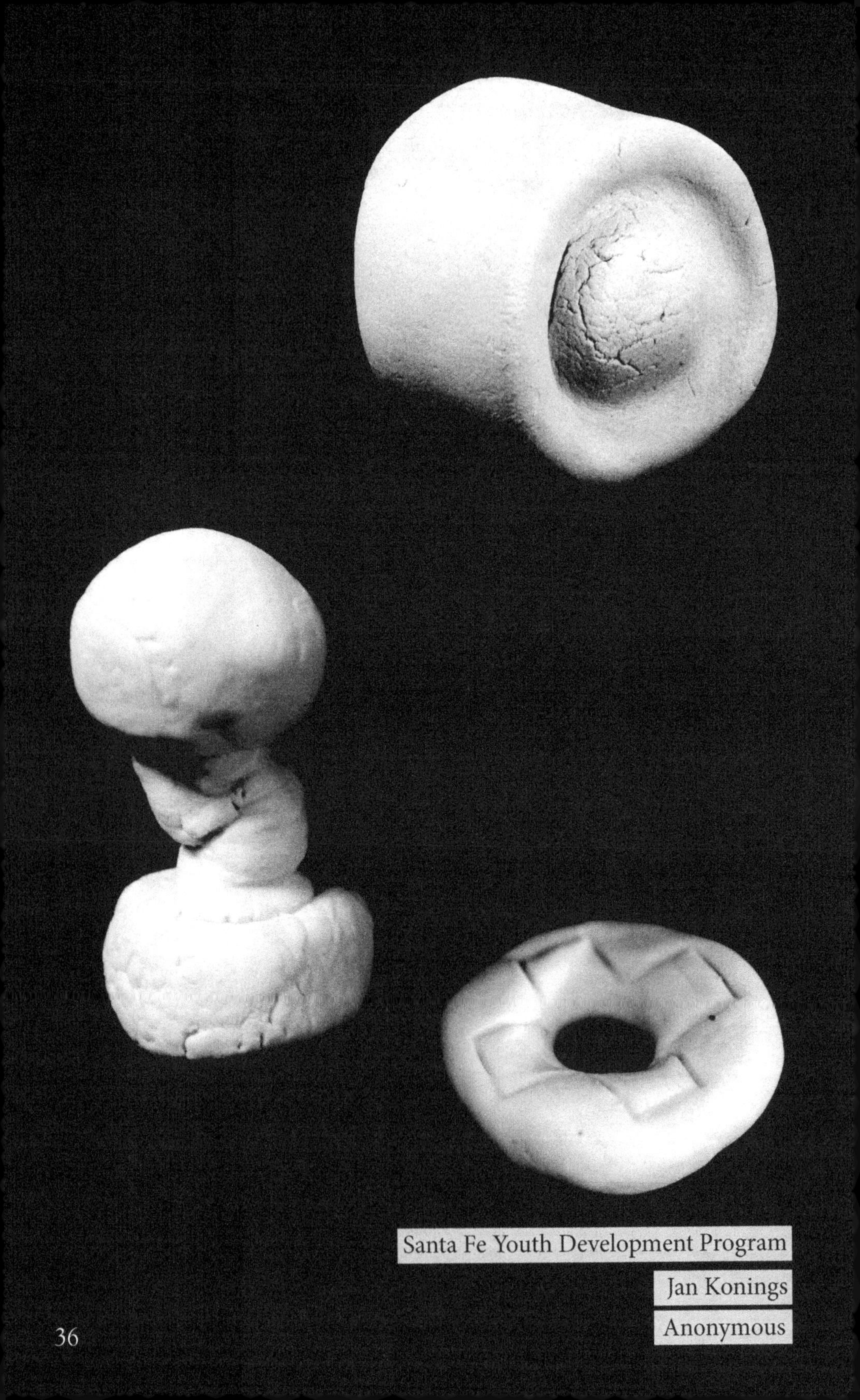

Santa Fe Youth Development Program

Jan Konings

Anonymous

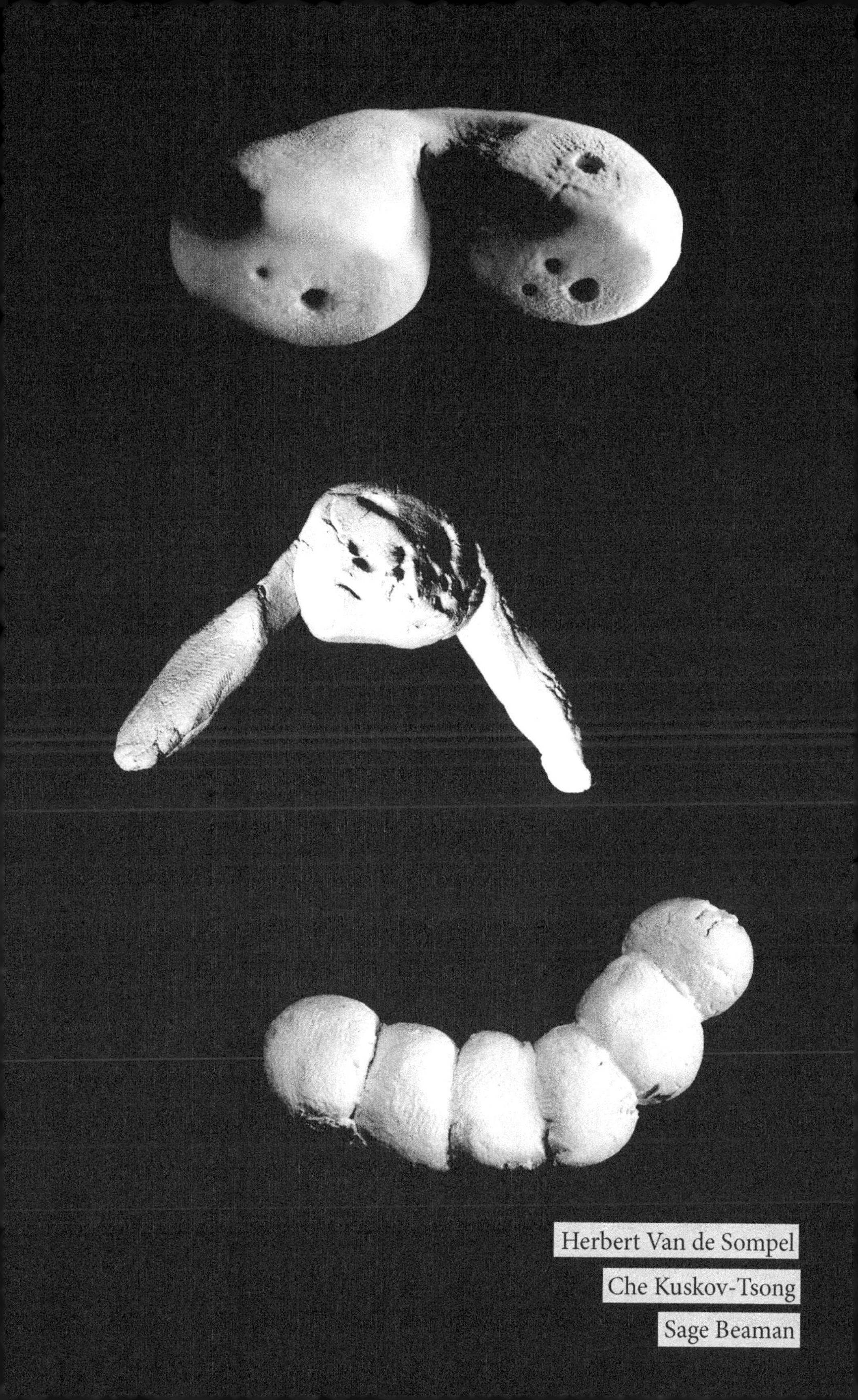

Herbert Van de Sompel
Che Kuskov-Tsong
Sage Beaman

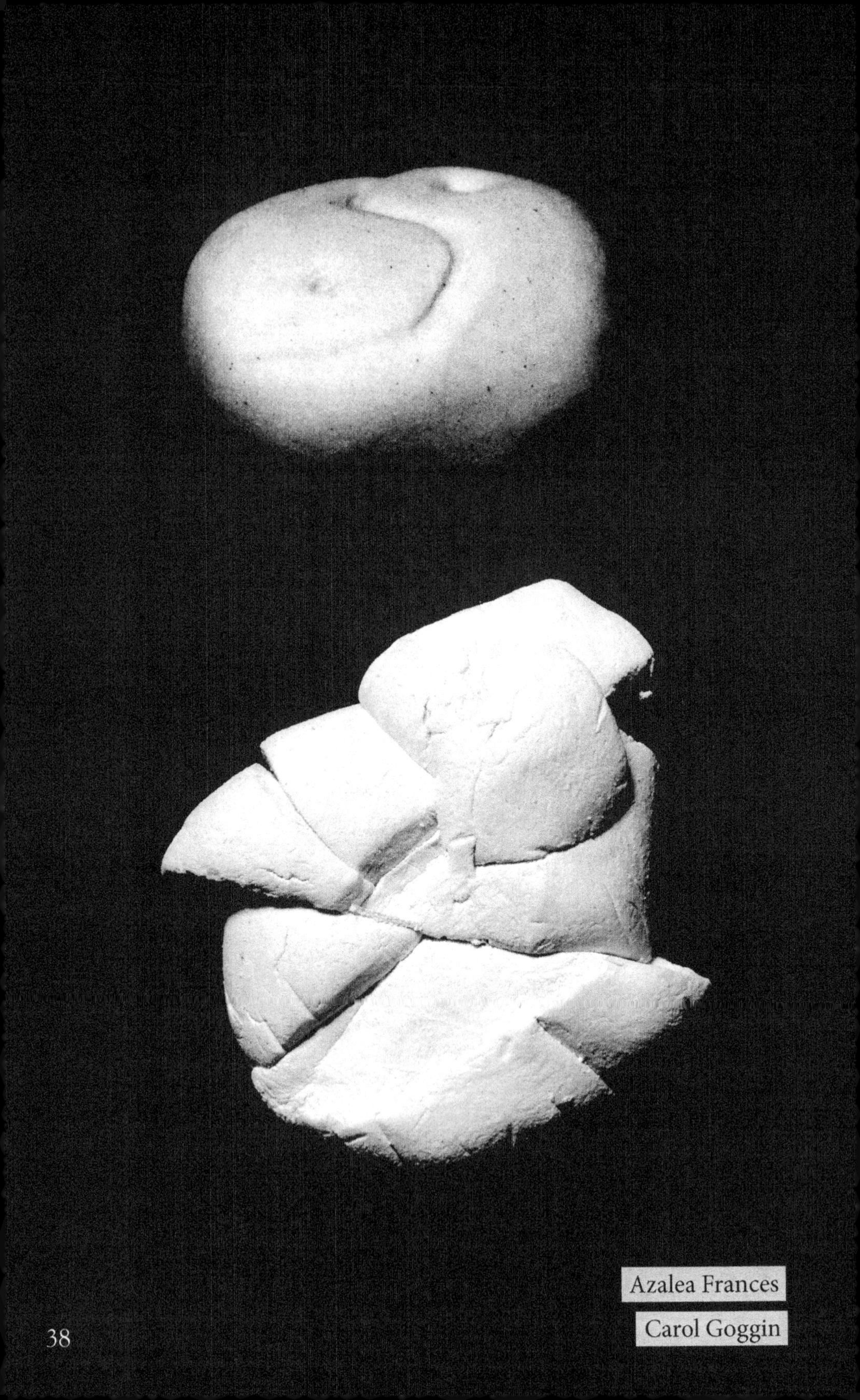

Azalea Frances

Carol Goggin

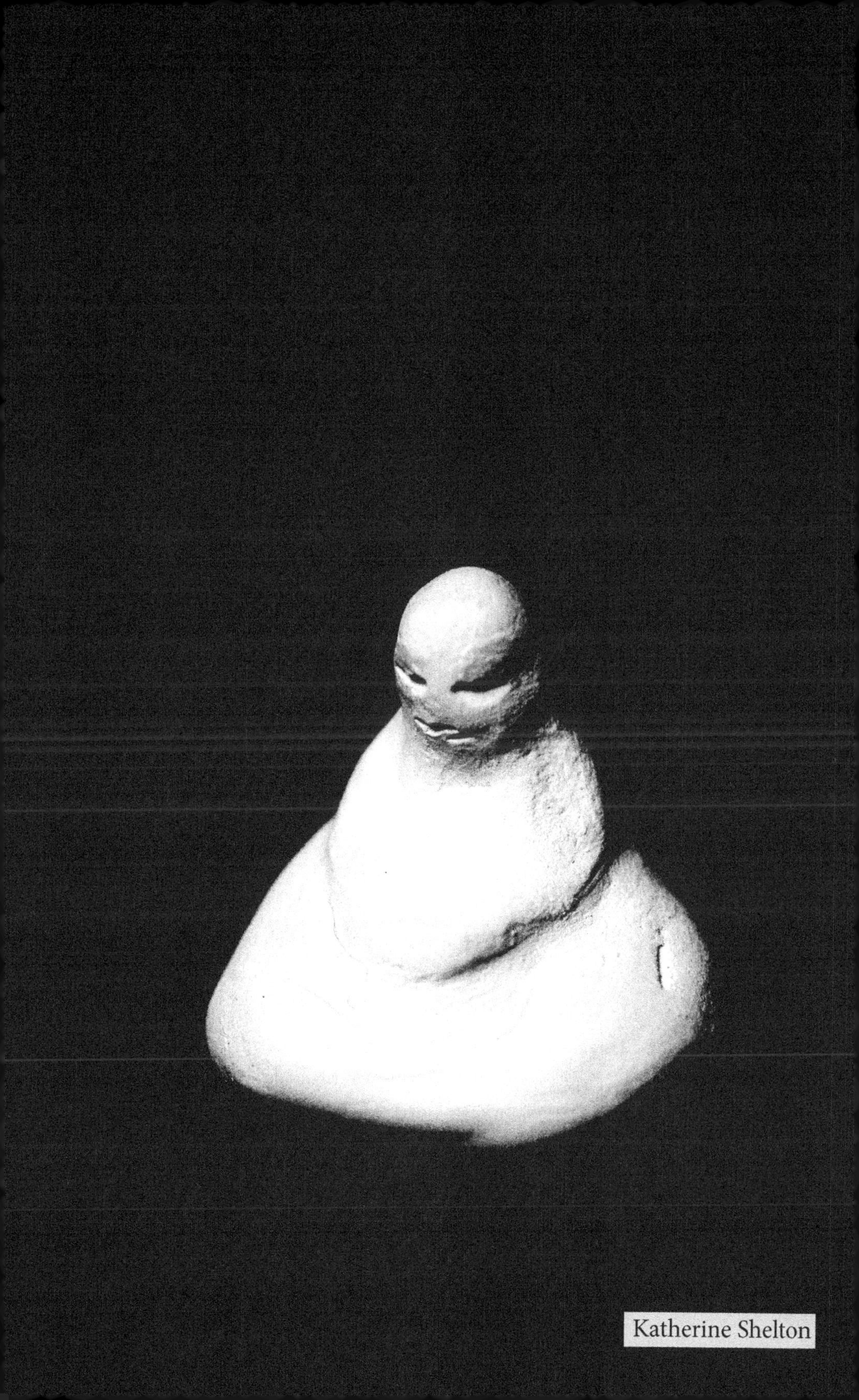

Katherine Shelton

My bread story isn't a happy one, but it does define me as an adult; where I came from. I grew up in the Bay Area in California. I was part of a middle class family with my mother and step-father. He was very strict, and I was a latch-key child. When I was between the ages of 7 and 14, I was by myself when I came home from school from about 3:30 to 9:00 pm. I wasn't allowed to eat anything until my parents got home and we had dinner so I would sneak slices of bread from the center of the loaf, then check to make sure no one could tell that a slice or two were missing and I would eat that as my afternoon snack. :(

-T. O'Harra Krebs

In 2009 I lived in a small Romanian village for about 6 months. The family I lived with was poor, and most meals consisted of bread and sour cream. I ate more bread during those 6 months than ever before in my life.

At Easter there was a woman in the village who made a very special bread, and everyone went to buy some from her. There was a cross on the top, I suppose for some religious significance. I left the village the day after Easter, and the family gave one of these special breads to take with me. When I got to Bucharest I gave this loaf of bread to the pigeons because I never wanted to eat bread again.

-Anonymous

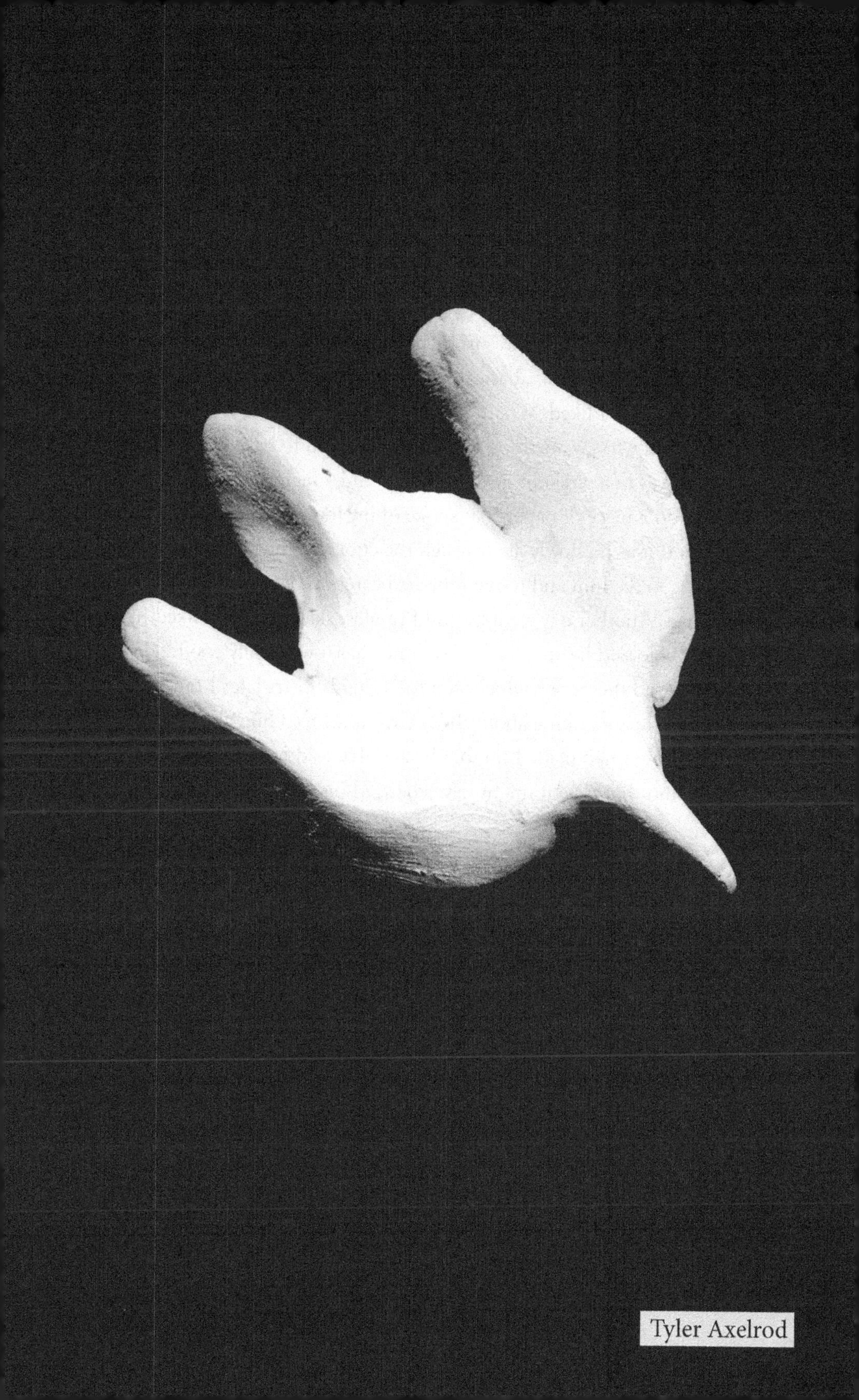
Tyler Axelrod

It reminds me of when I was in high school, I use to make these elaborate face cookies.....basically little sculptures. I would give them away to people I liked. There was a boy that I had a big crush on but I was too shy to say anything to him so I decided to bake him a cookie face. It was of a girl smiling at him but I hid a secret note inside the cookie on a piece of paper that spoke of my love for him. I figured he'd find it as he slowly ate through the cookie. The next day I was nervous to see him and to see if he had eaten his cookie yet. He said nothing. Another day went by and I finally asked him if he liked his cookie. He said he ate it right away and that it was really good. He never found the note having eaten too fast. 20 years later I ran into him and we got talking about those days and I told him about the cookie note I had made him that he ate. He told me he wished he had found that note it might have changed his life.

-Roxanne Swentzell

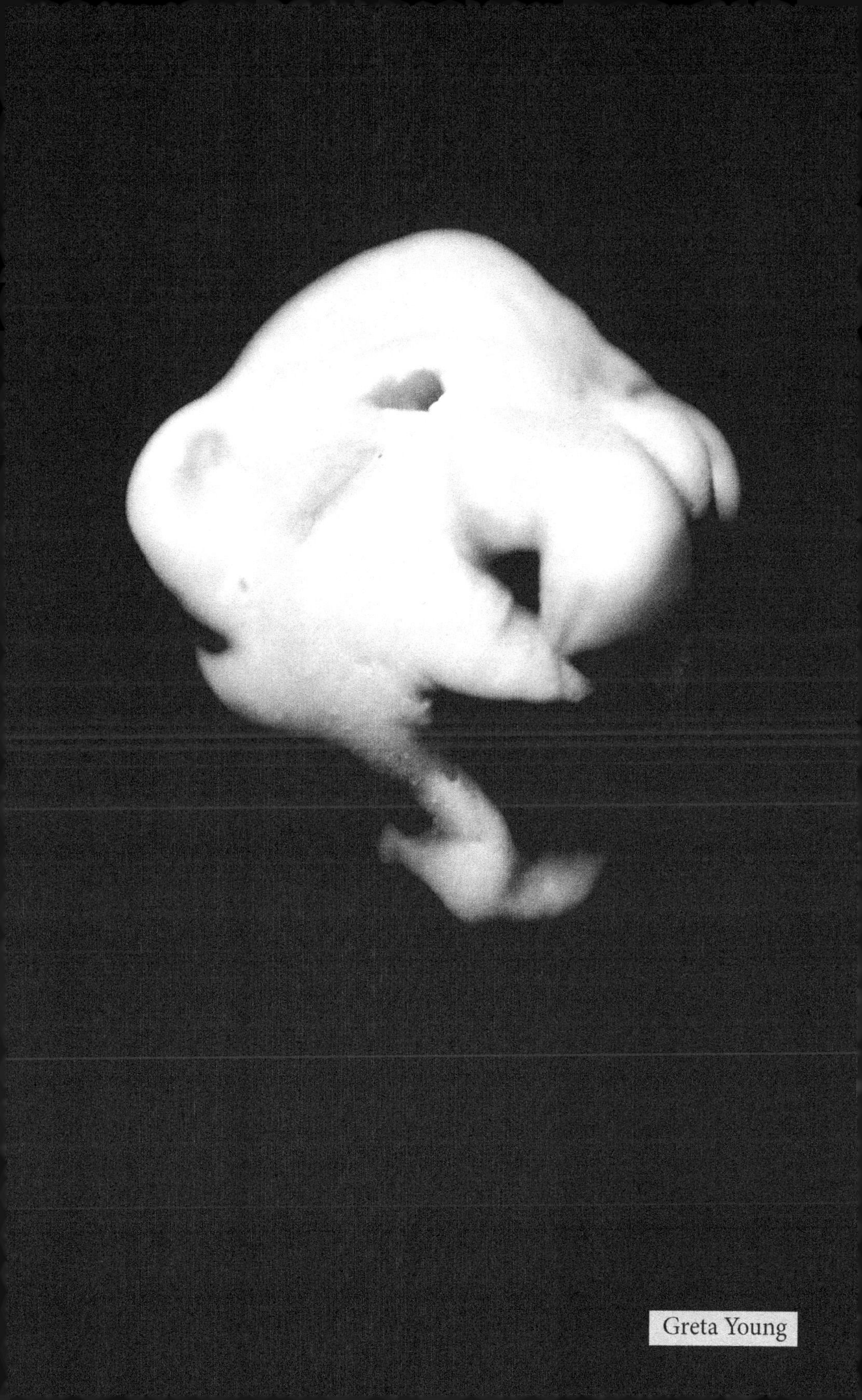

Greta Young

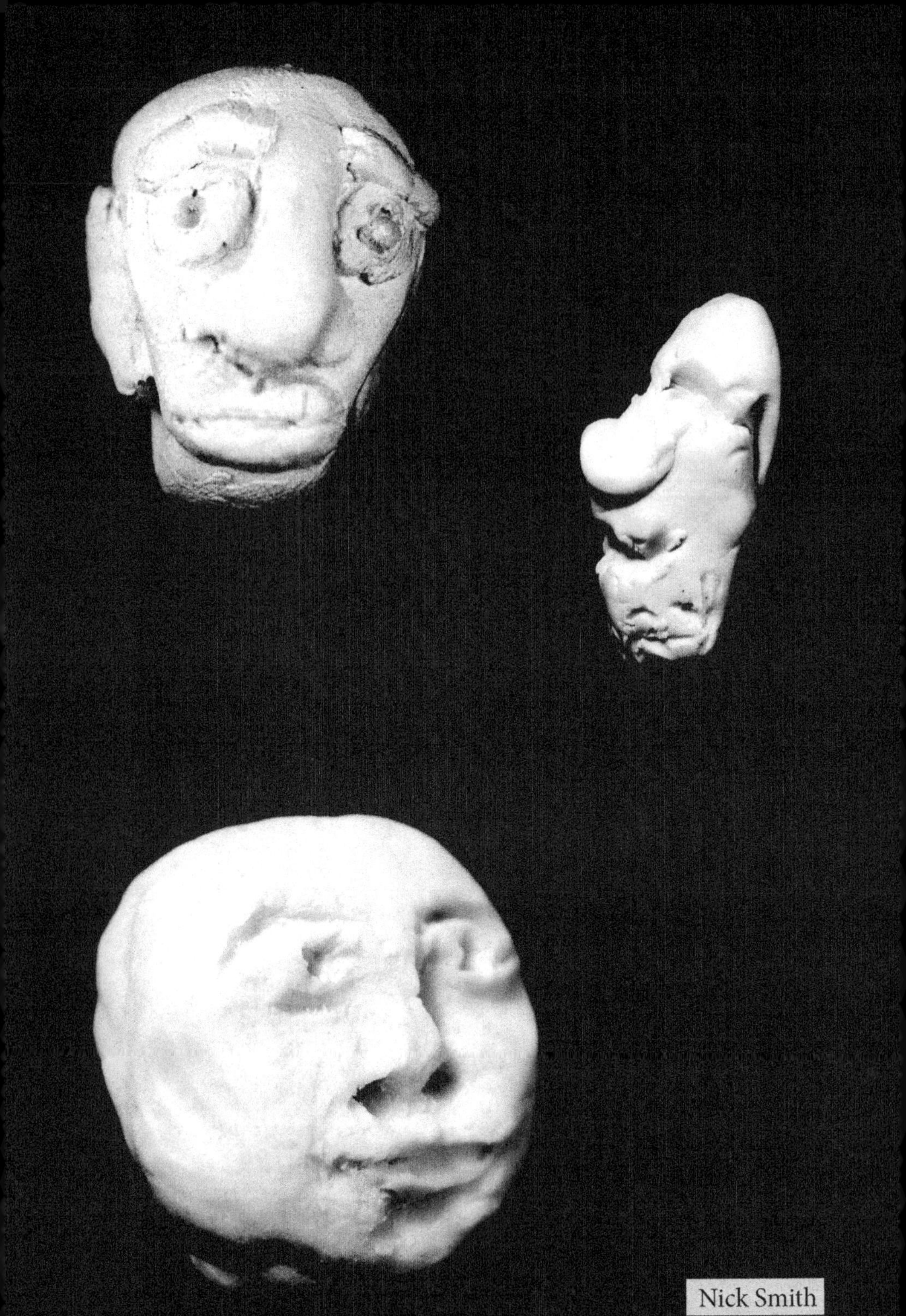

Nick Smith

Arlene Ory

Mindy Littman Holland

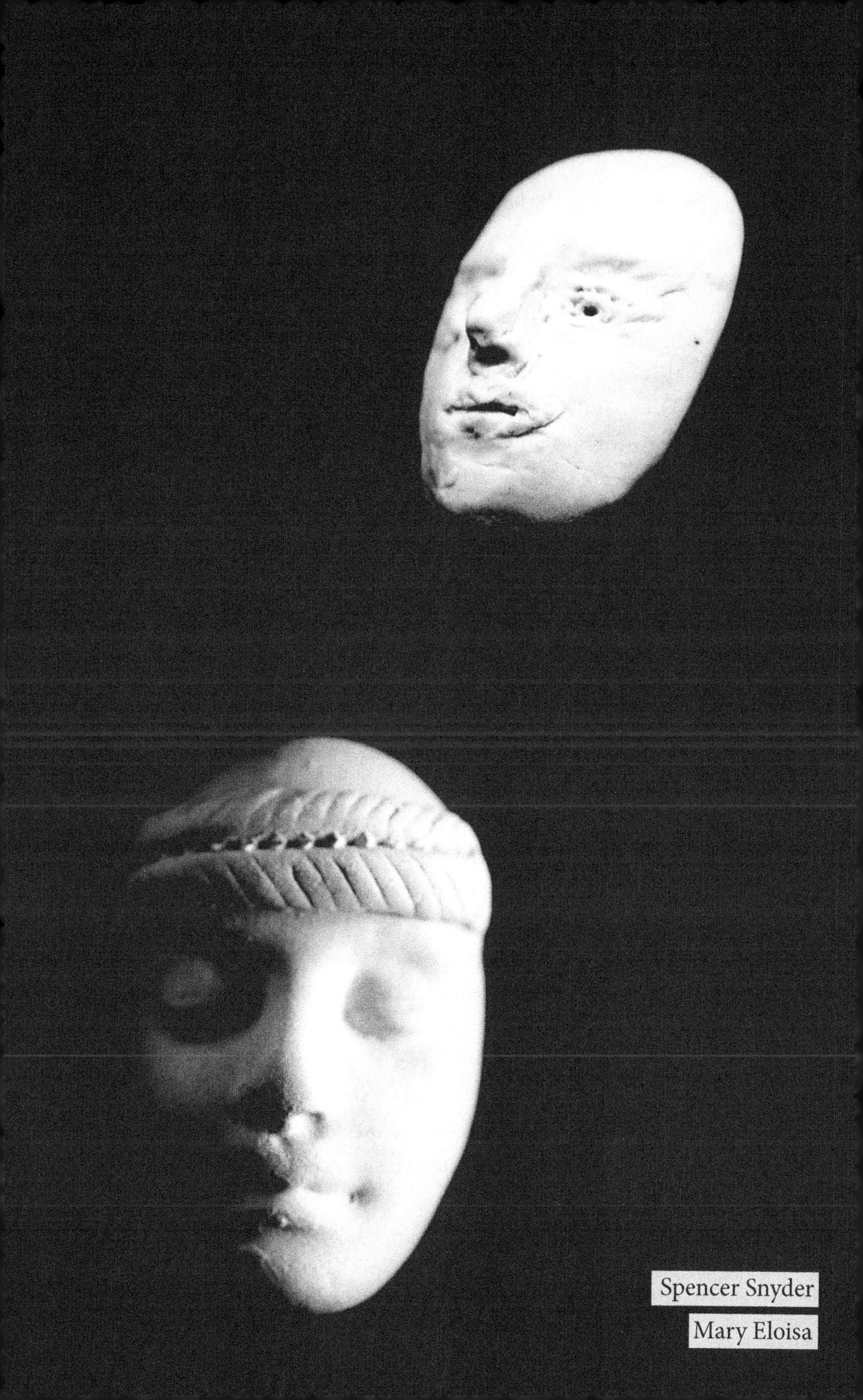

Spencer Snyder

Mary Eloisa

Former and Future Breadbasket of Agua Fria

Agua Fria Village was the literal breadbasket of the City of Santa Fe, the community stretching from Camino Carlos Rael (or Frenchy's Field Park) to San Felipe Road along the El Camino Real, was a series of farms irrigated by the acequias of the perennial Santa Fe River. The founder of the Villa of Santa Fe Don Pedro de Peralta in the period 1604-1610 complained in many missives to his superiors that the settlers of the capitol city were unable to sustain themselves and had to rely on surrounding communities. A place of recognized settlement since 1640, Agua Fria's place on a natural alluvial plain farmed by Native Americans since 3,000 BCE, lent itself to fill this void. The illegal closure of the acequias and diversion of the water from the wheat grinding mills in 1895 to fill the Santa Fe Reservoirs greatly reduced the planting of wheat after this date. However, of the 868.17 acres that were irrigated in the village 40.63 acres were in wheat according to the Office of State Engineer's Hydrologic Survey of 1914 (189.59 acres in corn and 72.62 acres in alfalfa). All this wheat was taken to the grinding mills on the upper Santa Fe River and was used for bread, mainly for personal use or barter.

This continued until sliced bread loaves[i] appeared at a price of 19 cents in 1928 with commercially produced loaves going for as little as 6 cents a loaf in 1913 and later 5 cents in 1933.[ii] How could any farmer compete with that? The time, money and energy put into planning, fertilizing, planting, harvesting and grinding wheat into flour--all before the bread is even baked then sliced. There is no way for the family farmer to compete with the factory farmer.

Also, the values of society and people changed. People started going to chain grocery stores instead of farmer's markets; besides a lot of that local farm stuff had some dirt on it and did not stay as fresh as long or have all that fancy packaging. World War Two forced young people off the farm because Agua Fria farms were so small they were not considered "essential" to the War Effort and the farmers did not get a military draft exemption. Older farmers were told to move and work in defense plants. Most Agua Frians went to work at the naval shipyards in Oakland. After the war, without a dependable supply of water from the acequias for farming and a local market, people could no longer make a living from farming.

The Good News is that the values of people have changed again. Those things we use to do as traditional communities were actually kind of smart and take us away from the dependence on corporate masters. Home and community gardens, shopping at the Farmers' Market all lead to New Mexico's independence from factory farms and foreign markets. Instead of the average item traveling to our table from 2,500 miles away, it will come from places like Dixon, Embudo, Santa Cruz, La Cienega and maybe one day Agua Fria. Where I live was a wheat field, maybe one day it will be again.

-William Mee

[i] http://en.wikipedia.org/wiki/Sliced_bread
[ii] http://www.gti.net/mocolib1/prices/1933.html. Retail food prices of bread range 6-8 cents in 1914 and 1924: http://historicaltextarchive.com/sections.php?action=read&artid=418.

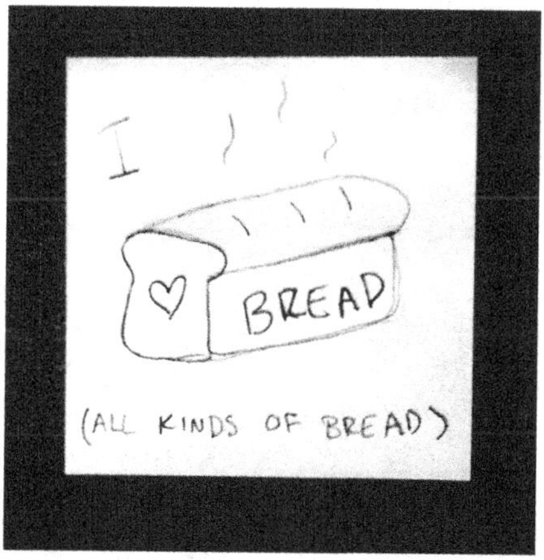

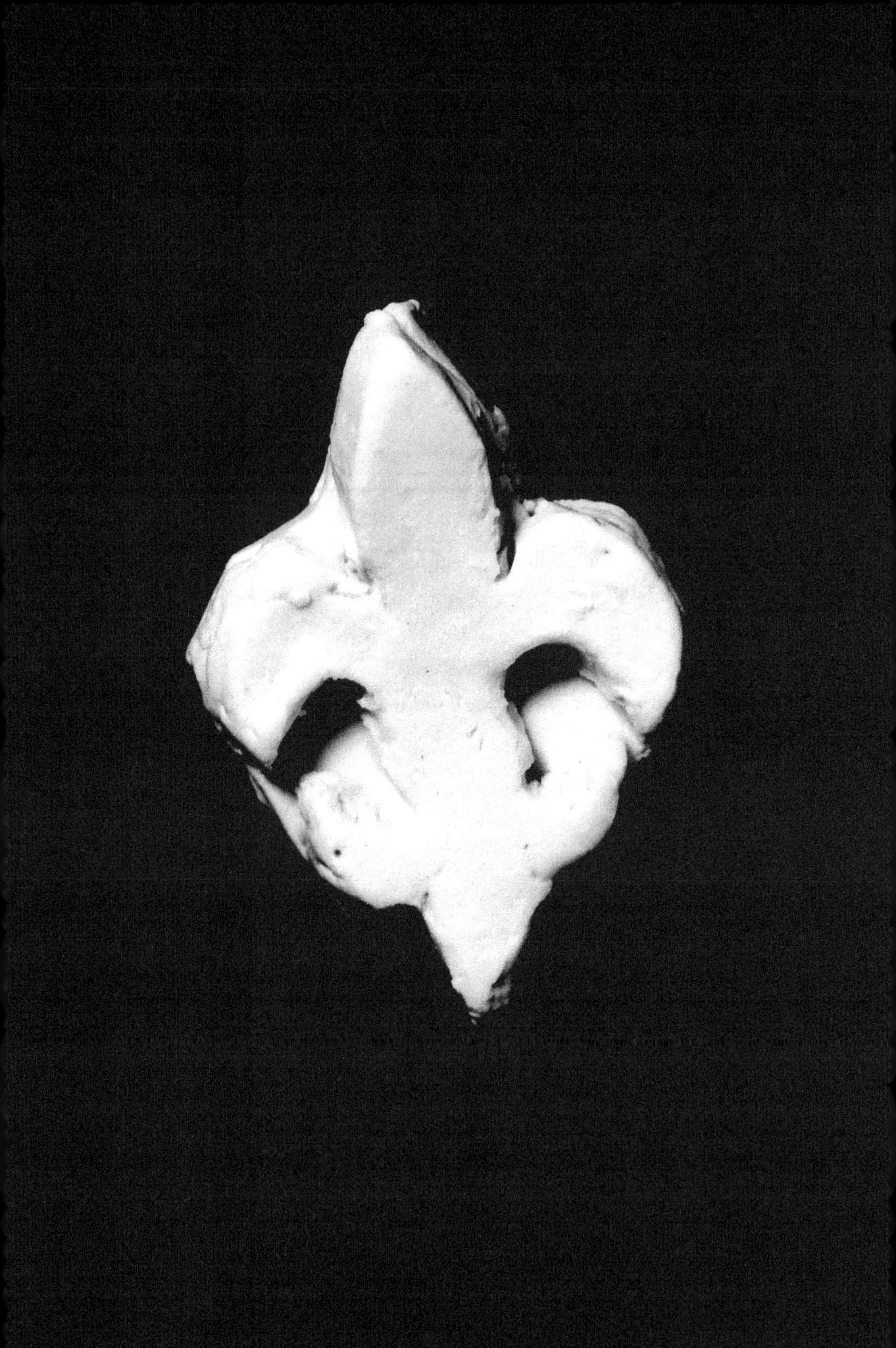

Synpliné Sorina

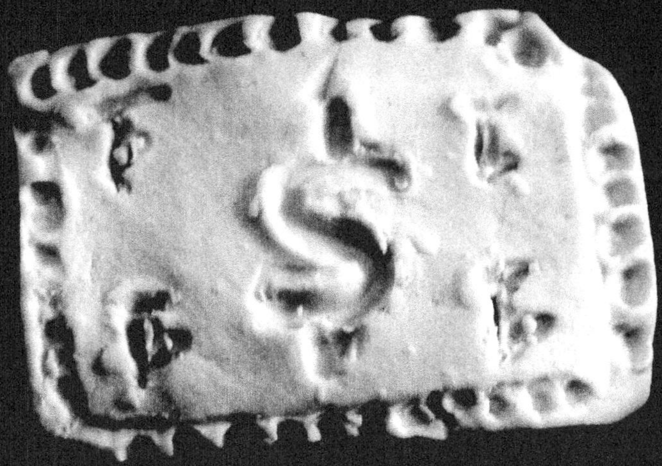

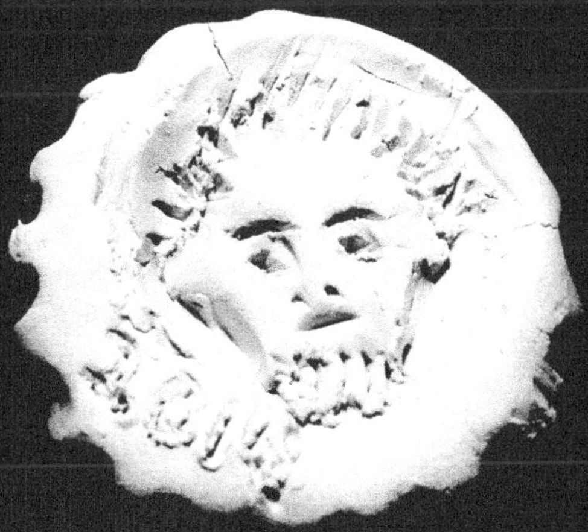

Dianne Stromberg

John Littrell

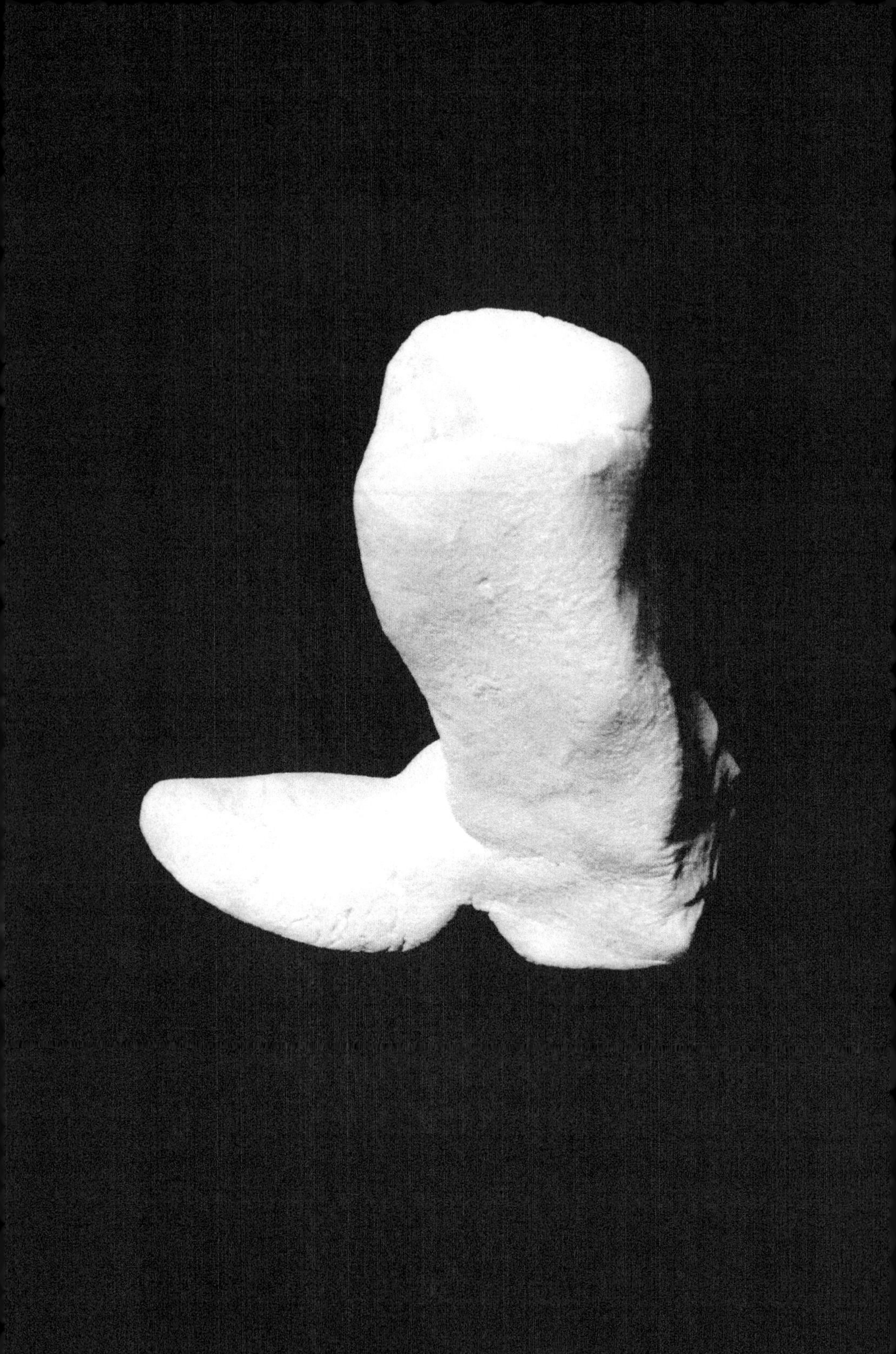

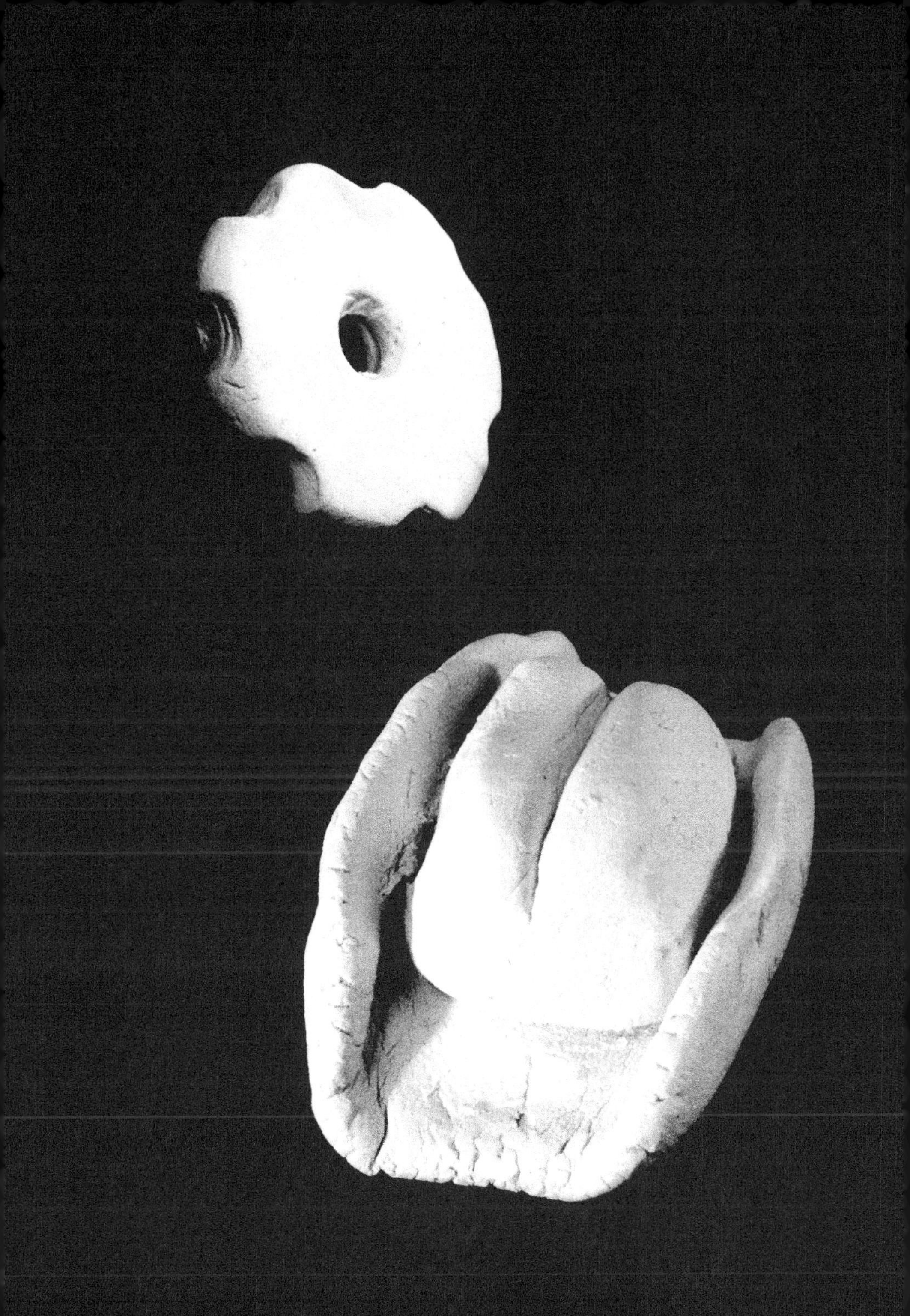

Alessandra Haines

Santa Fe Youth Development Program

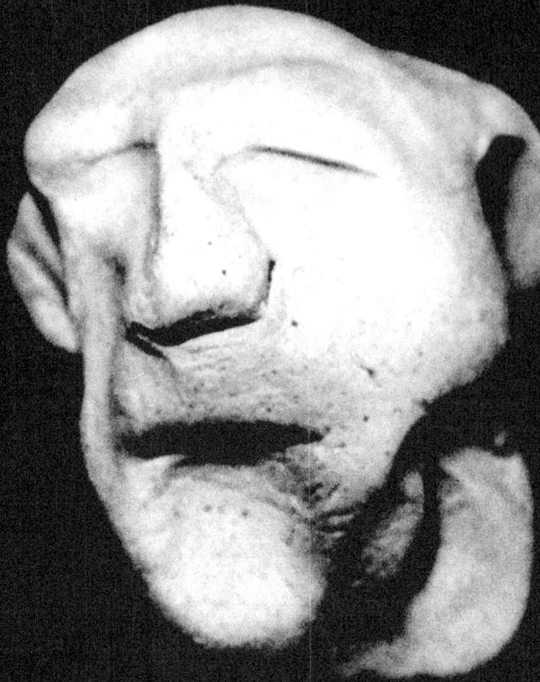

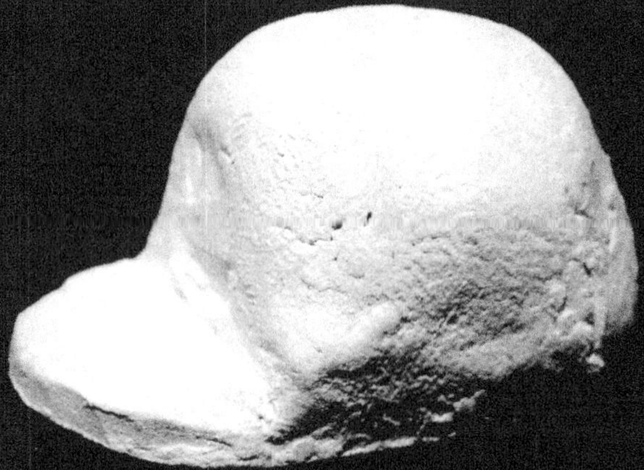

Conor Flynn

Lonnie Lopez

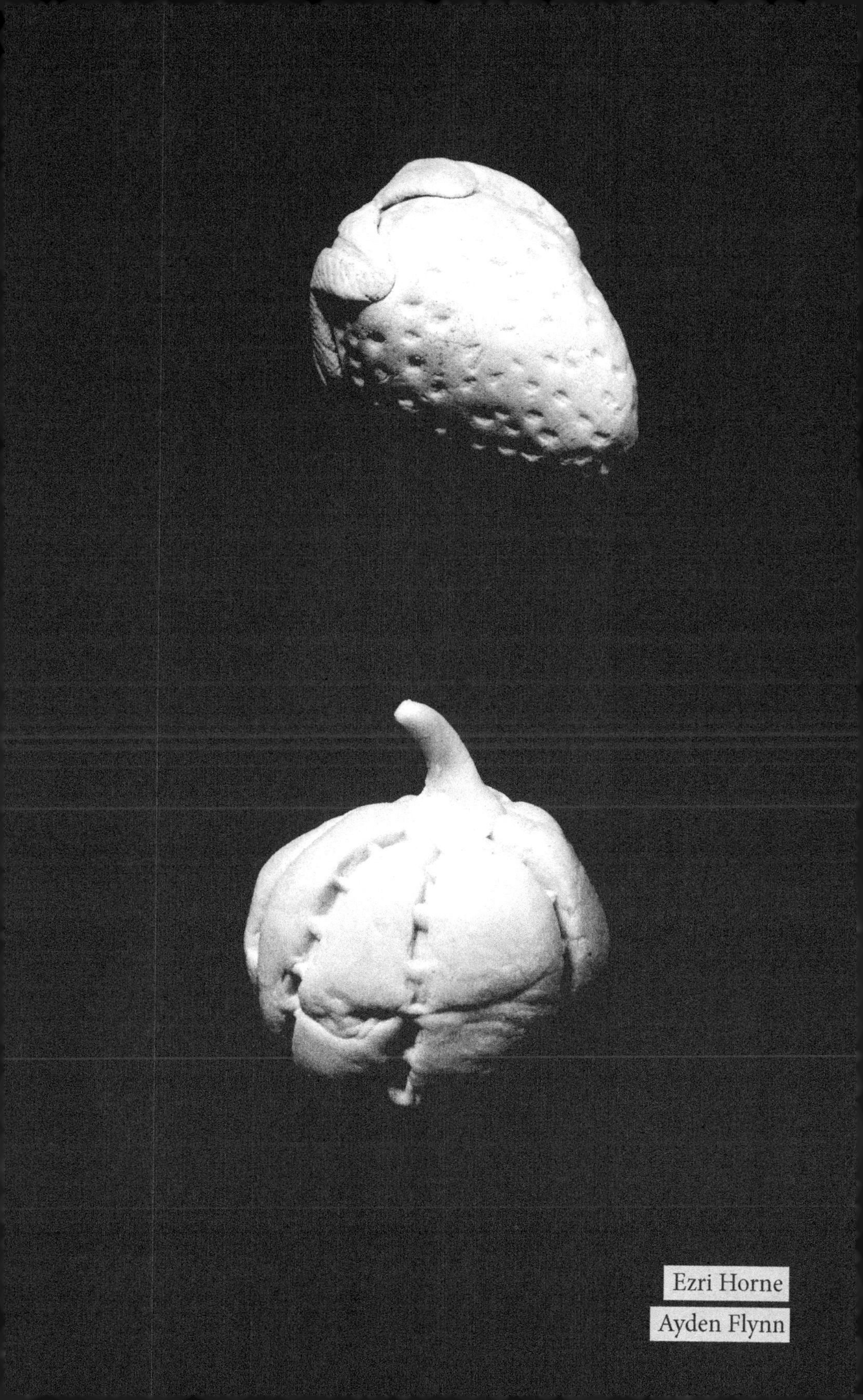

Ezri Horne
Ayden Flynn

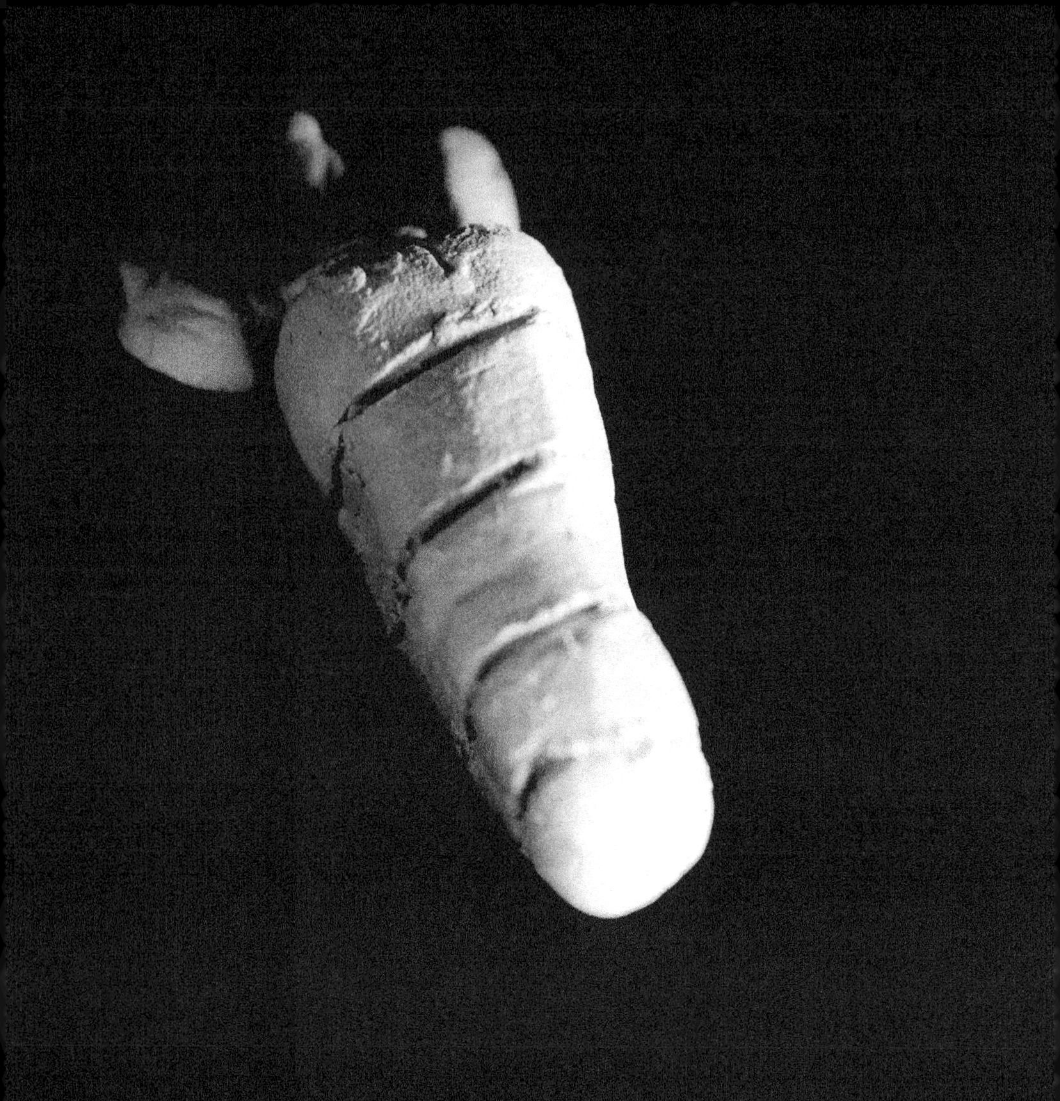

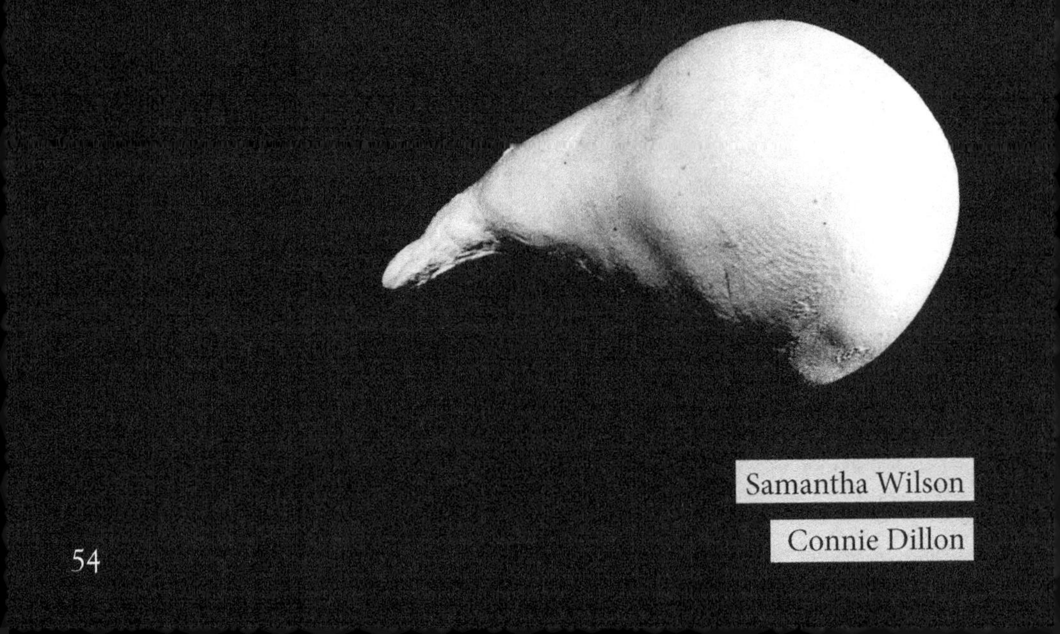

Samantha Wilson

Connie Dillon

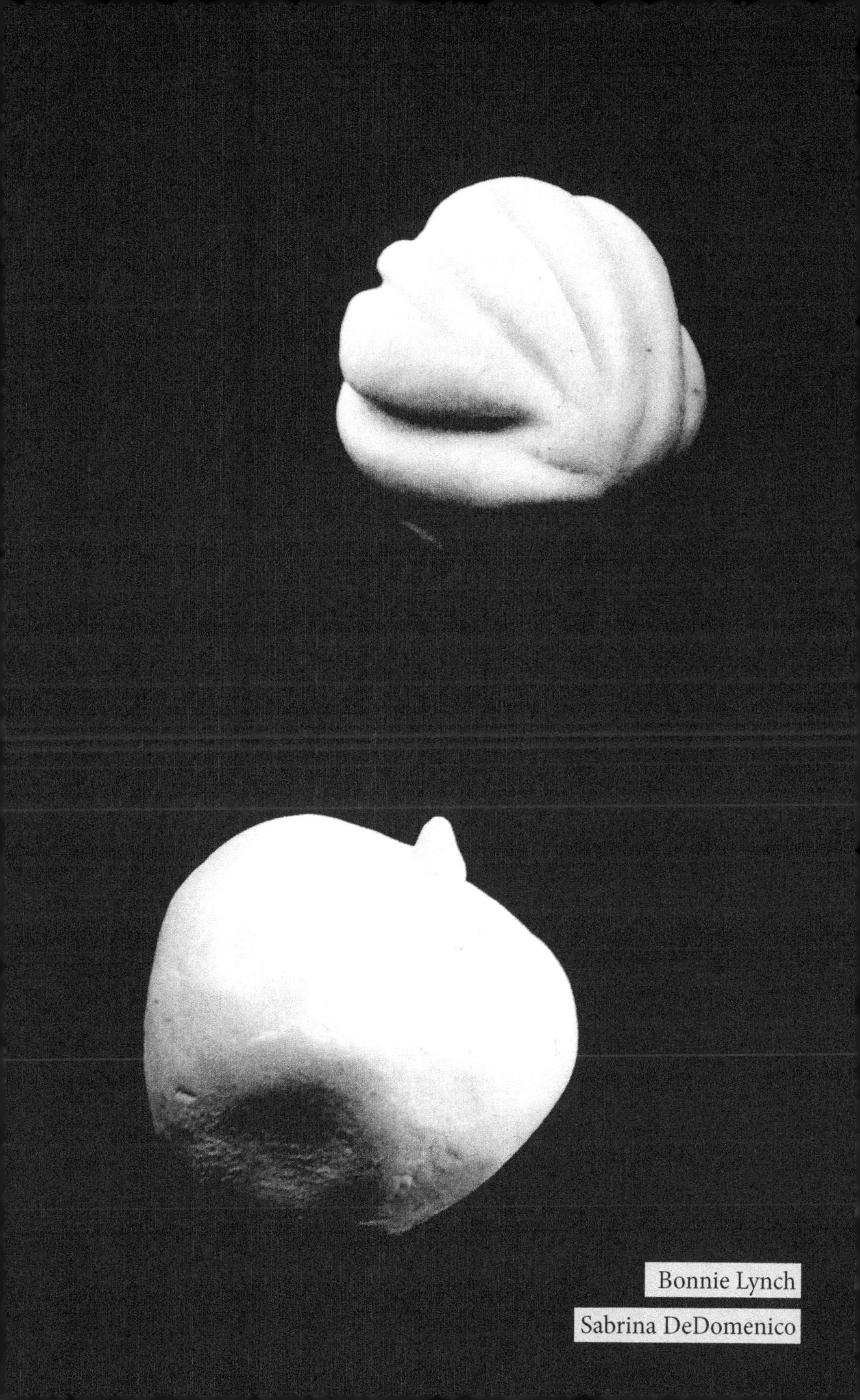

Bonnie Lynch
Sabrina DeDomenico

Paradise

the natives laughed at the hardtack like coral rocks but
after sailors built an oven and gave away fresh bread all
the tieties obtained from sex came pouring back: strings of
beads, iron hoops, clothes and bottles re-traded for a slice.

Chiefs carried fruit and hogs across mountains for a warm loaf
shoals of women swarmed to the ships during mealtimes: breasts bobbing on
waves, toes treading shark teeth, tattooed hands
raised for half eaten rolls tossed down by the ship's nouveau riche

-Emily Severance

This poem is based on events described in "Journal of a Cruise Made to the Pacific Ocean" by Captain David Porter, 1822. I recently learned that dough and paradise have a linked etymology.

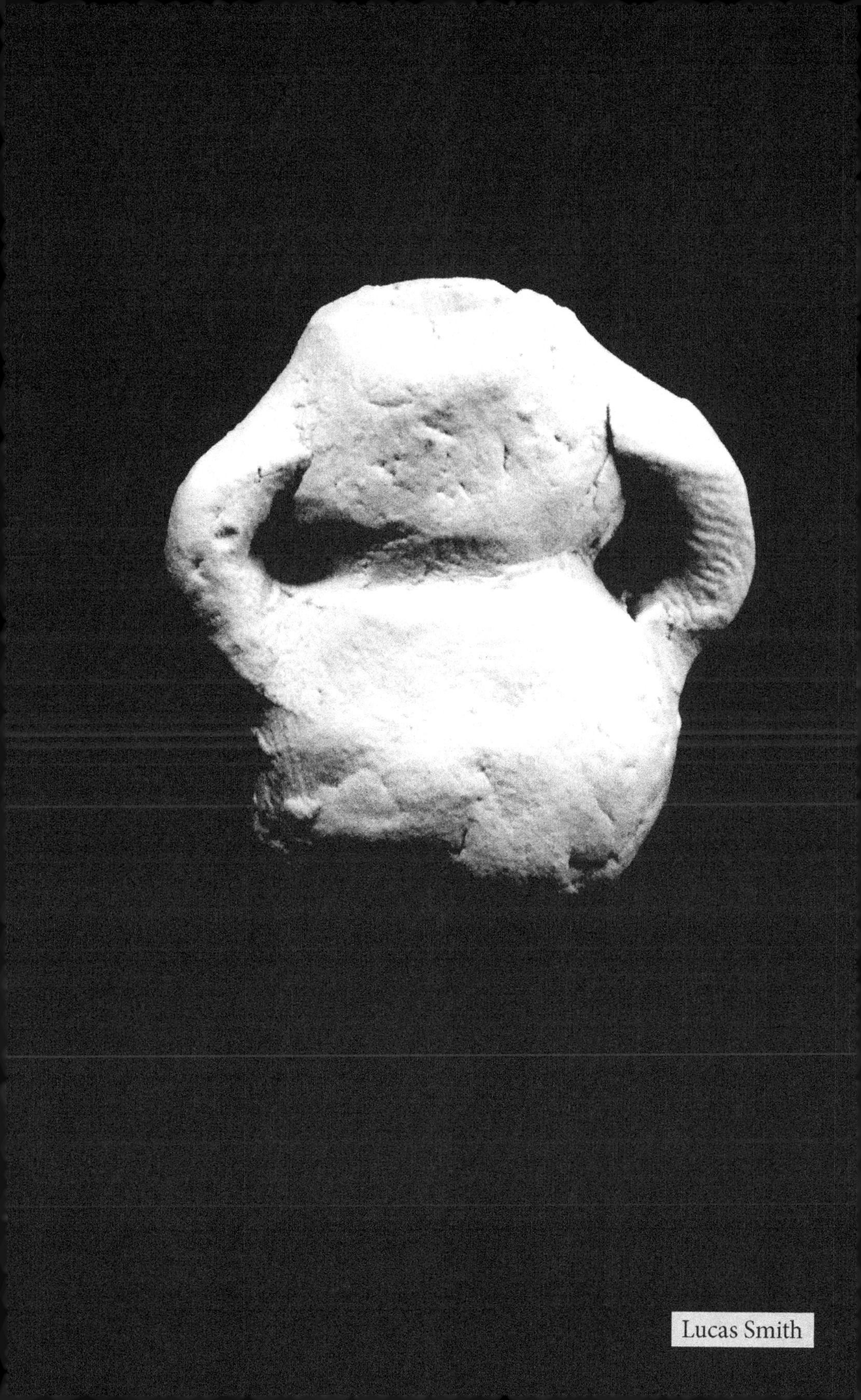

Lucas Smith

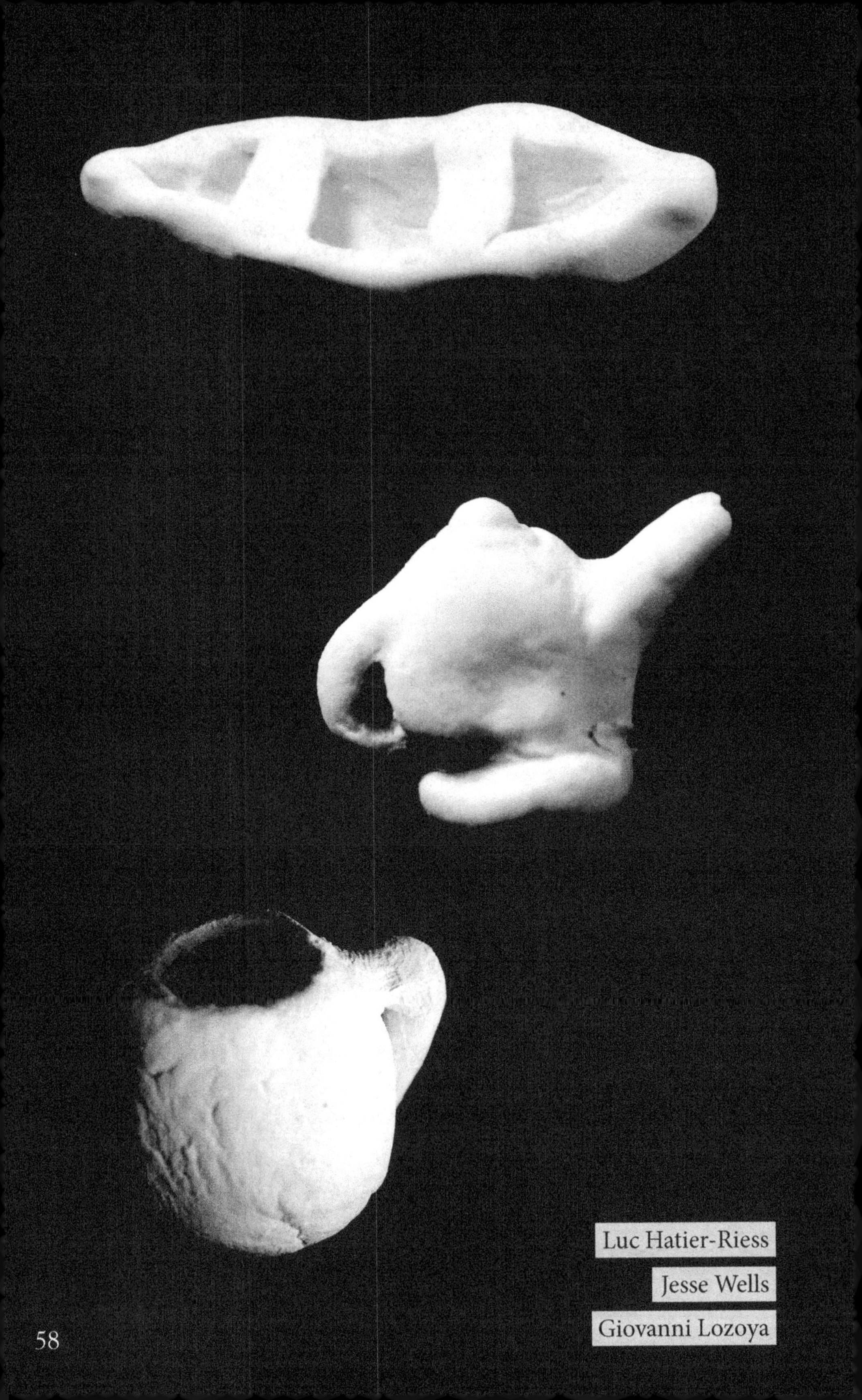

Luc Hatier-Riess

Jesse Wells

Giovanni Lozoya

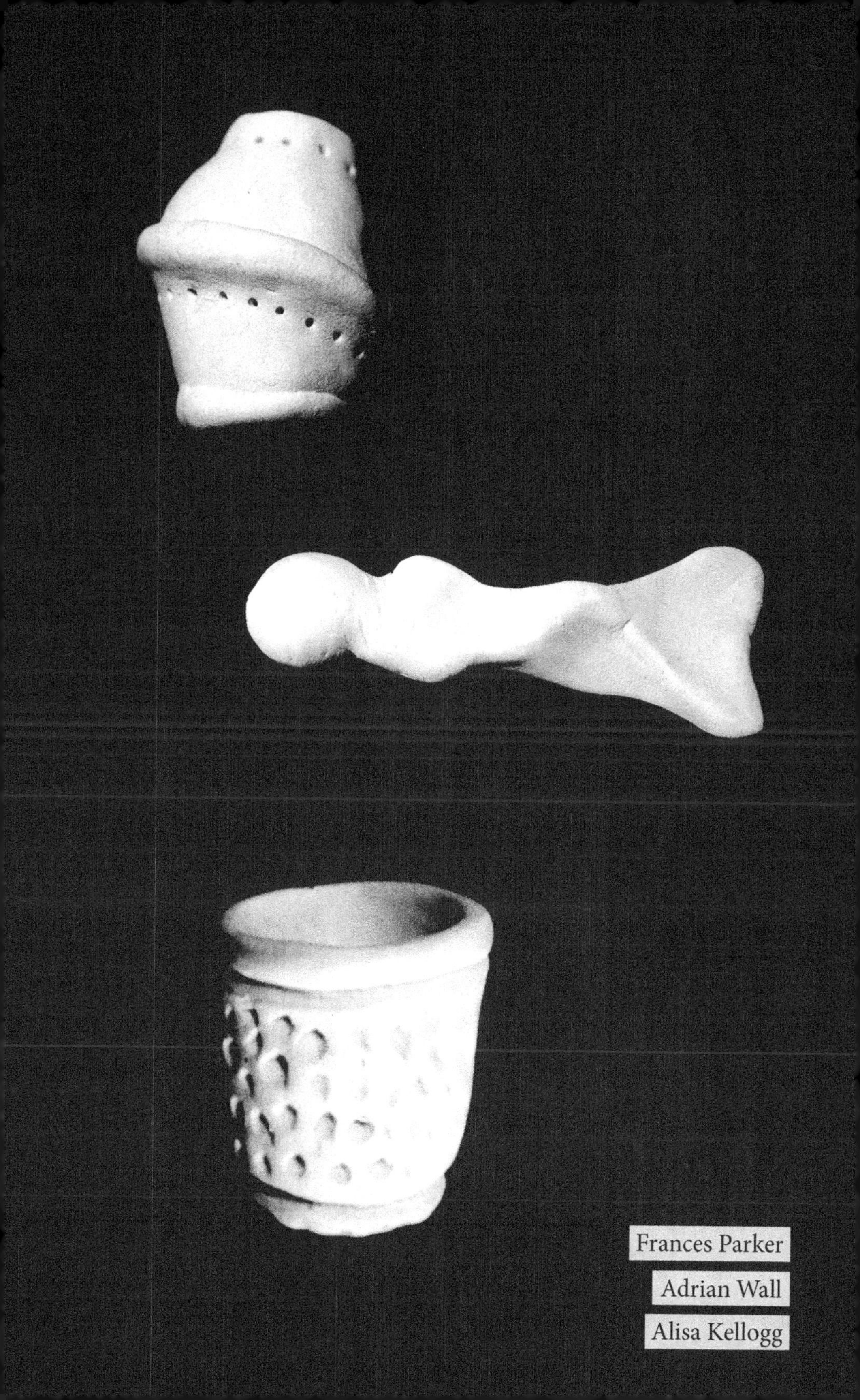

Frances Parker

Adrian Wall

Alisa Kellogg

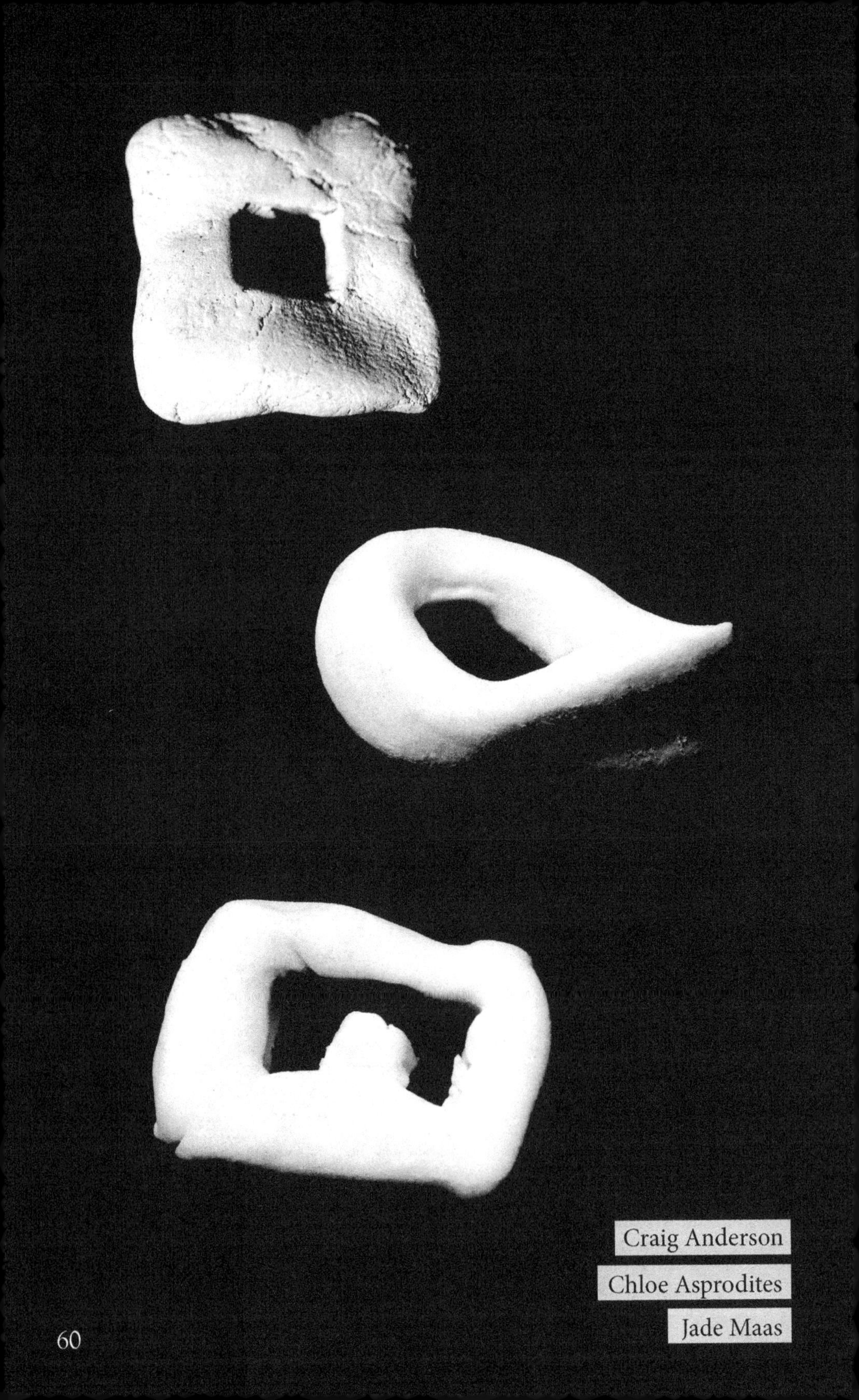

Craig Anderson

Chloe Asprodites

Jade Maas

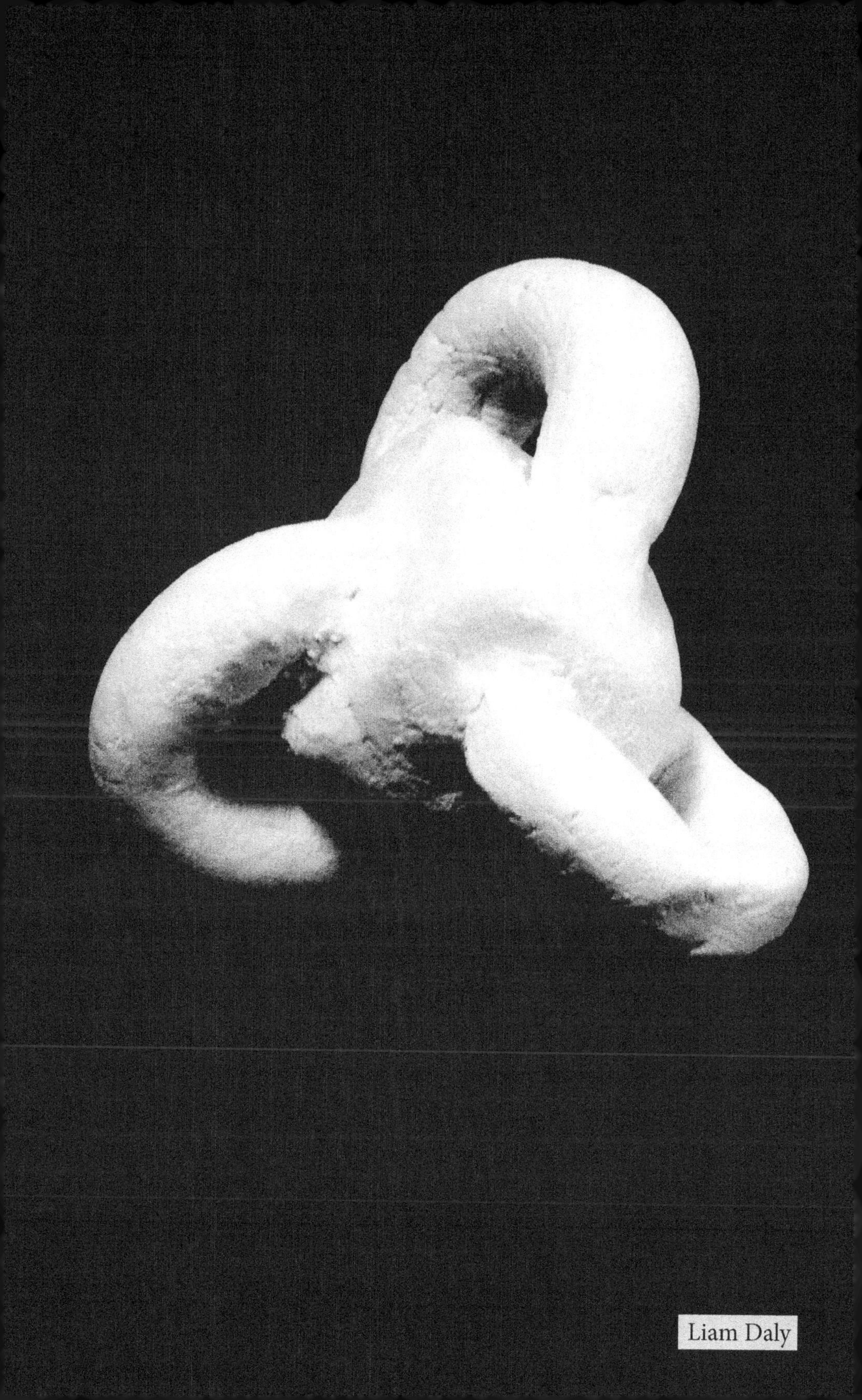

Liam Daly

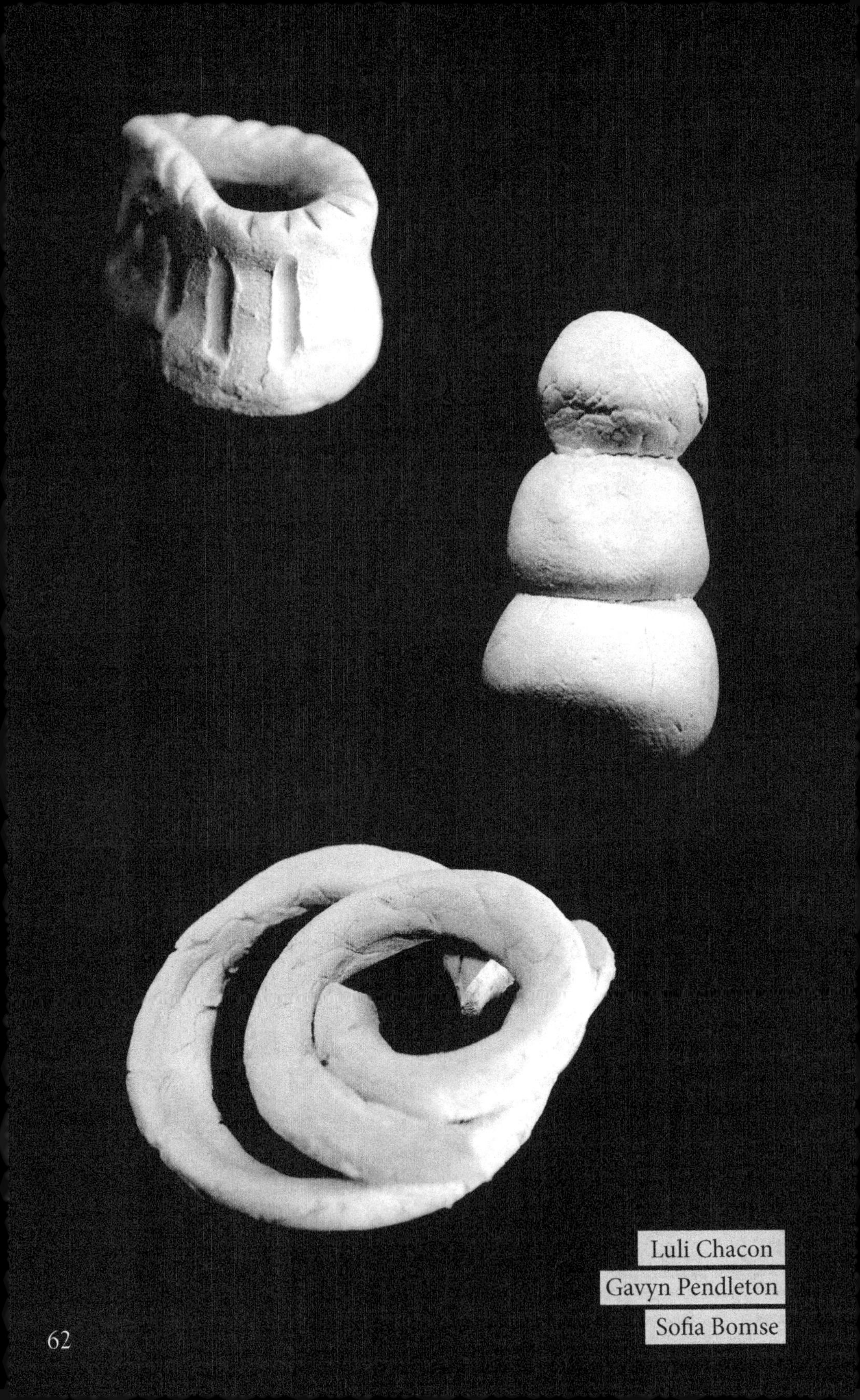

Luli Chacon

Gavyn Pendleton

Sofia Bomse

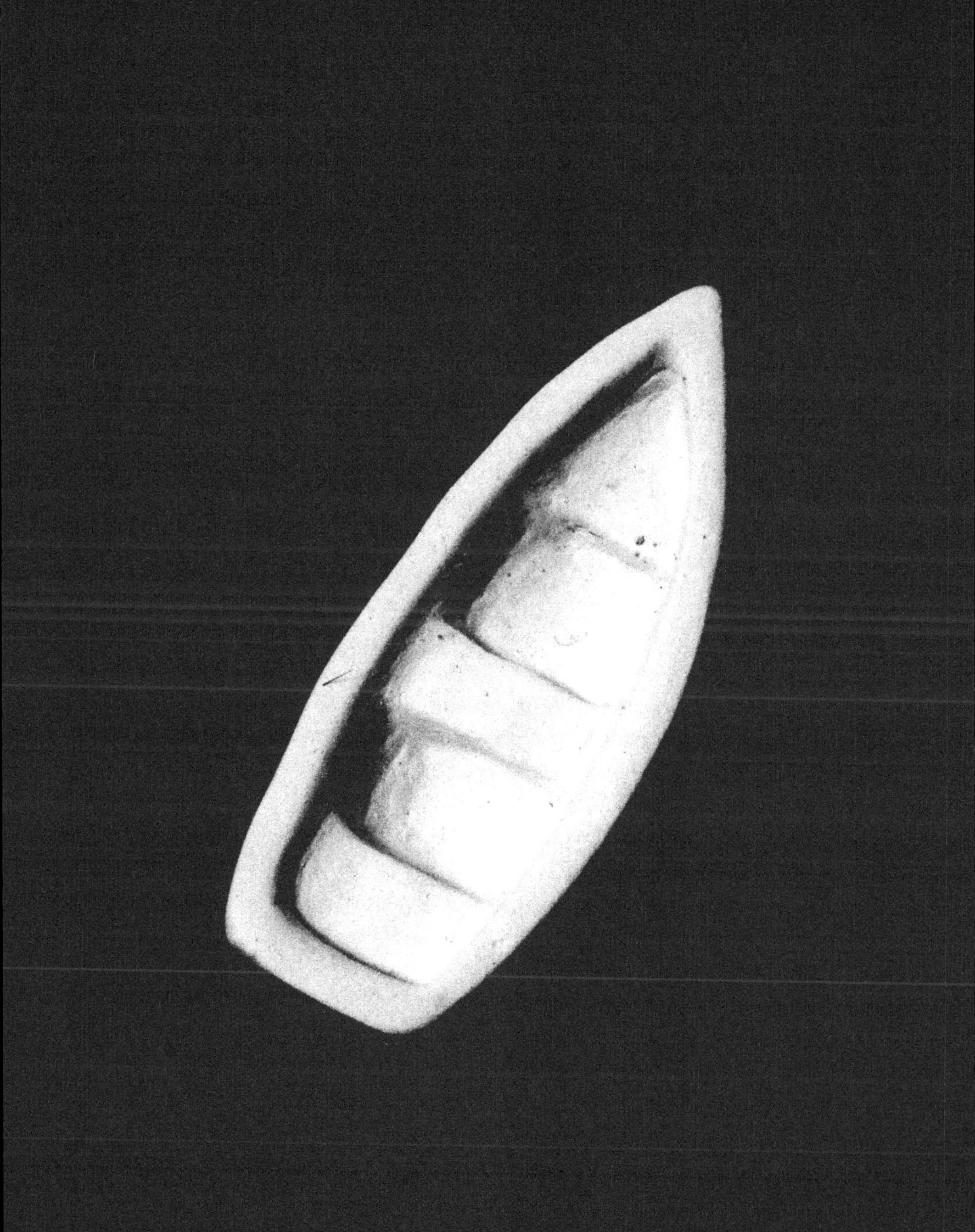

Dana Chodzko

Be as a Fresh Baked Loaf of Bread

Consider the loaf
rising, browning in the heat
as it bakes.

Consider each footstep
rising, falling in the snow
as you walk home.

Consider the dark muck of frozen soil
below a field of red winter wheat.

Consider the farmer, growing and harvesting
the baker, grinding and kneading
your lover, your friend, cutting and buttering
your mother, knitting and napping.

Consider also the hungry and the lonely,
the food line at the local shelter,
the fast-talking saleswoman
making her phone pitch on Christmas Eve.

Consider wolves and prisoners,
the boundaries of their knowledge,
and your own limited time
walking on this great blue earth
inhaling fragrant piñon
burning bright in the kiva fireplaces of Santa Fe.

Then sit at your kitchen table,
take a bite and be happy.

Be as bread, as tender and warm
as you want your home,
your family, your community,
the whole world to be.

-Ann Filemyr

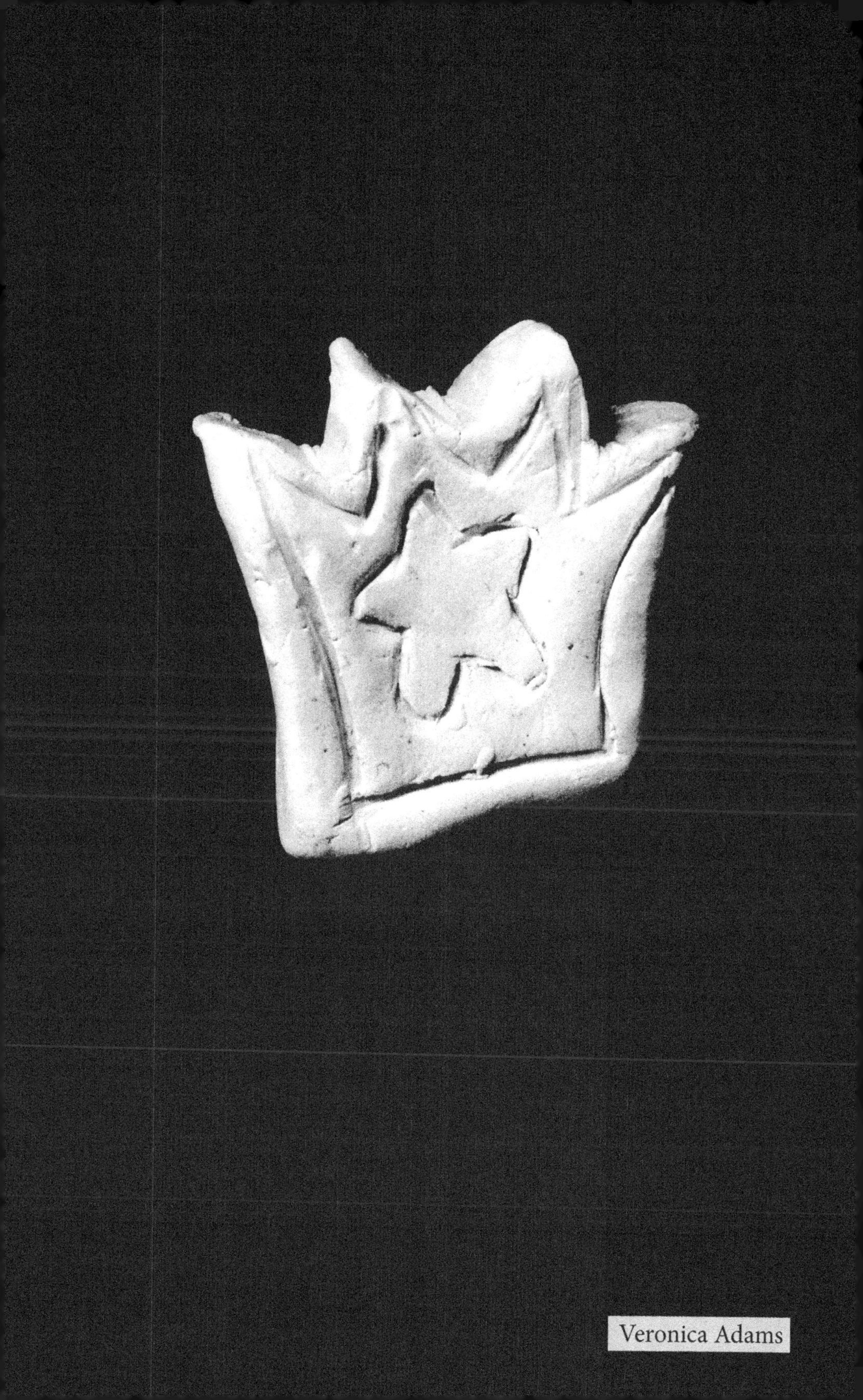

Veronica Adams

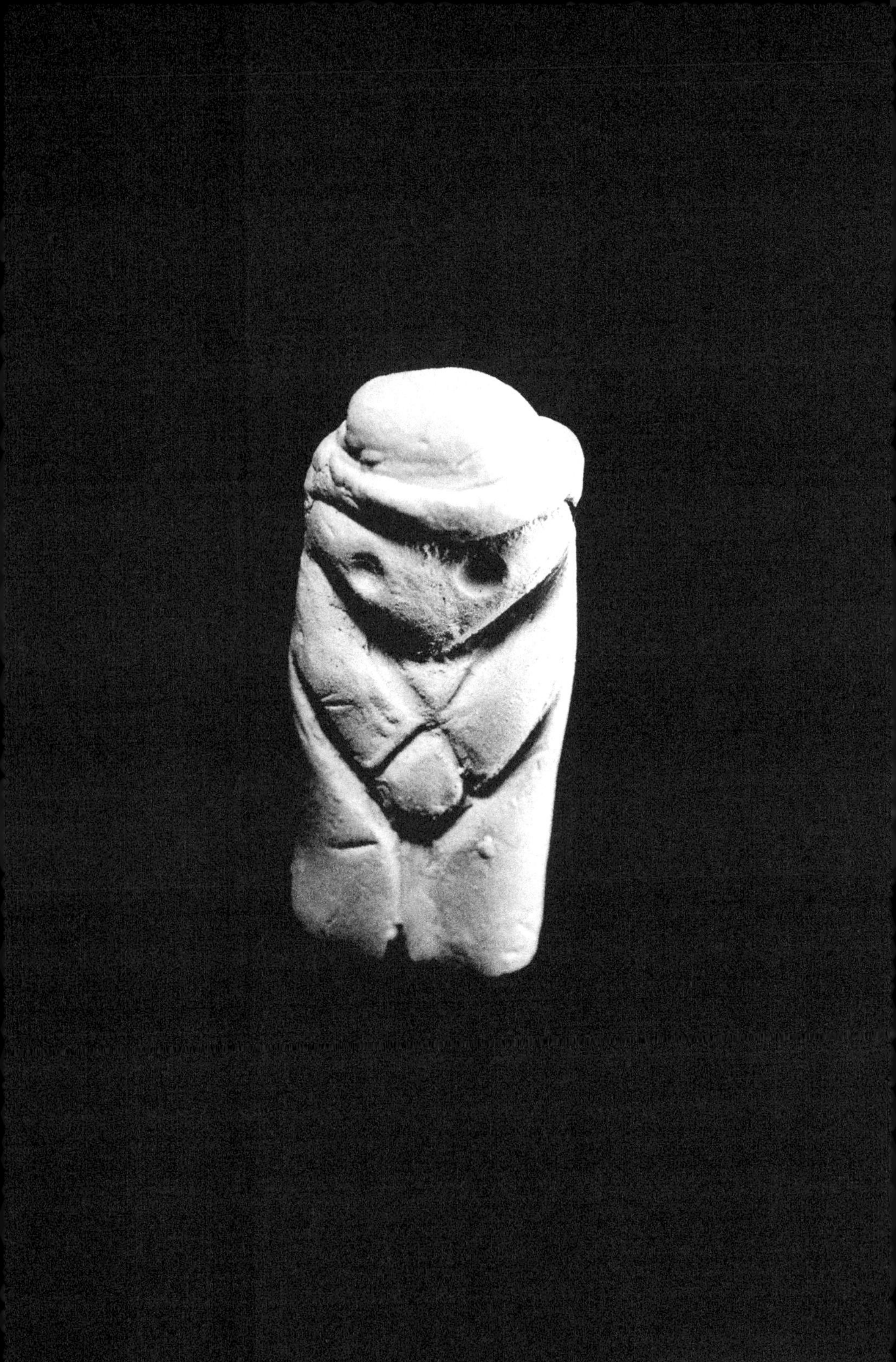

Mildred Farris

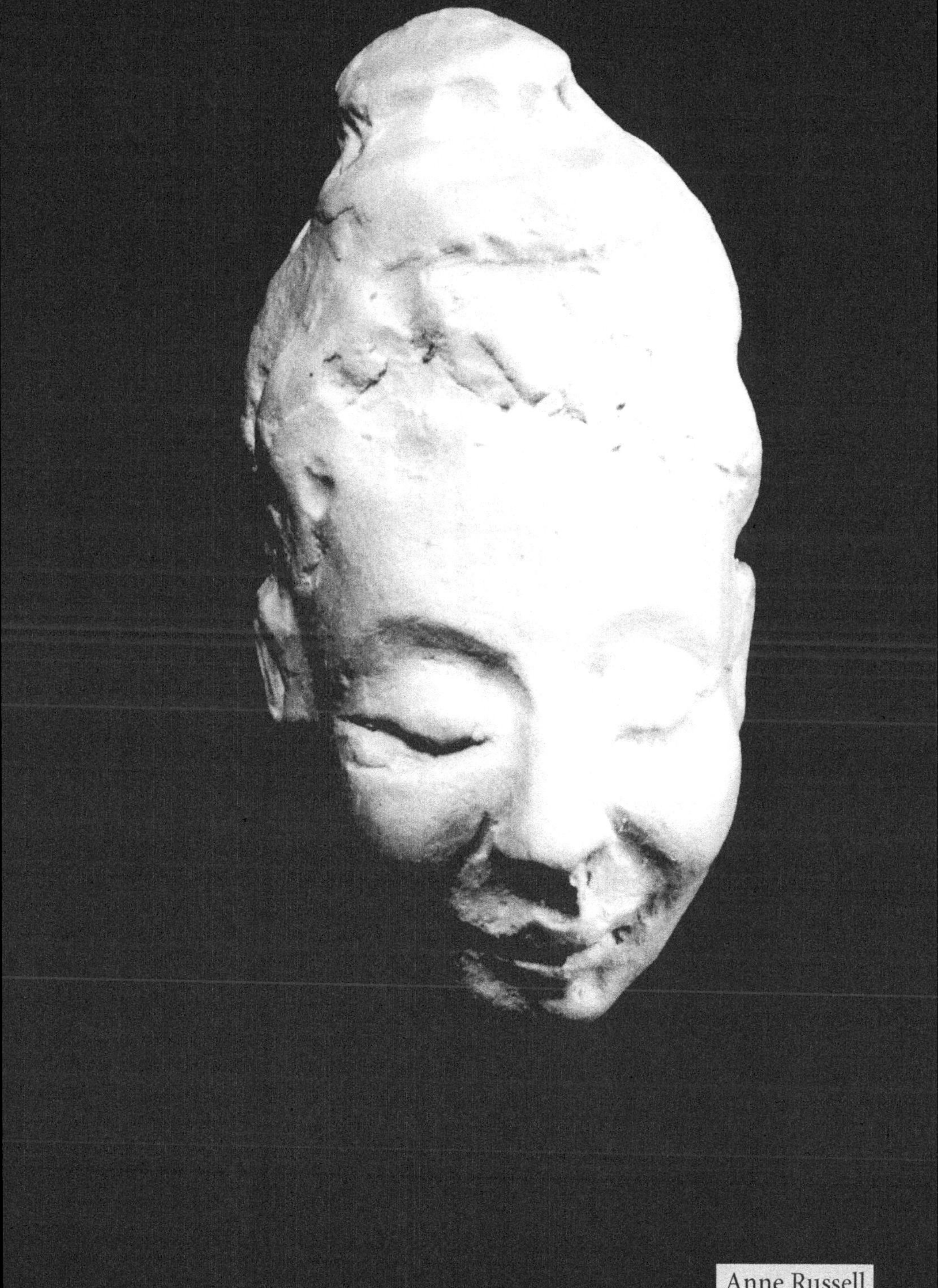

Anne Russell

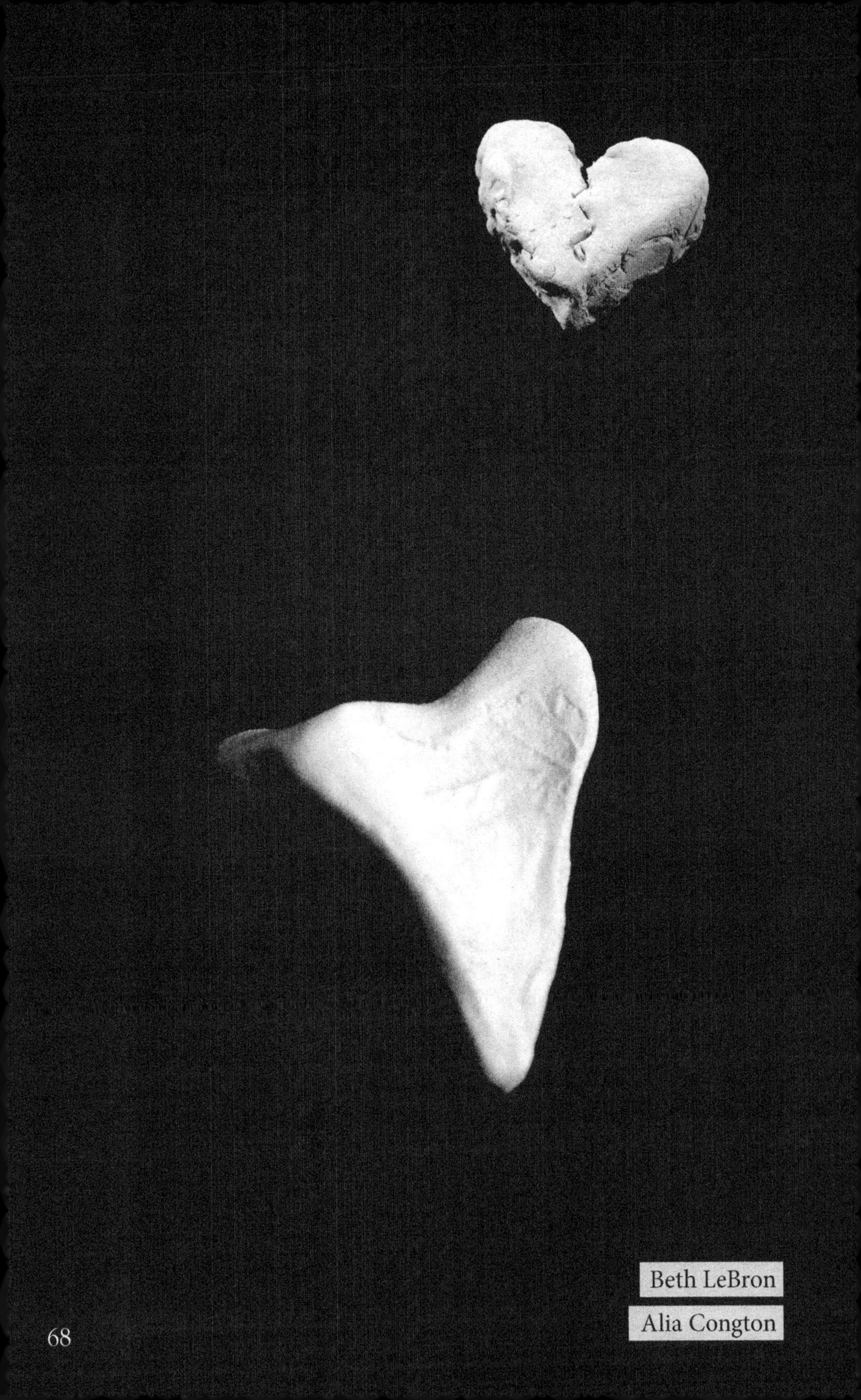

Beth LeBron

Alia Congton

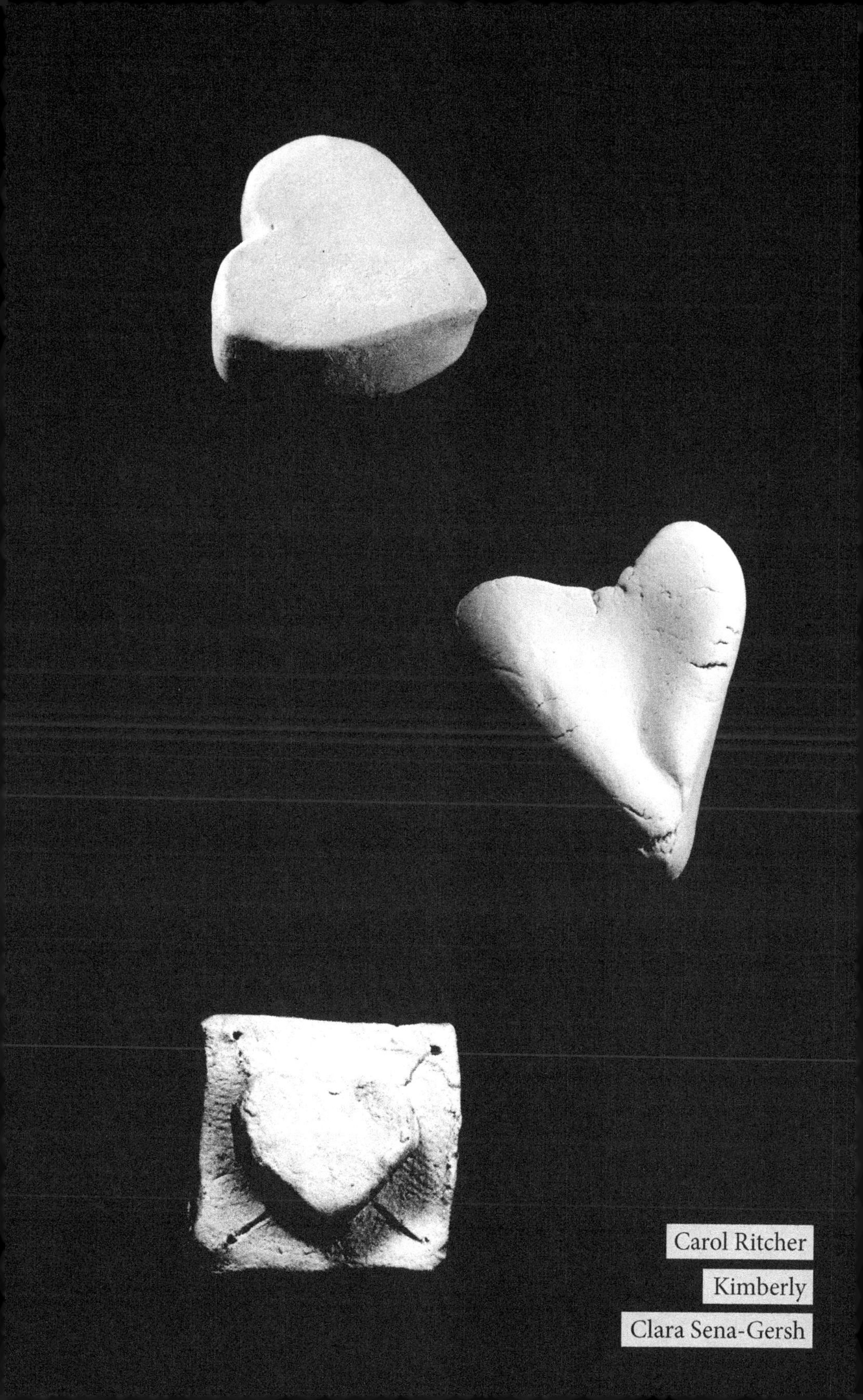

Carol Ritcher

Kimberly

Clara Sena-Gersh

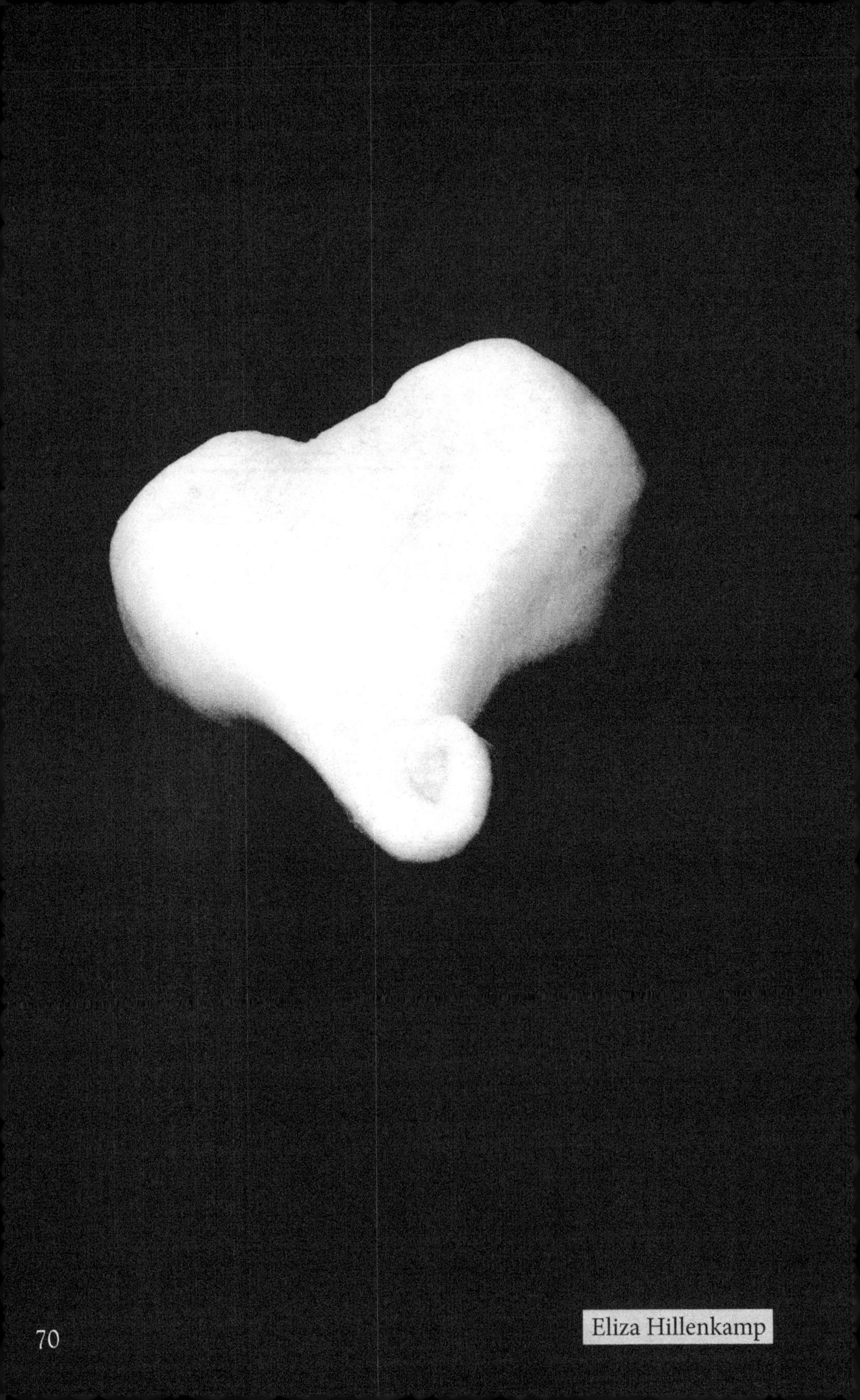

Eliza Hillenkamp

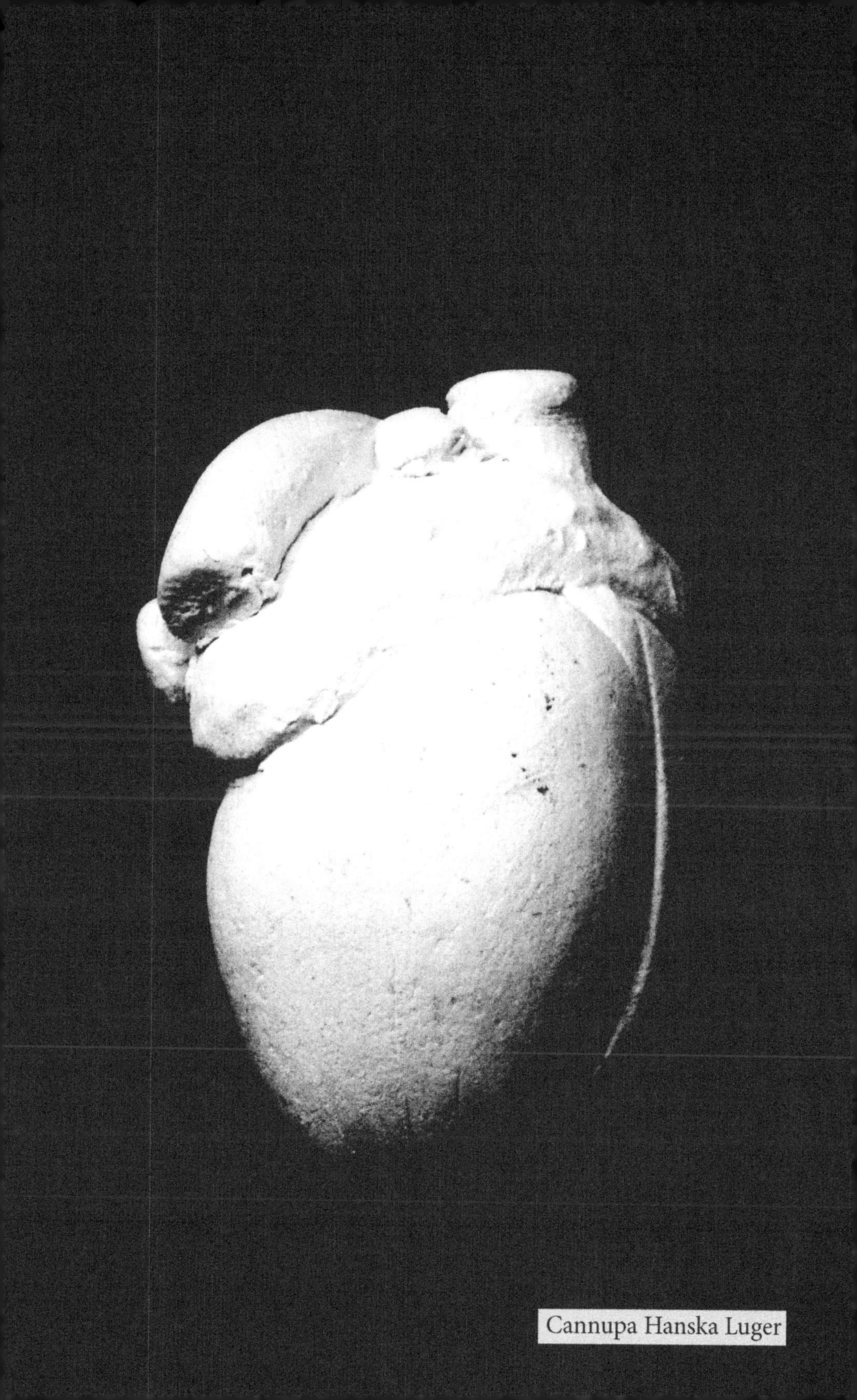

Cannupa Hanska Luger

BREAD is LIFE

Nourishment.

The making of bread represents primal, tribal urges to sustain and satisfy.

The Royal Bread Project potentially nurtures the body and soul, the heart and spirit, symbolically.

The project denotes age-old endeavors, celebrating the essential and ritualistic experiences of providing nourishment, hospitality, generosity and the 'hand' made.

It most artfully mixes unexpected creativity into the dough. Originality and invention are offered to creatively feed all who are receptive to the unexpected.

It invites a shared sensual experience for the maker and the audience, a personal opportunity to mark one's own participation as artist, leading to the the discovery of a secreted object through another's investigation.

Bread dough and porcelain clay, primary, seductive materials of undefined sculptural promise, provide the means to explore a parallel, potentially sustaining, tactile experience.

Muse on the power of an intimate object, a tiny, unidentified form secreted in the bread and then in one's palm. The as-yet undiscovered, unseen, minute forms hold limitless possibilities.

The results at their best are intimate tokens of remembrance, unexpected, hand scale objects which identify and mark this unique communal occasion.

The random experience may be surprisingly meaningful.

These objects could become important personal tokens and treasured amulets- modest keepsakes to memorialize this exceptional, thoughtful, creative project.

Anticipate the occasion, both the domestic and the artistic, for what awaits is a heightened, indelible, re"mark"able experience: one in which to participate, observe, share and savor!

Thank you for delicious expectations.

-Gail M. Brown

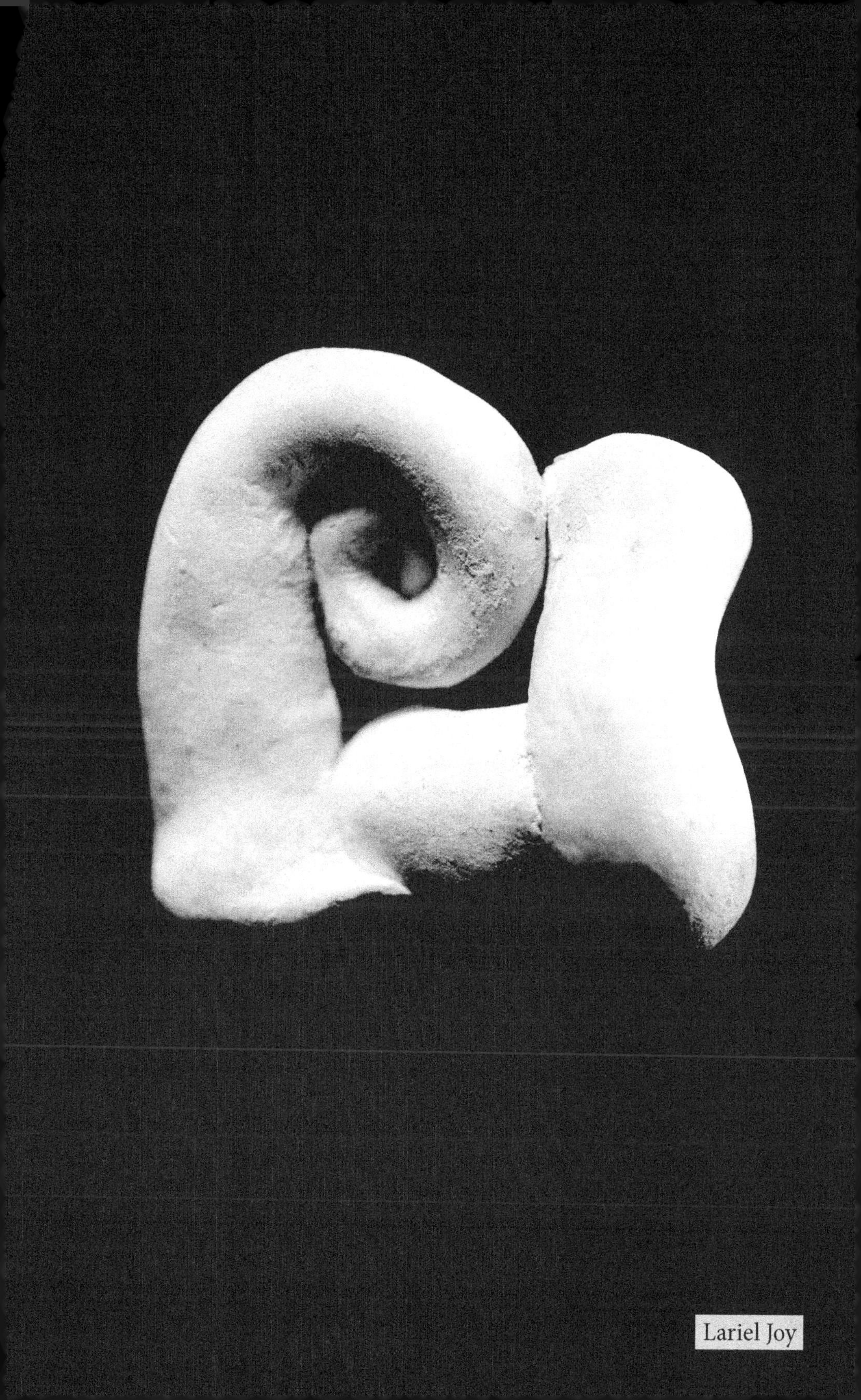

Lariel Joy

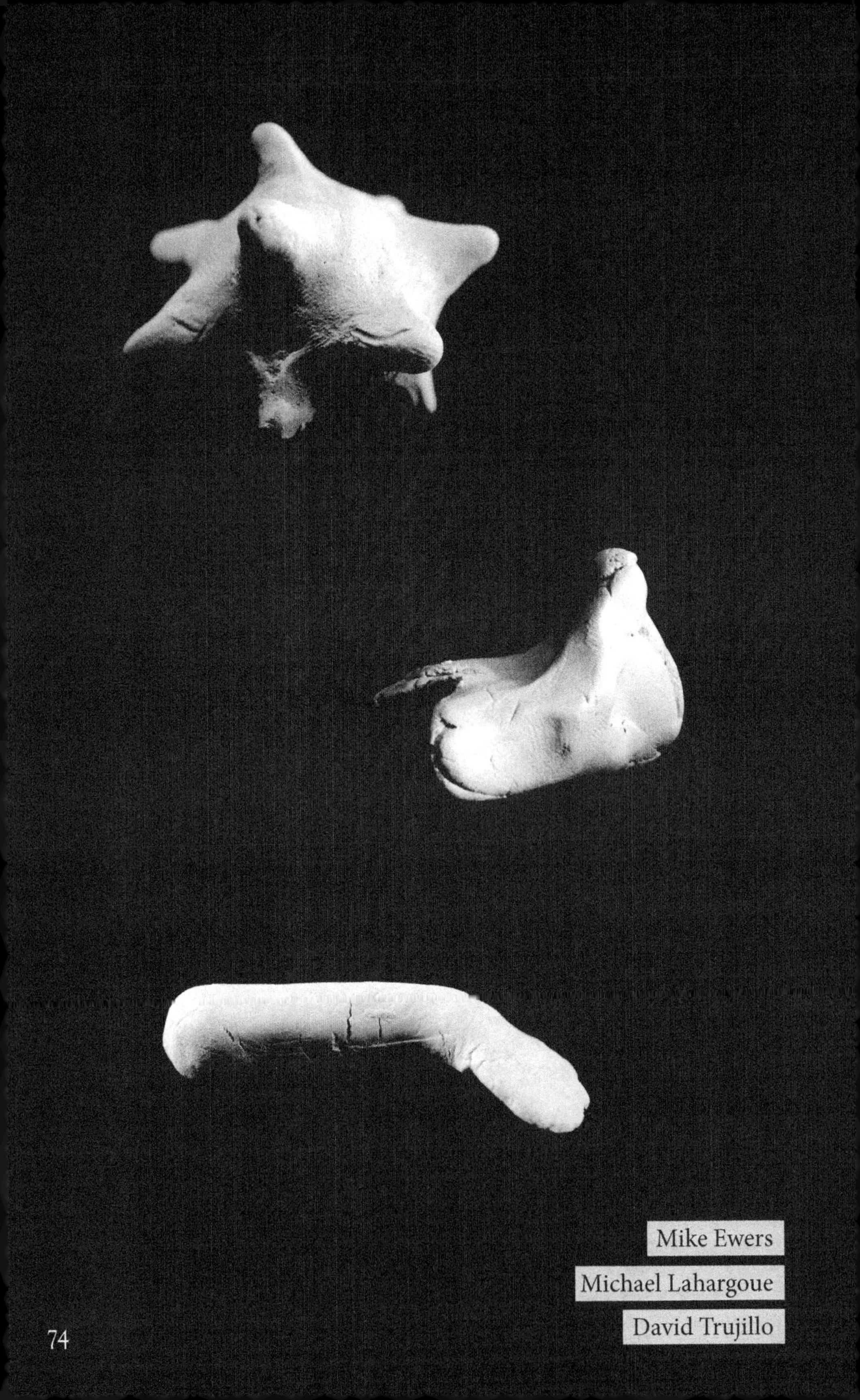

Mike Ewers

Michael Lahargoue

David Trujillo

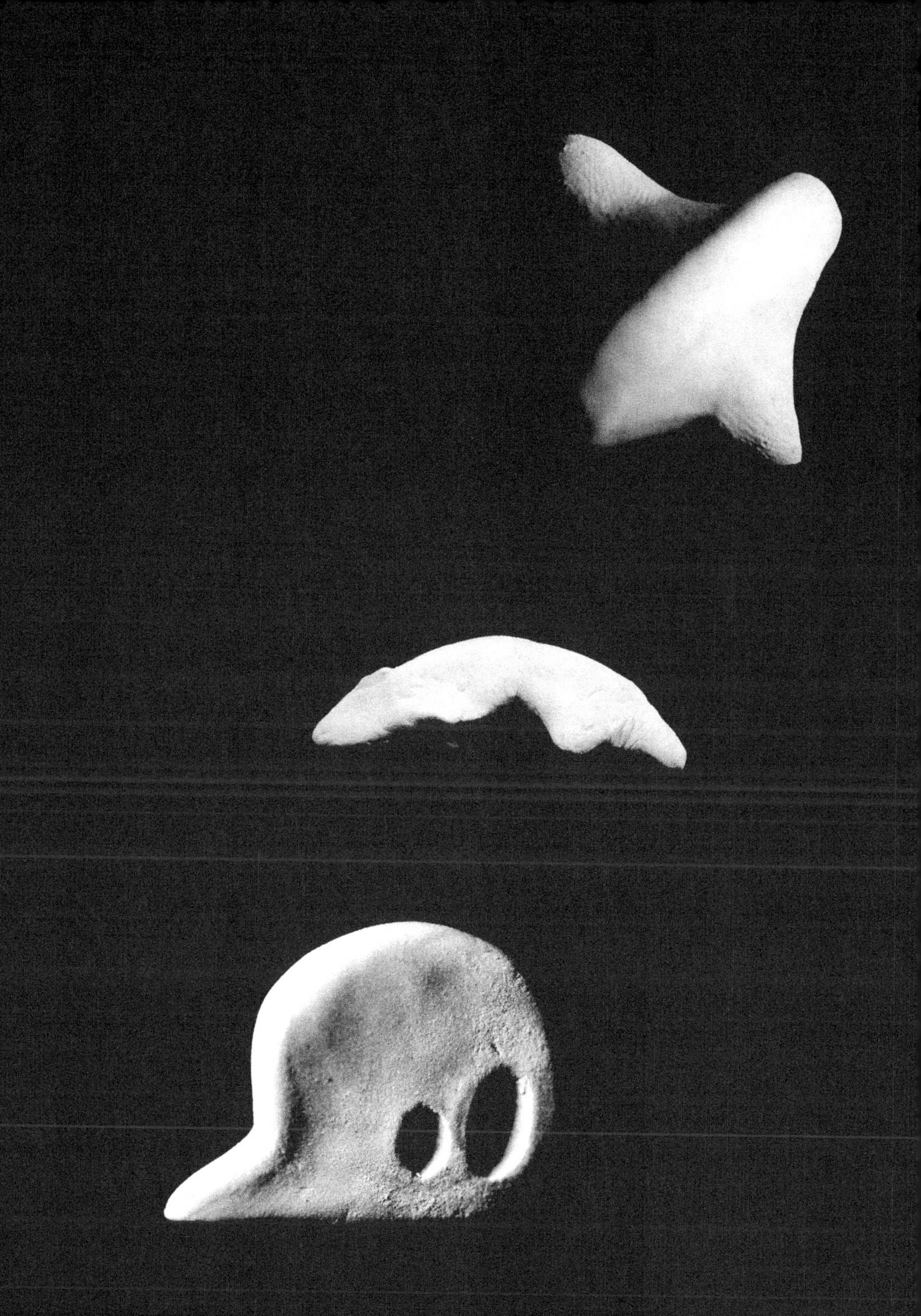

Mary Grace Kelley

Adam John Melk

Matt Donovan

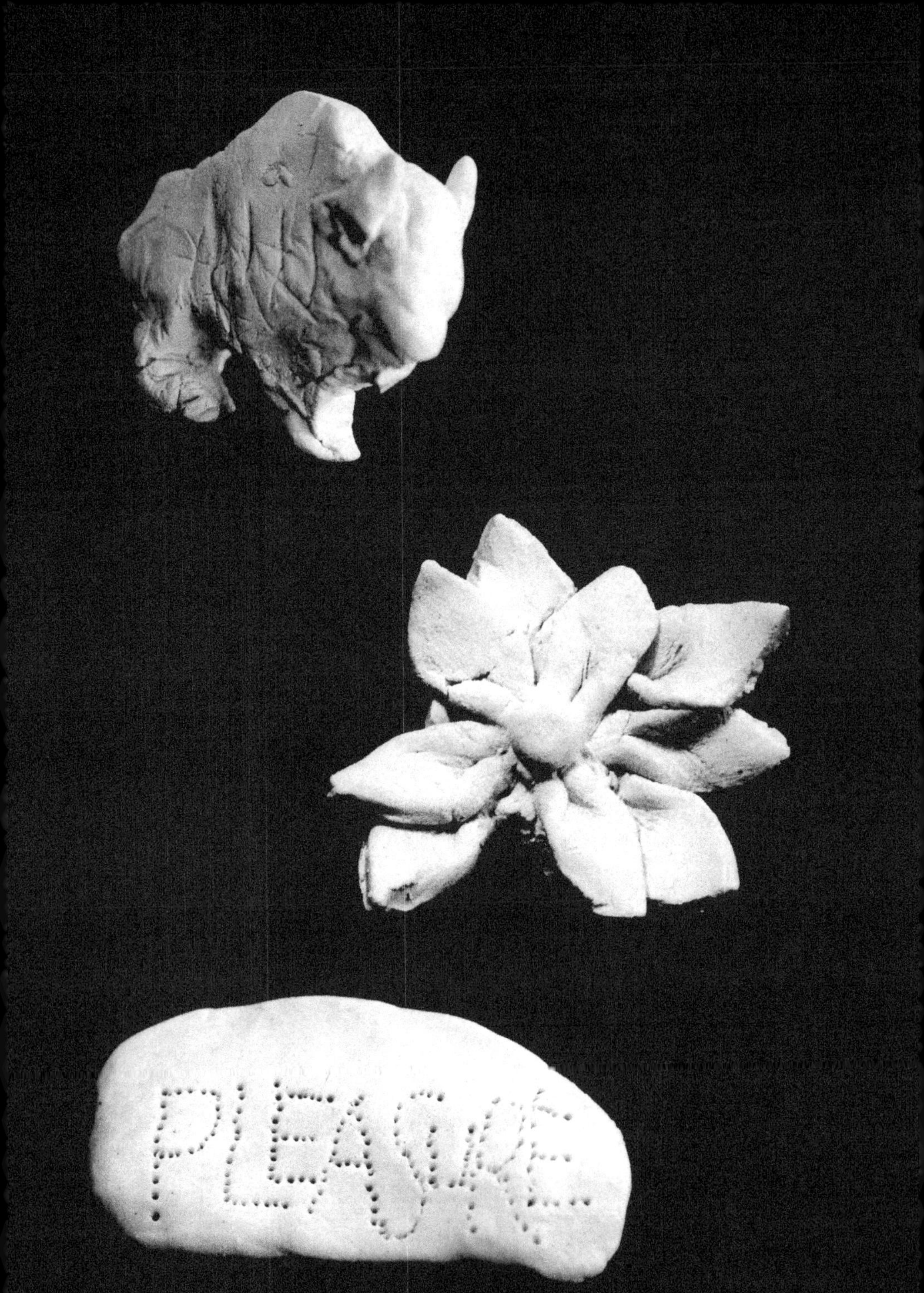

Yvette Tapp
Isabelle Ruesch
Conrad Skinner

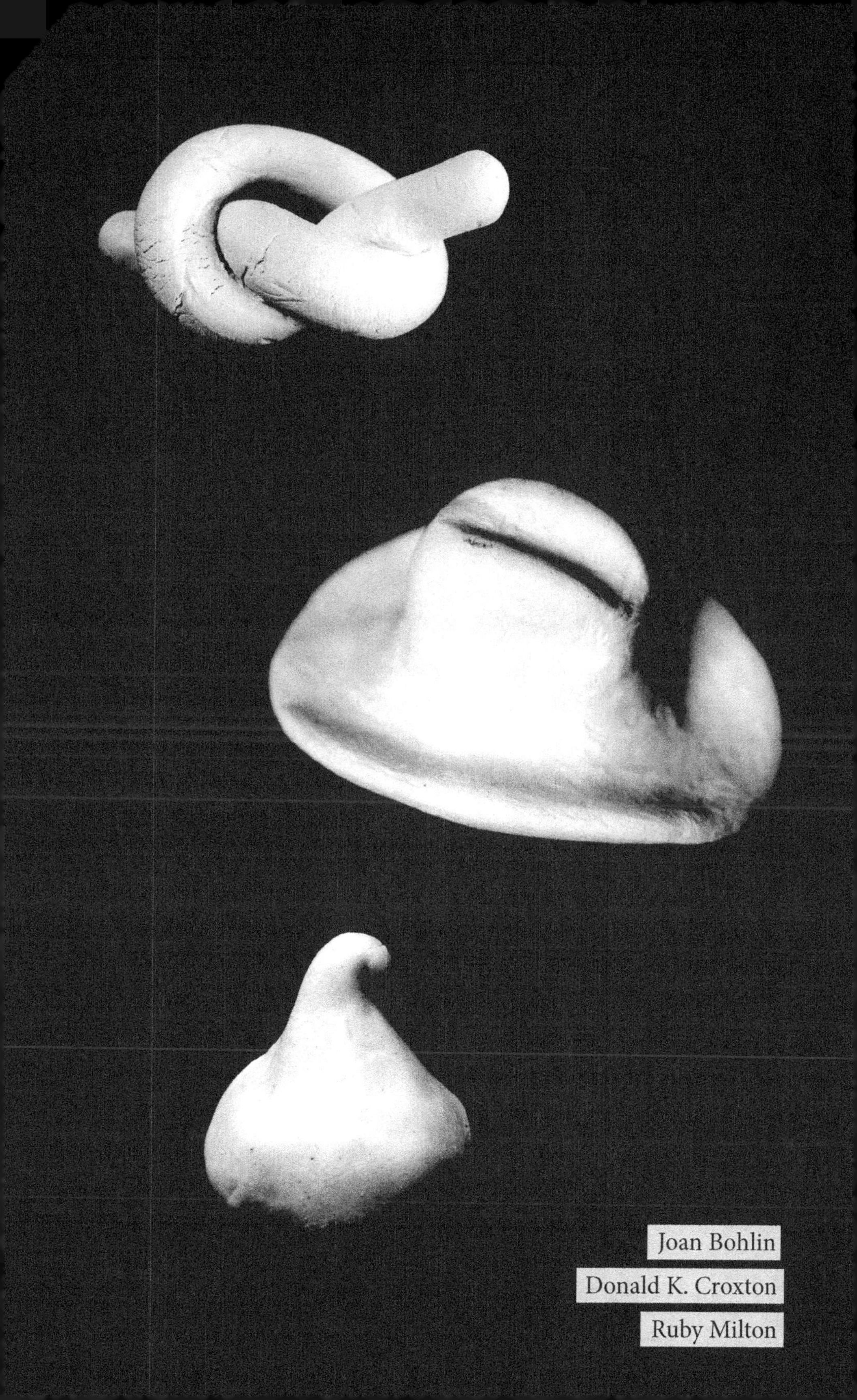
Joan Bohlin
Donald K. Croxton
Ruby Milton

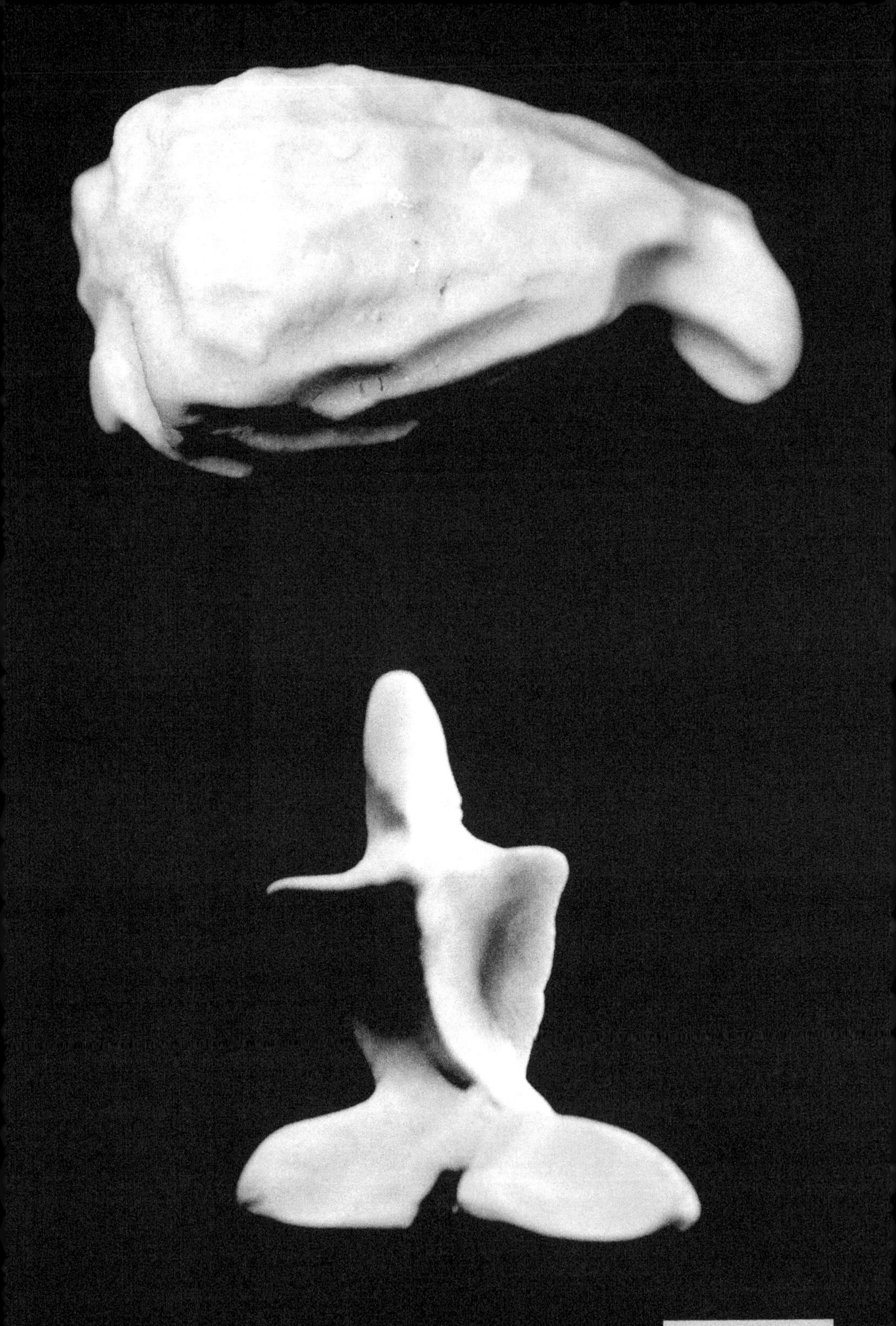

Linda Oldham

Sara Dawes

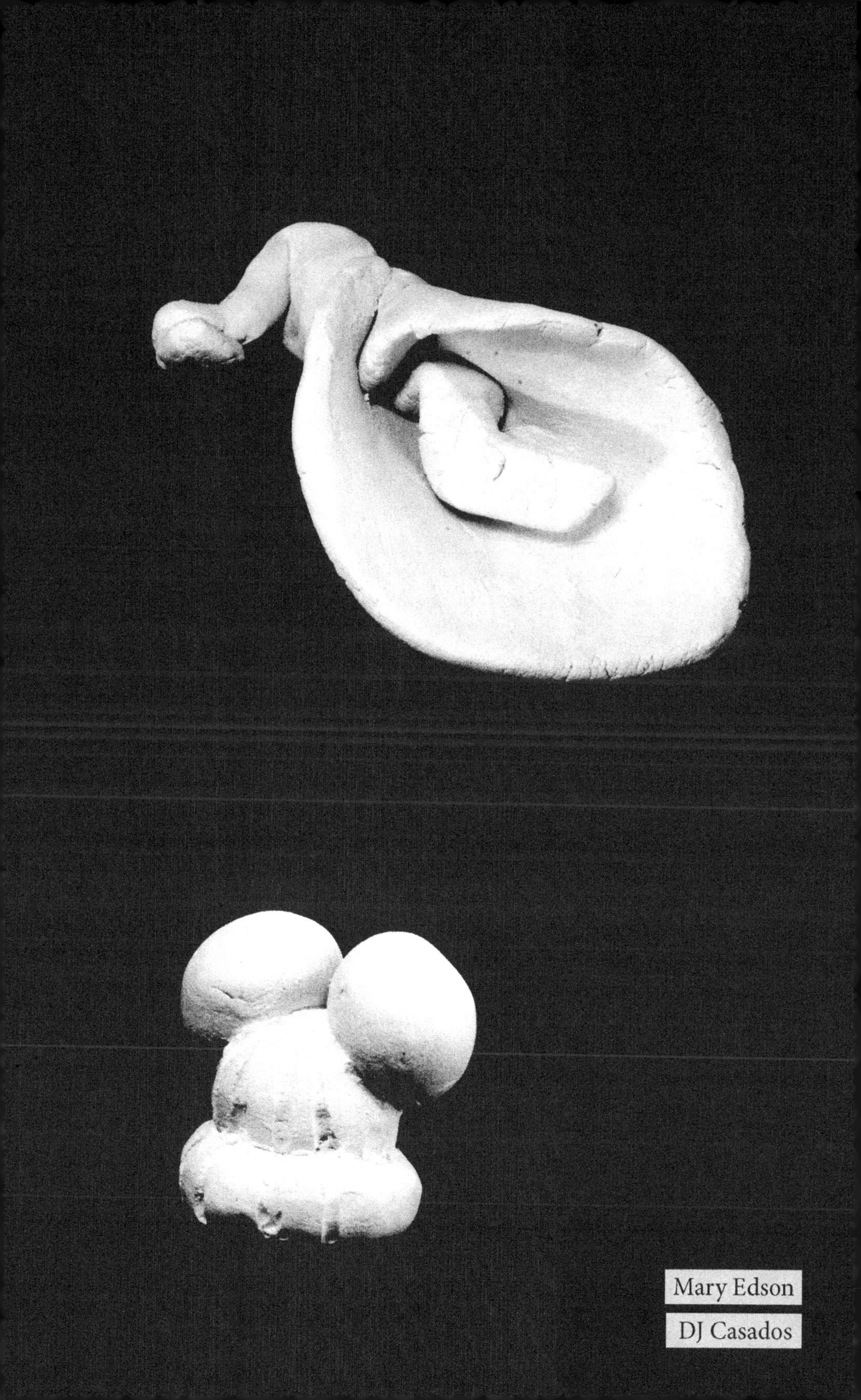

Mary Edson

DJ Casados

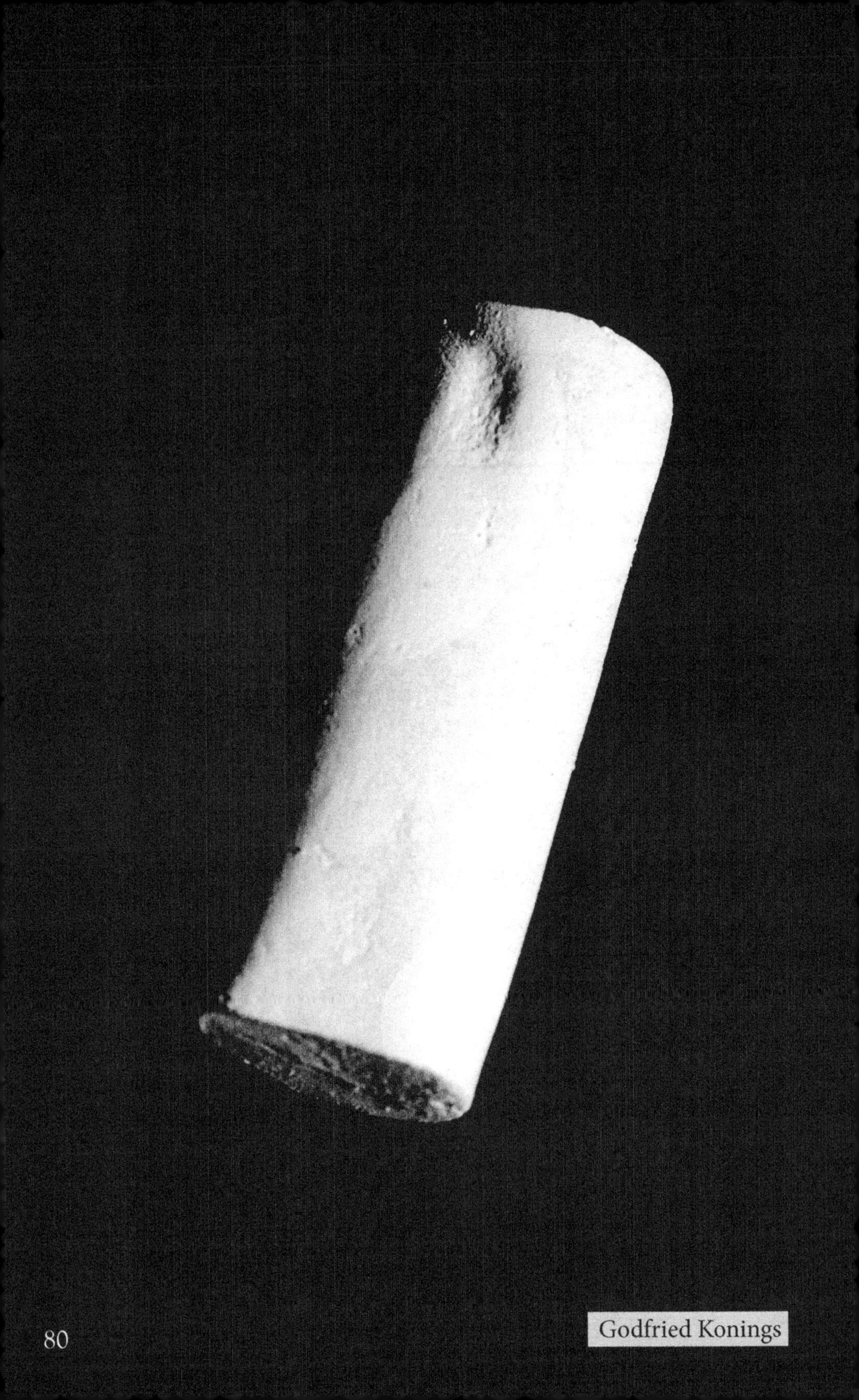

Godfried Konings

Archeological Blessing

Like festive, King Cake in New Orleans
— a holy bread hiding baby Jesus,
cast as the plastic sacrament of fun—
a chance to be taken with a bite.

the holiness of bread
the hominess of bread
the community of art-bread partakers,
relish the hidden blessing.

A secret—until it is quietly located,
and delicately removed, like a lost tooth in the
batter, or
like an archeologist working in South Africa
down, down, down through the tiny seven-inch
diameter hole,
at shoulder level, leading into
a vast 1.9 million-year-old cave—
and locating, for the first time,
the magic left by the hominids.

-Sally Blakemore

Bread provides a commonality across cultures at the table. Whether tortilla, chapati, pizza dough, or one of the ubiquitous varieties of baked bread, everyone loves its place in a meal both as a condiment and as a staple.

May the many forms of bread remind us of how similar we are as humans, just as the many names for the divine allow us to honor it in so many interesting ways.

-Nicolai Bachman

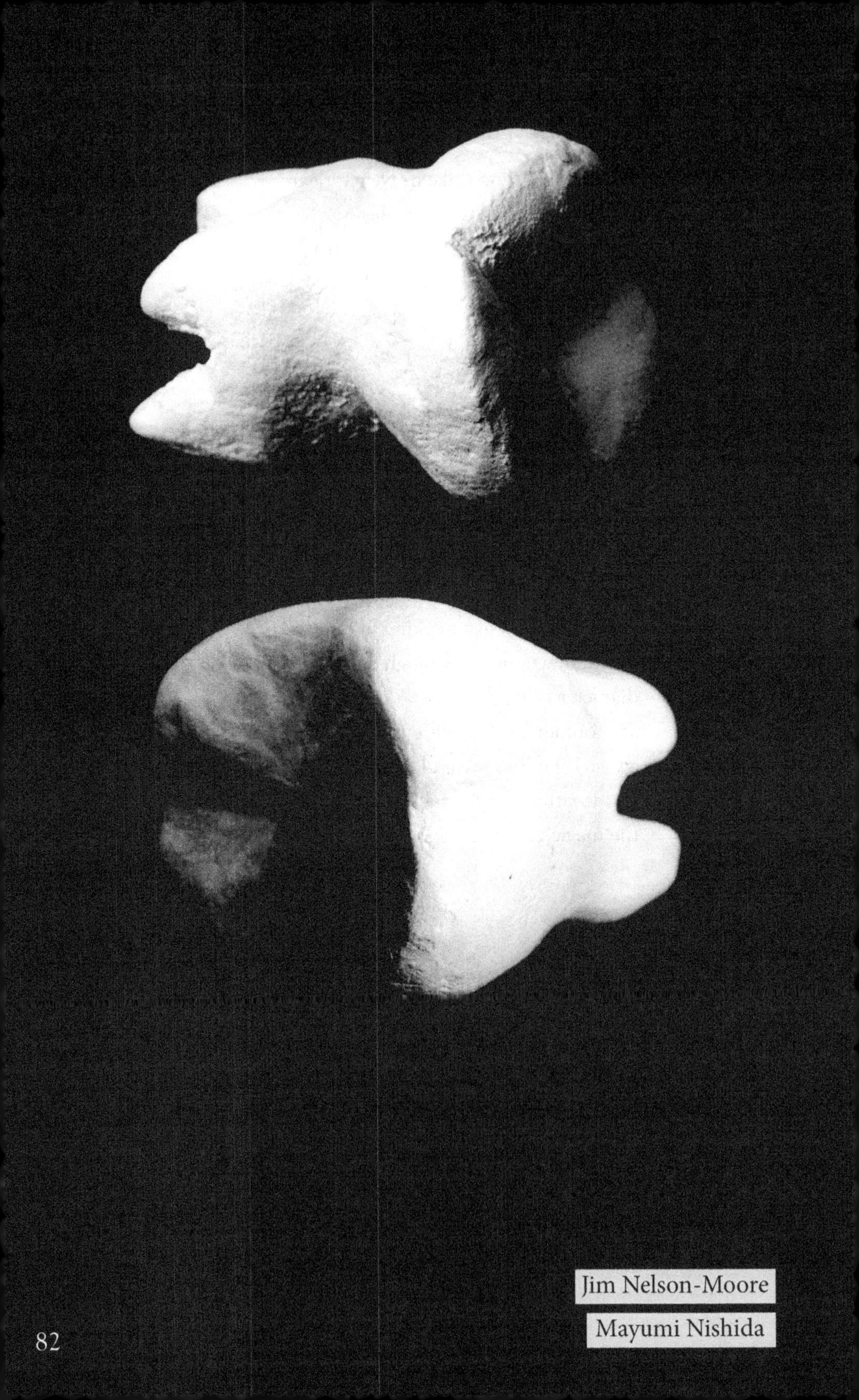

Jim Nelson-Moore

Mayumi Nishida

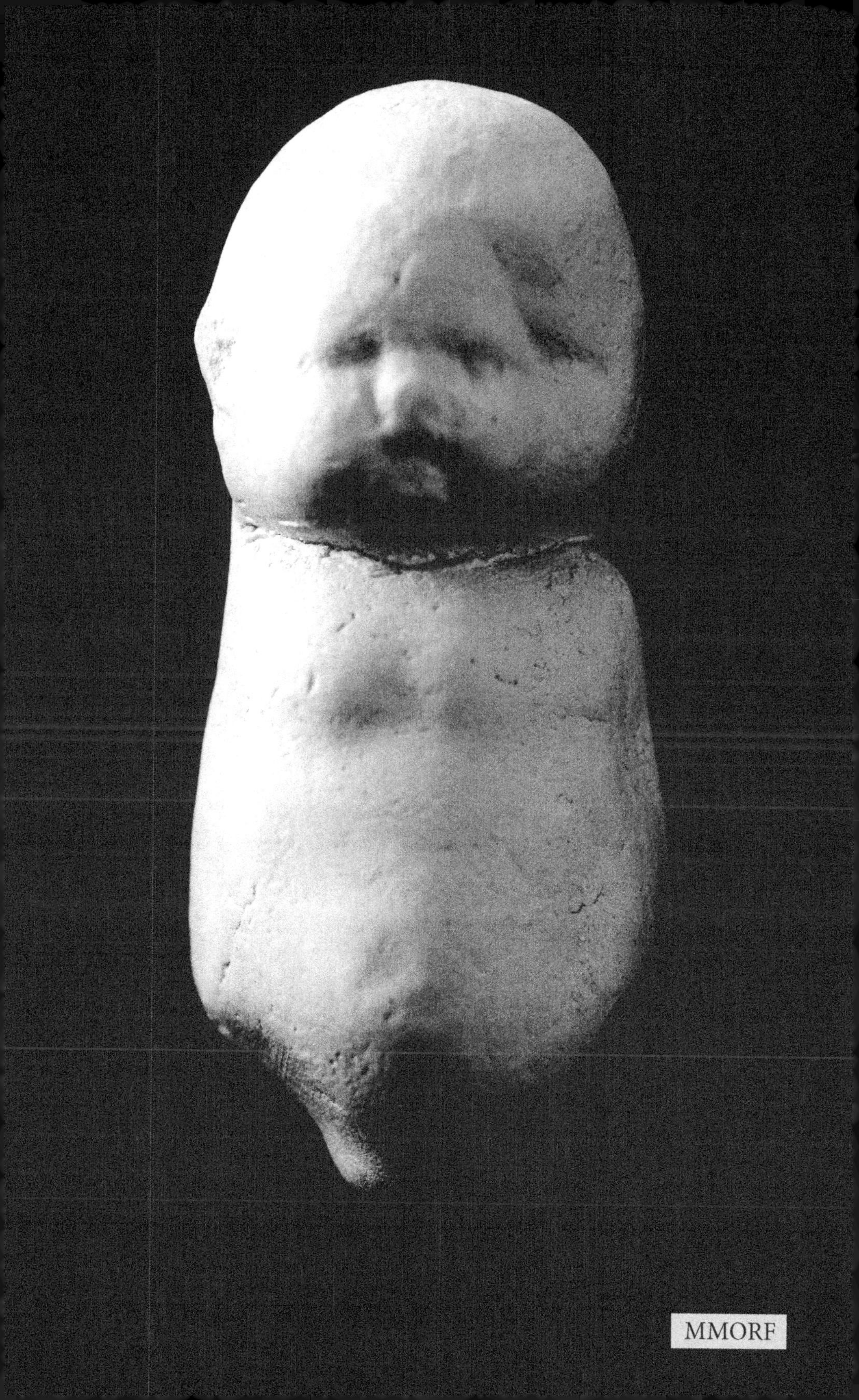
MMORF

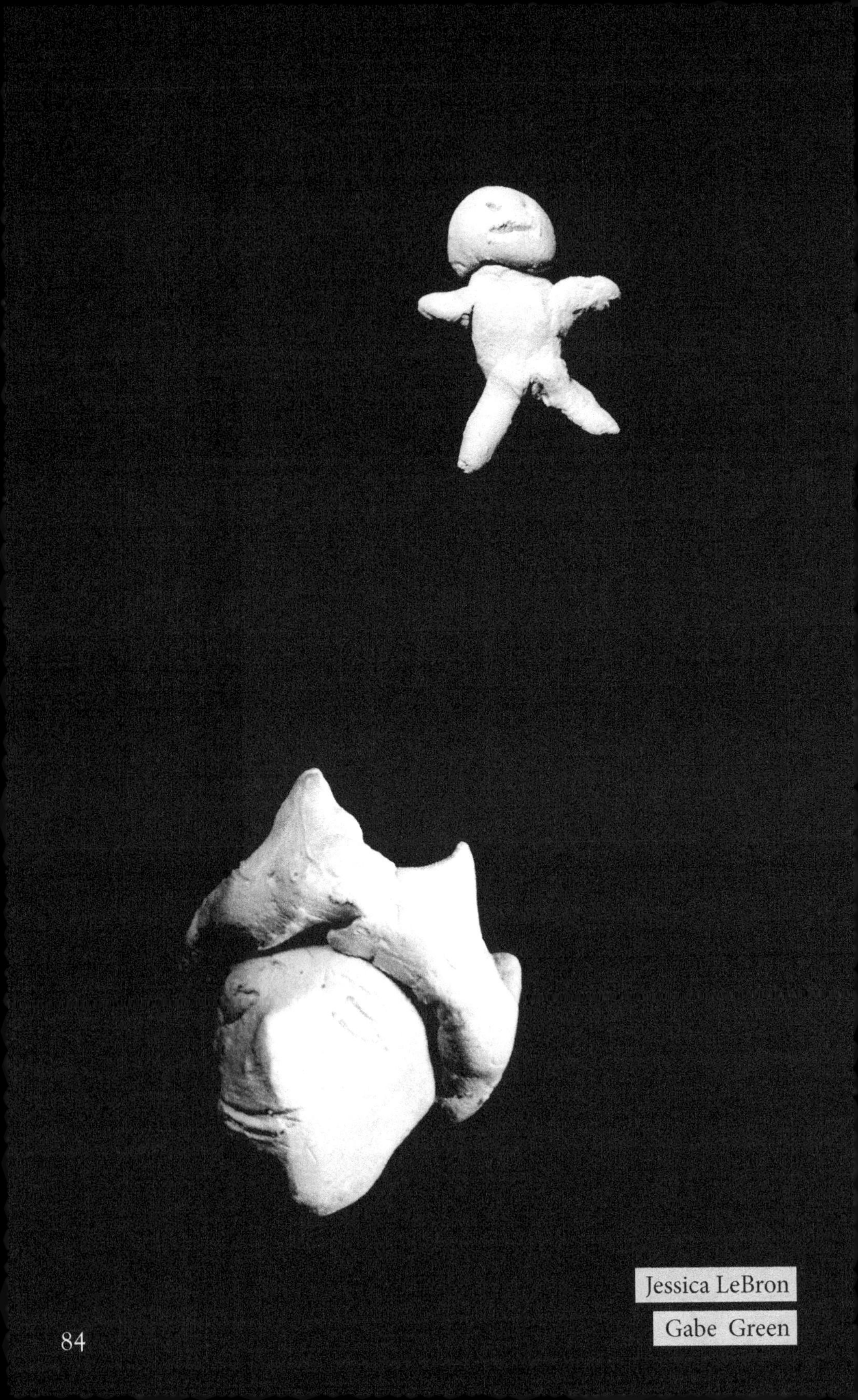

Jessica LeBron

Gabe Green

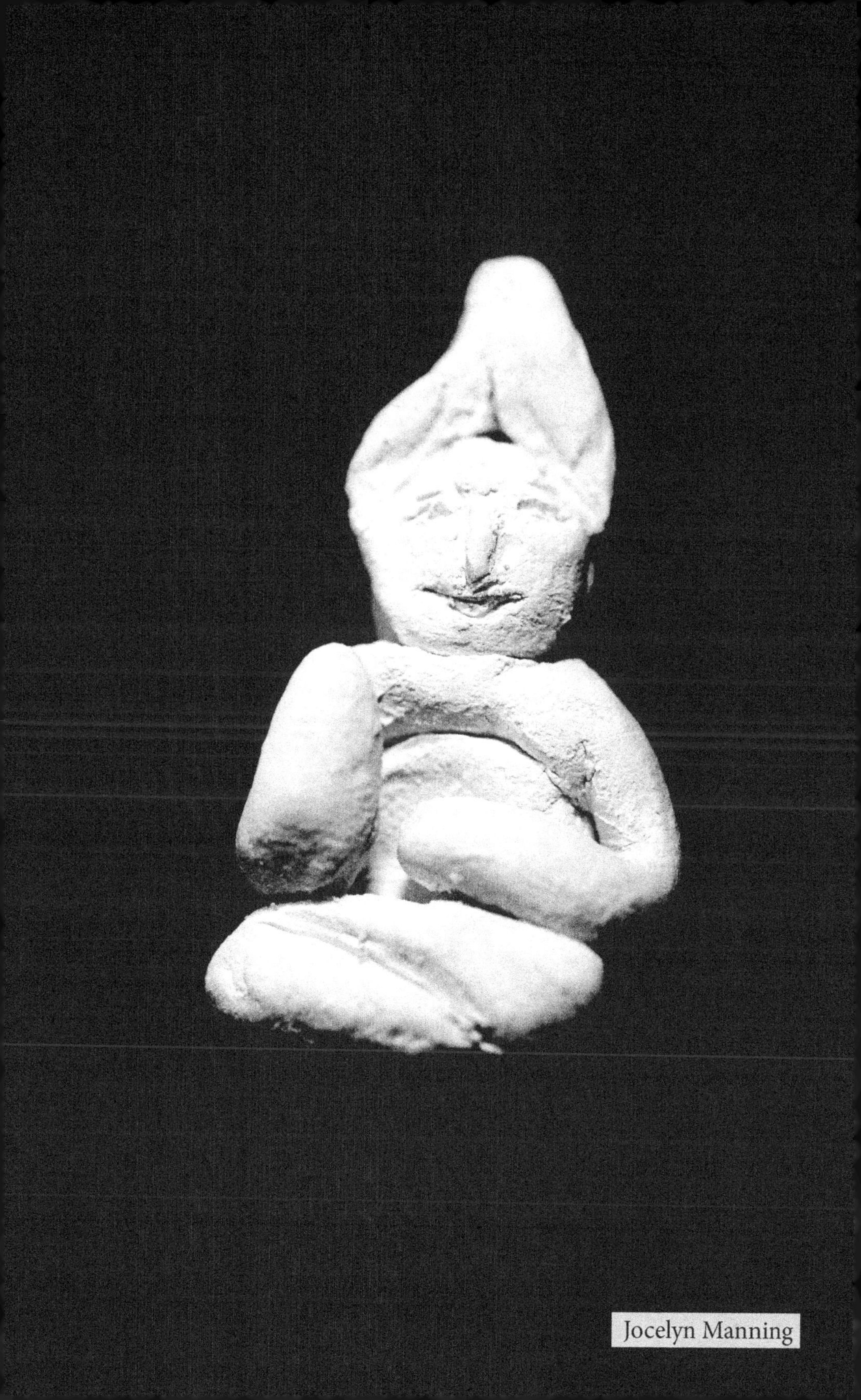

Jocelyn Manning

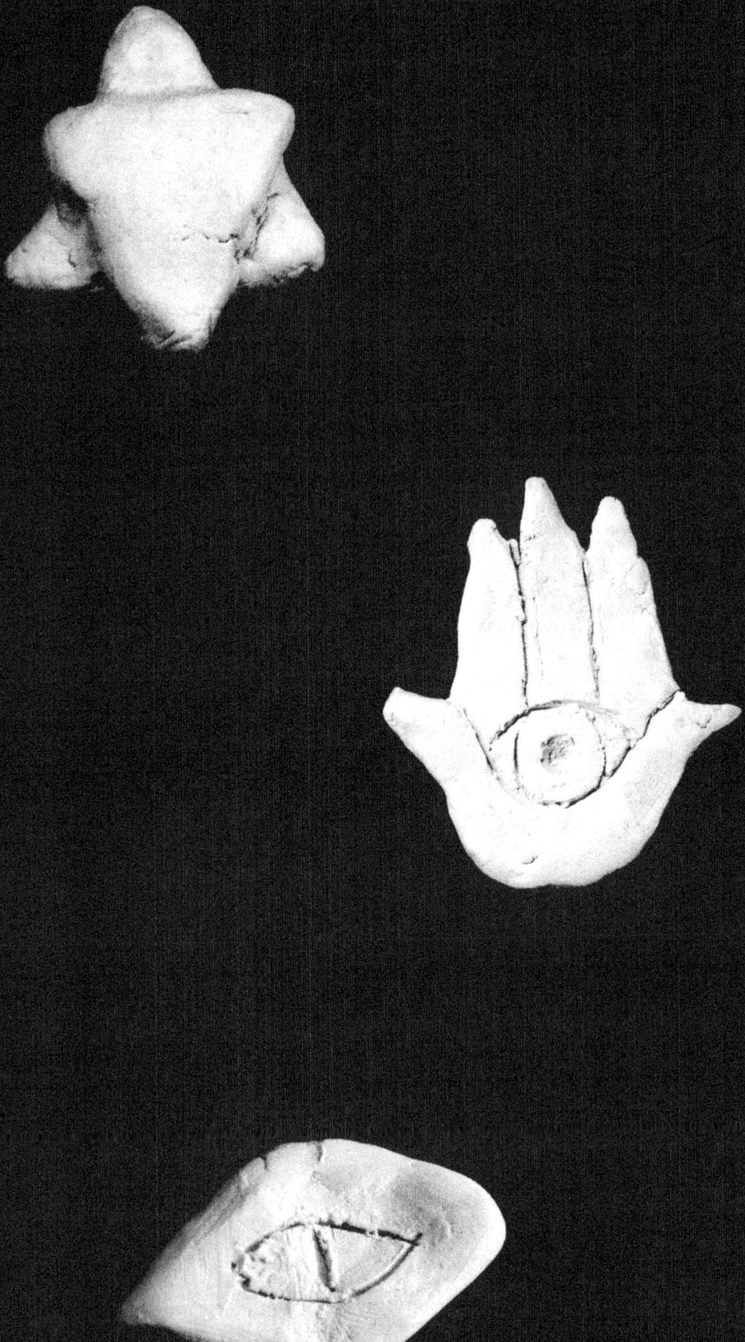

Sarah Sze

Virginia Adams

Max Spatz

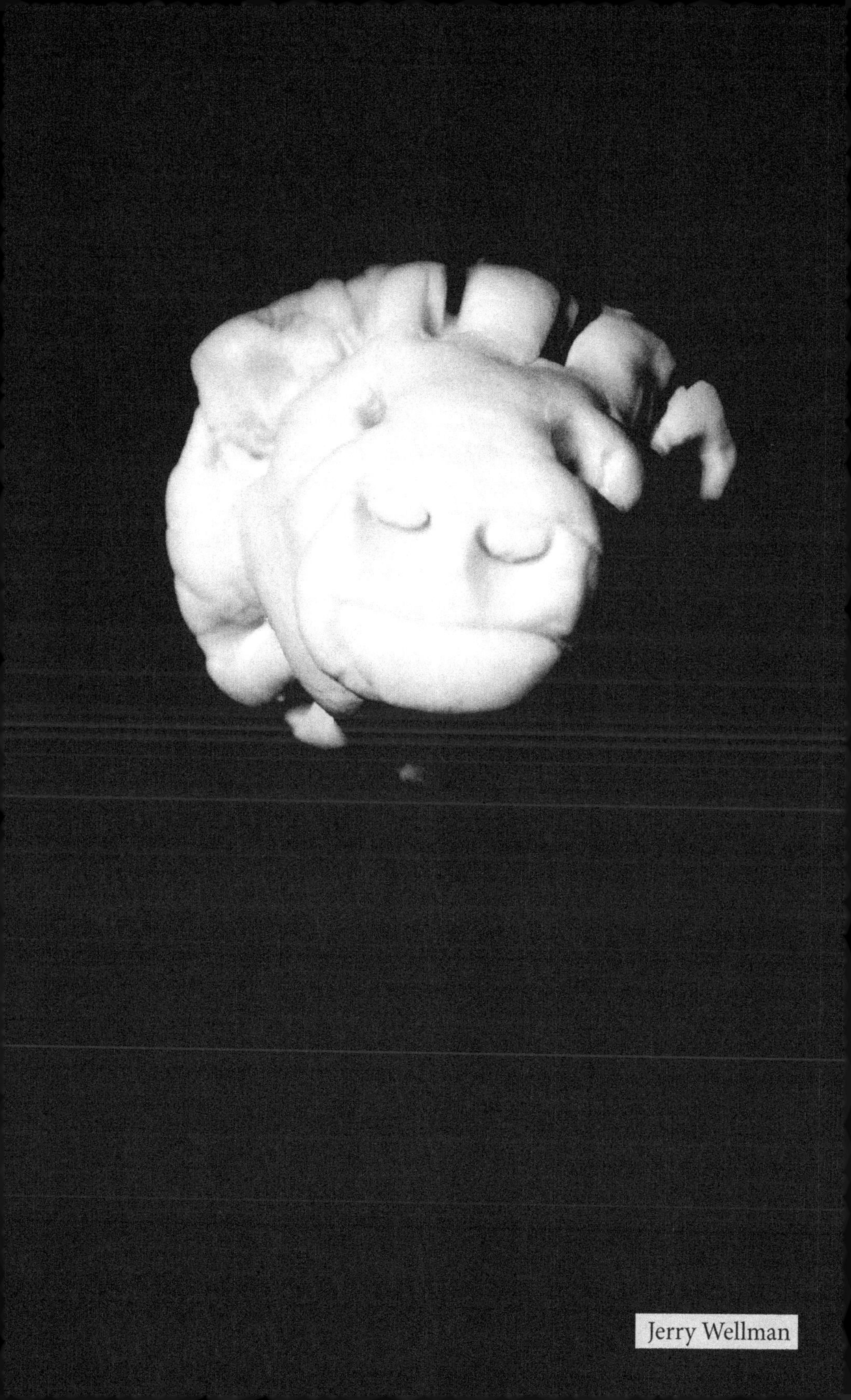

Jerry Wellman

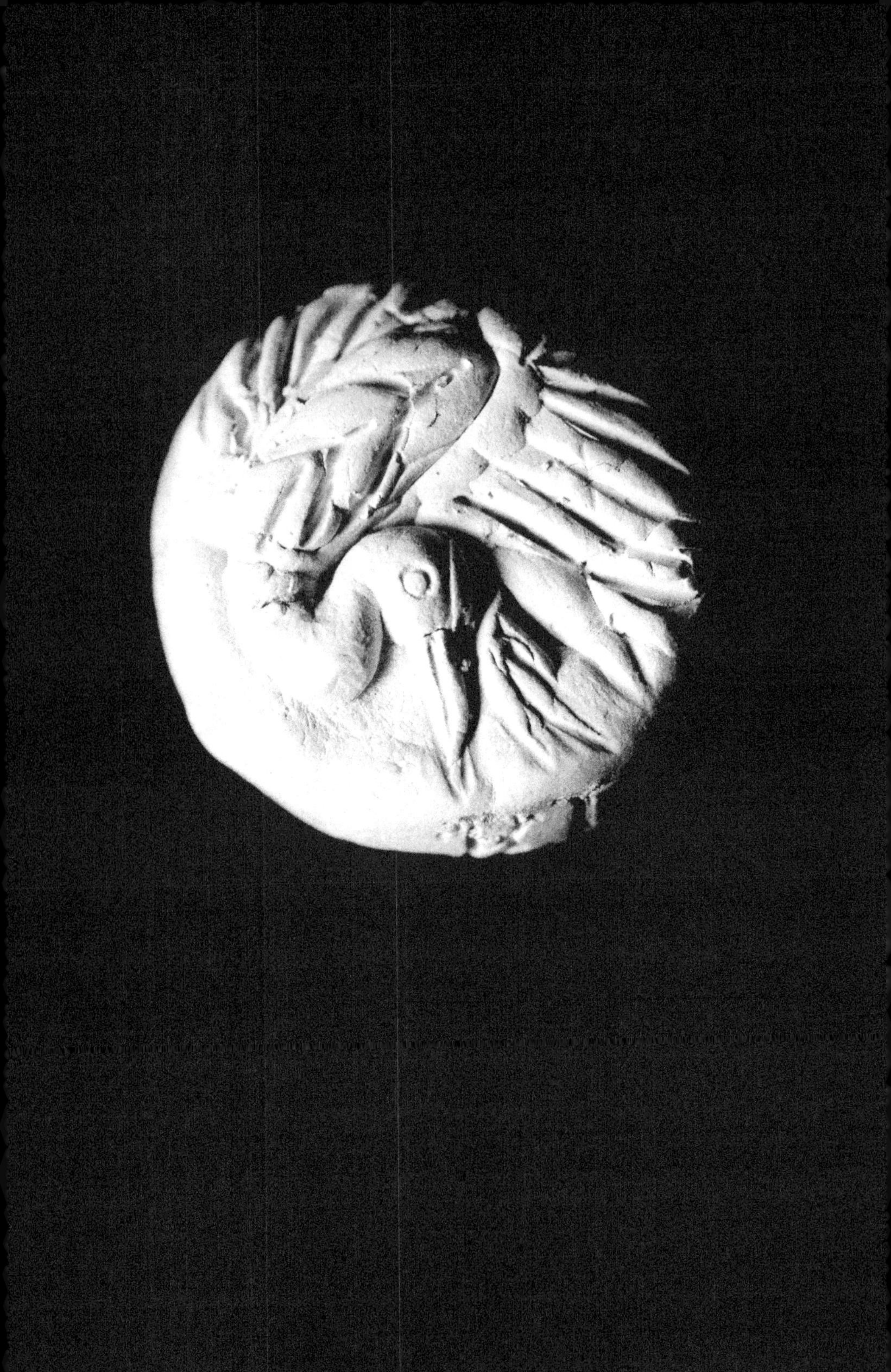

Barbara Ingram

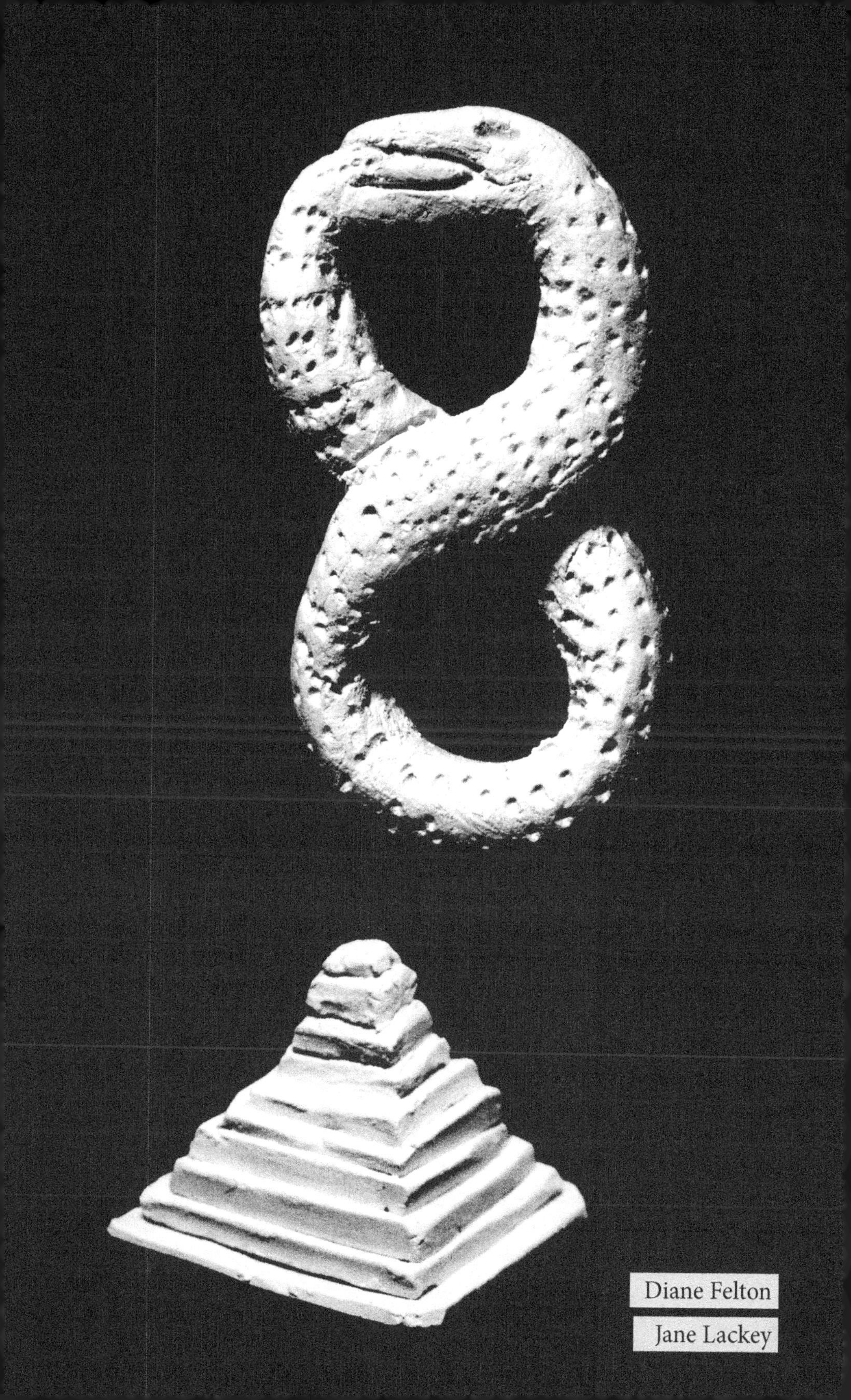

Diane Felton

Jane Lackey

BREAD MYSTERY

in the uncountable alphabet
bitter pine forest of words
sans serif
without butter or jam

one day we'll eat earth
and cry for more!
drink tea through a sugar cube
in italics

how is the strand of wheat
bent heavy with seed
supposed to speak
without being ground?

the night was aphasic
and the day
also said nothing
had nothing to say

it's winter, and the wild
girl goddess has gone under~
"why me" is not a question
that bears repeating

this dough will rise
in the starter of spring
and its crust can be opened
by the mouse teeth of desire

white bread like the moon
in the eastern sky
full, sliced, gone~
round again.

-Miriam Sagan

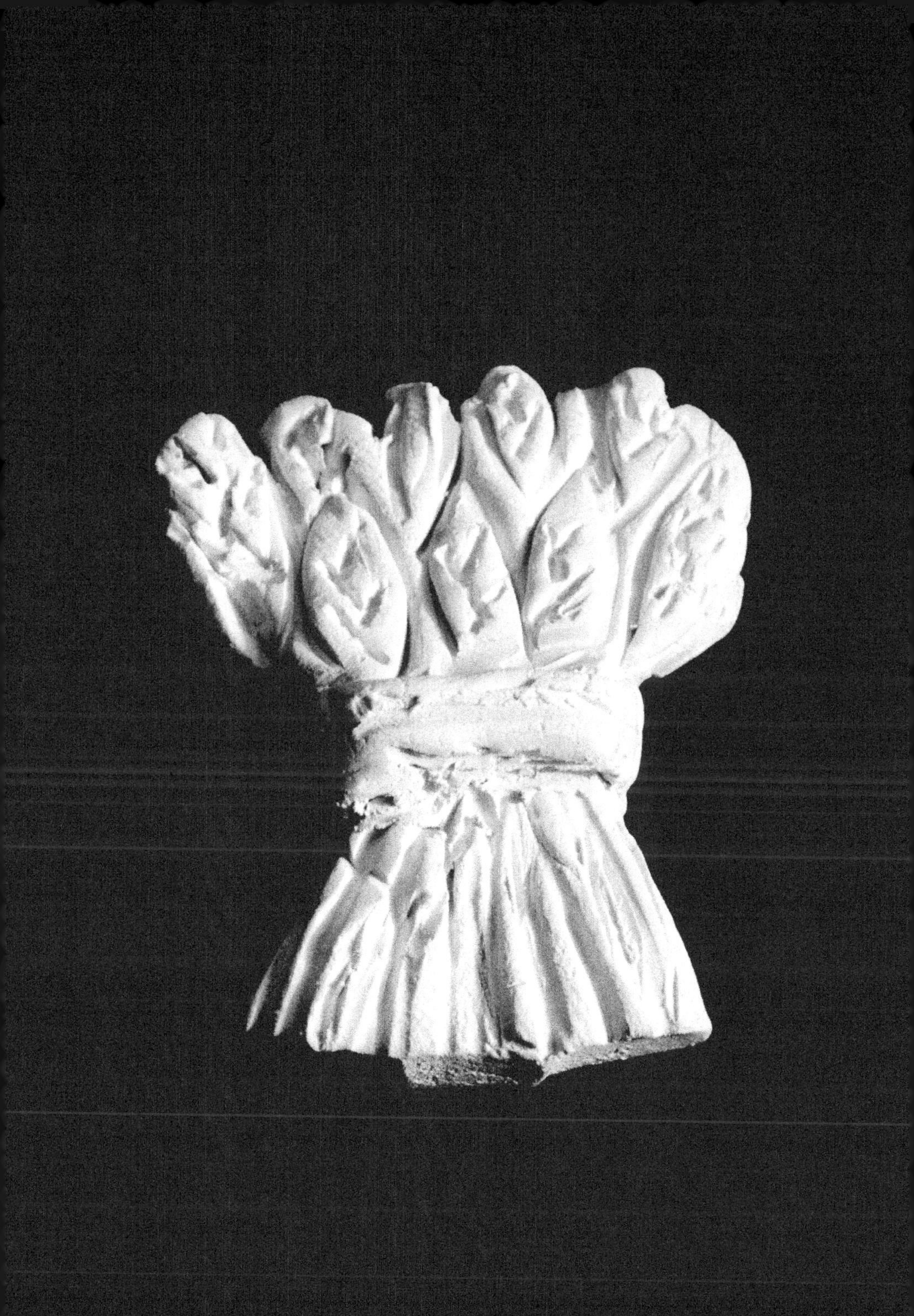

Julia G. Swab

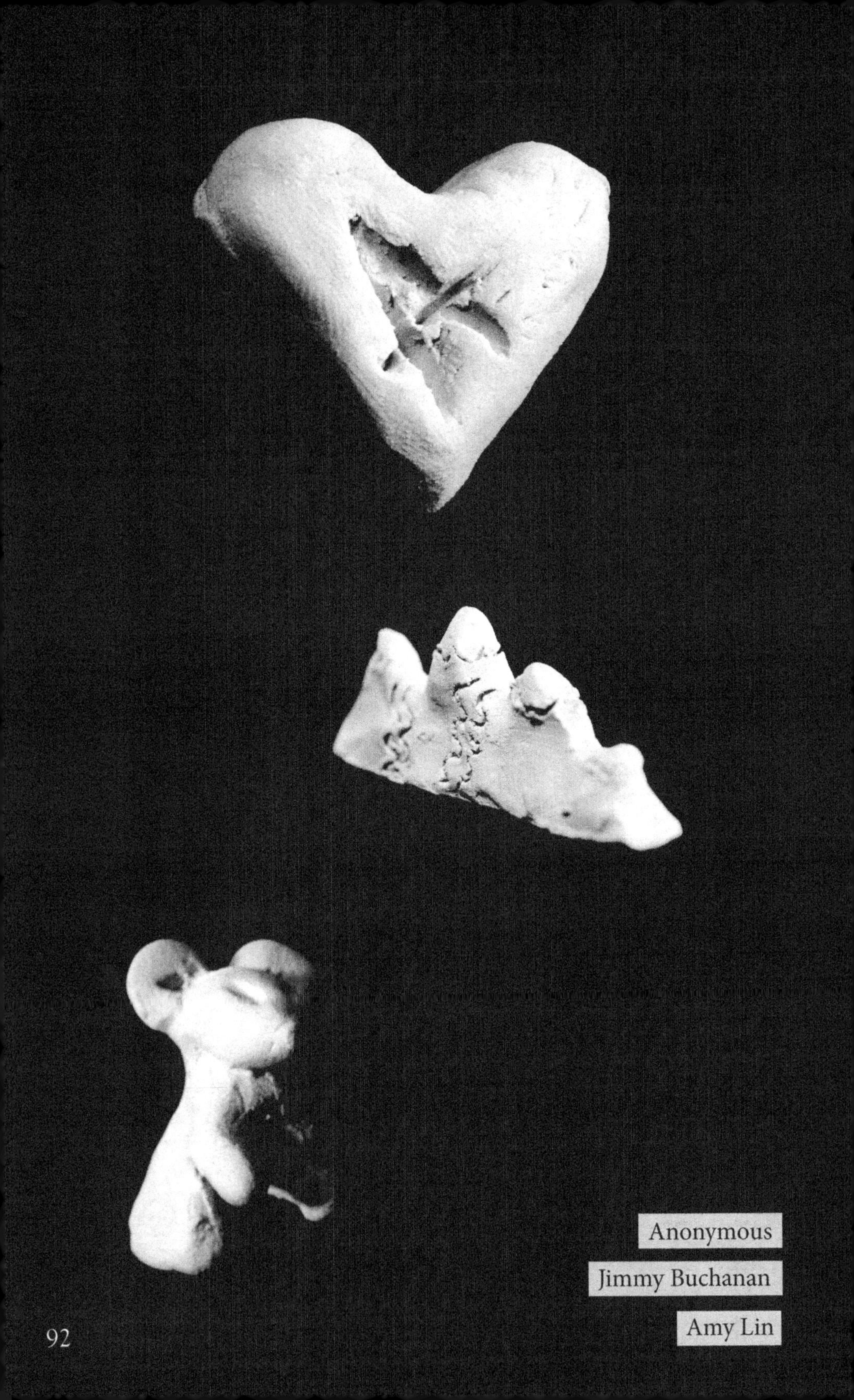

Anonymous

Jimmy Buchanan

Amy Lin

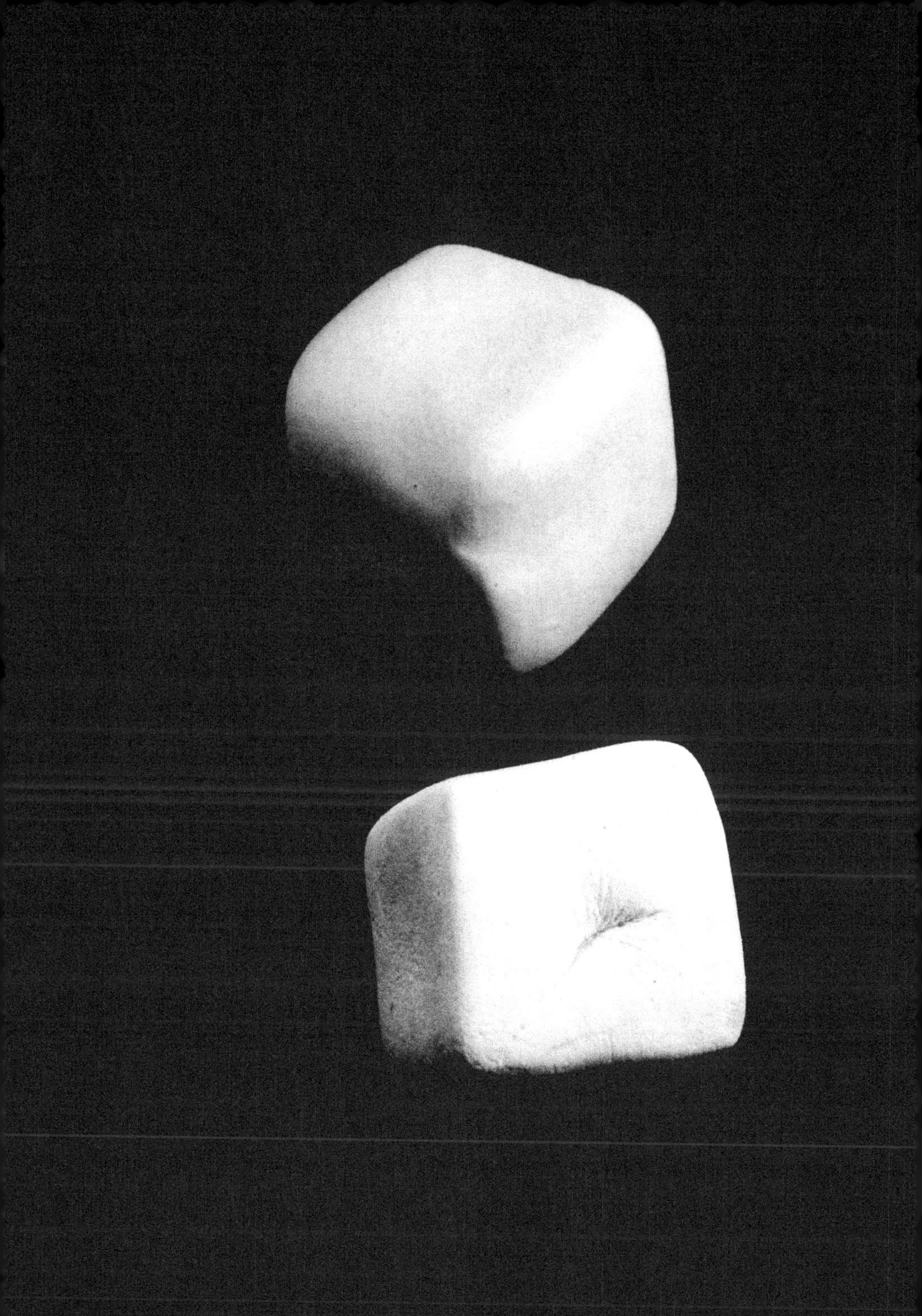

Santa Fe Youth Development Program

Santa Fe Youth Development Program

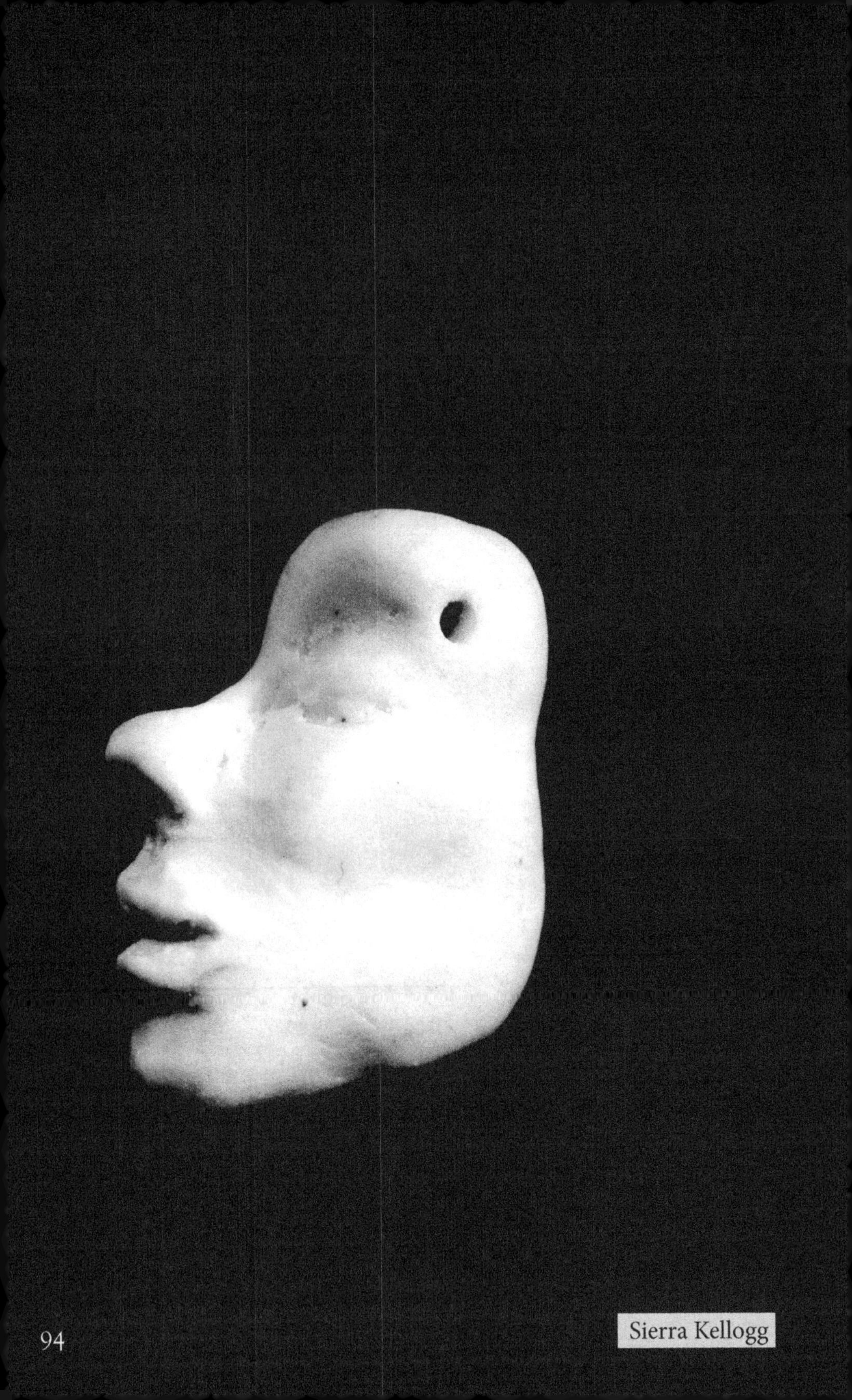

Sierra Kellogg

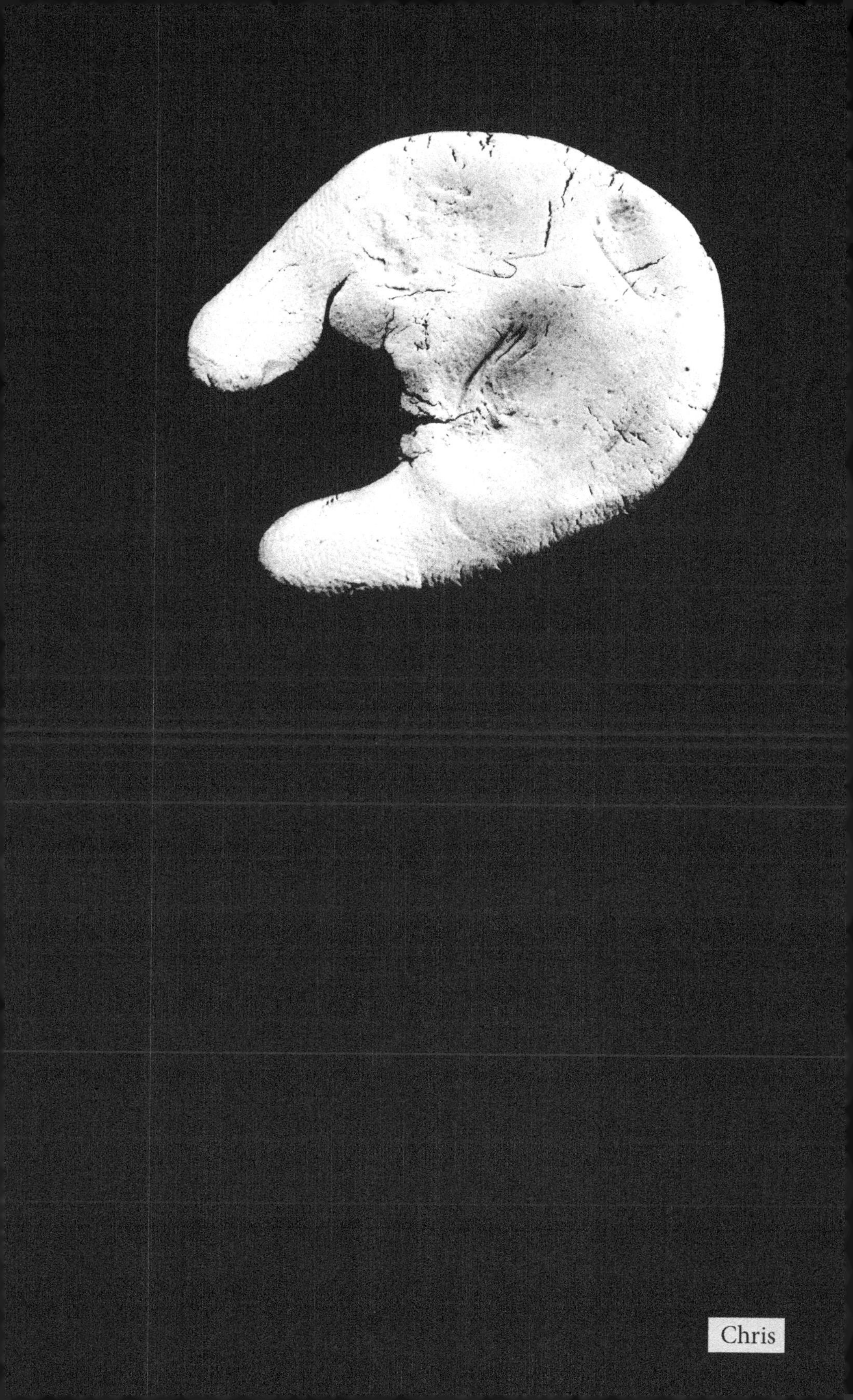

Chris

baking bread

there's many a grandmother
who'd surely think less of me,
measure the cups,
rely on the recipe;

stir salt and sugar
along with the yeast,
punch down the volume
before it's increased;

open the oven with
some trepidation,
inhale warm aroma,
exhale my elation! - - -

no one's more shocked
to unloaf such a miracle,
sweet fortress of crust
capped hemispherical!

-Darla Graff Thompson

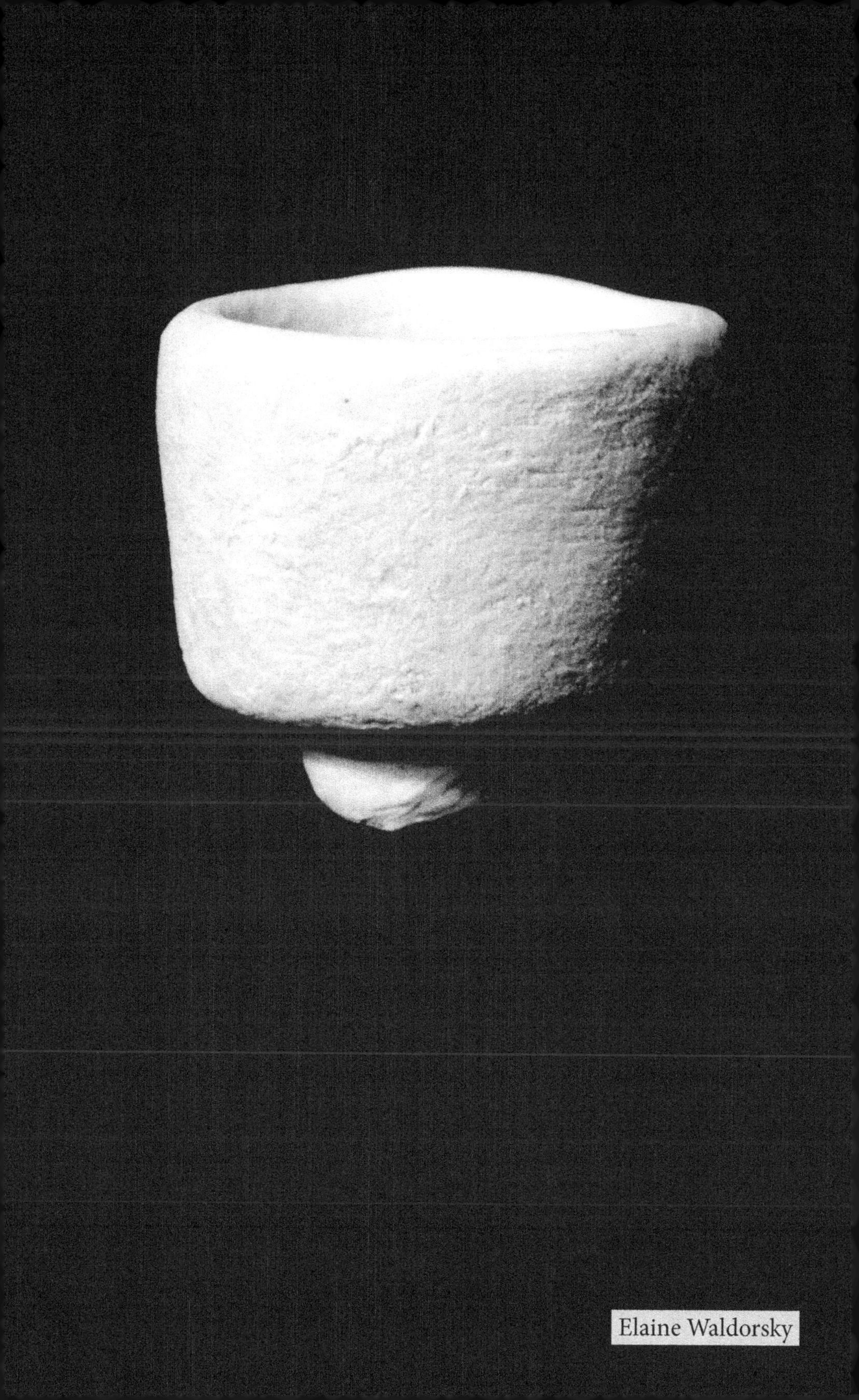

Elaine Waldorsky

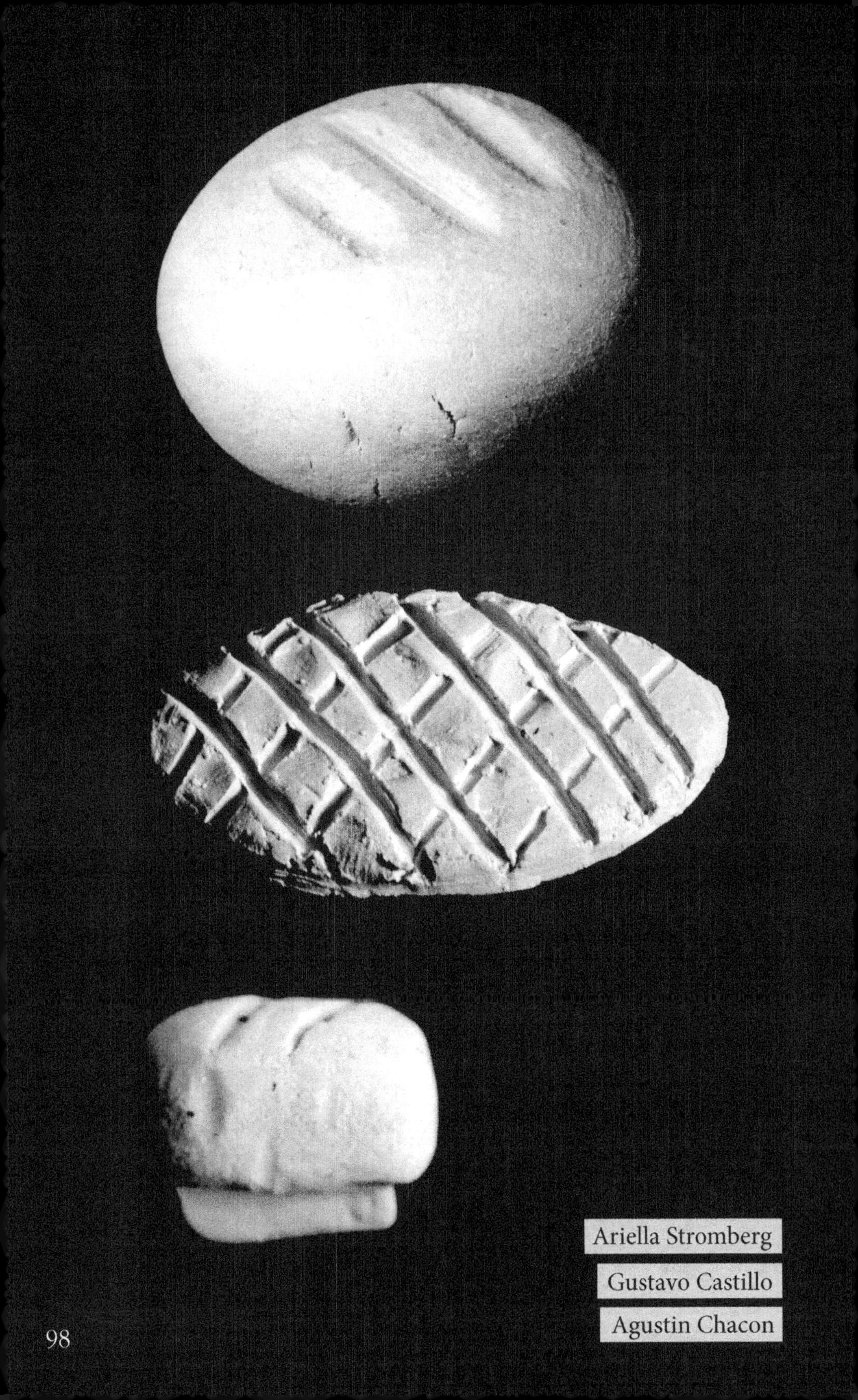

Ariella Stromberg

Gustavo Castillo

Agustin Chacon

Barm Brack

Old Irishwomen punch down the dough
over and over, and golden
raisins stick to their knuckles;

and sometimes, through a morning window,
sun lights their hands:
sudden jewels are there

where a poor anger lives.
Another left hook to the bread–
the need to eat goes on forever.

-Zoe Bird

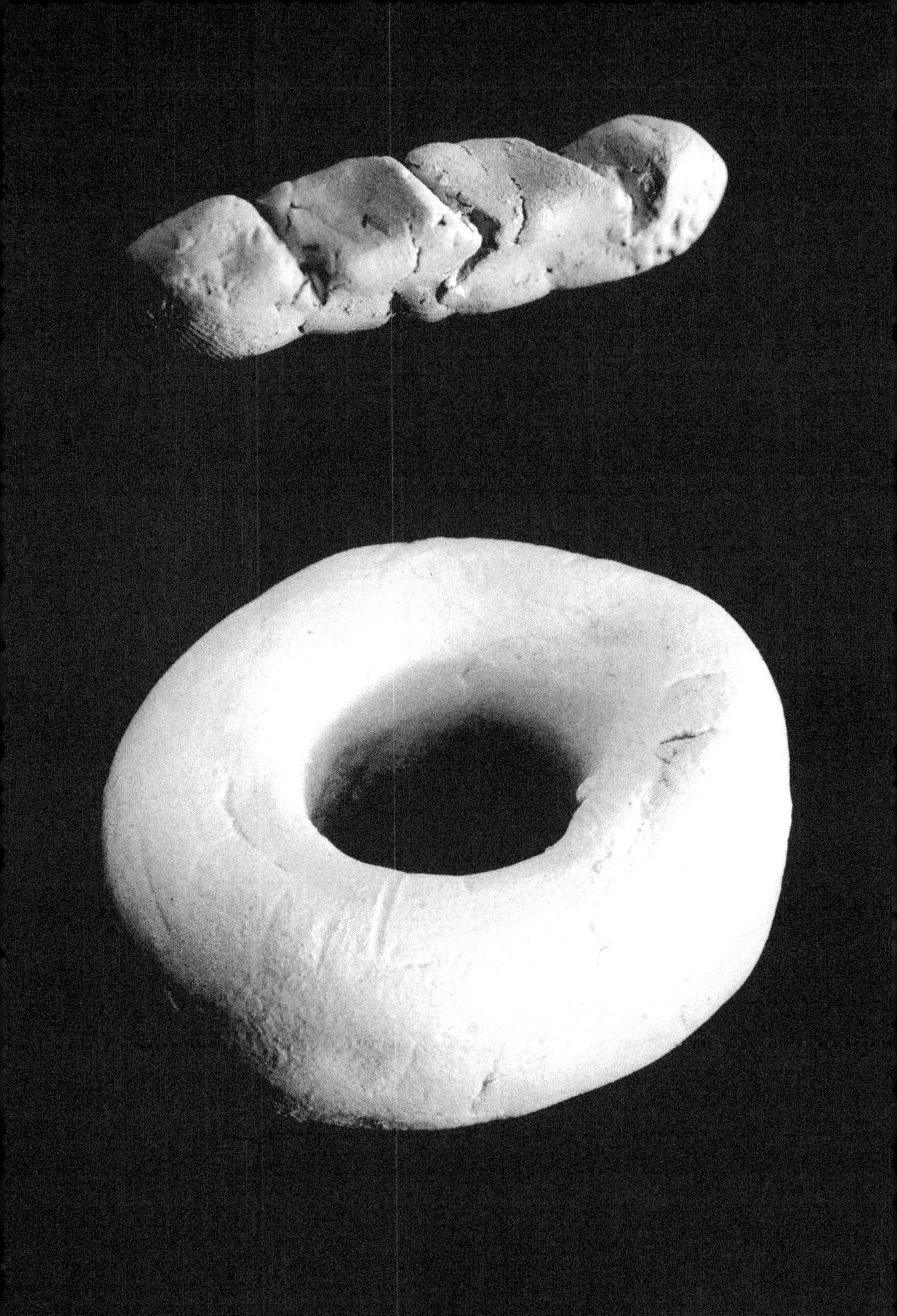

Jesse Glass

Sophia Livingston

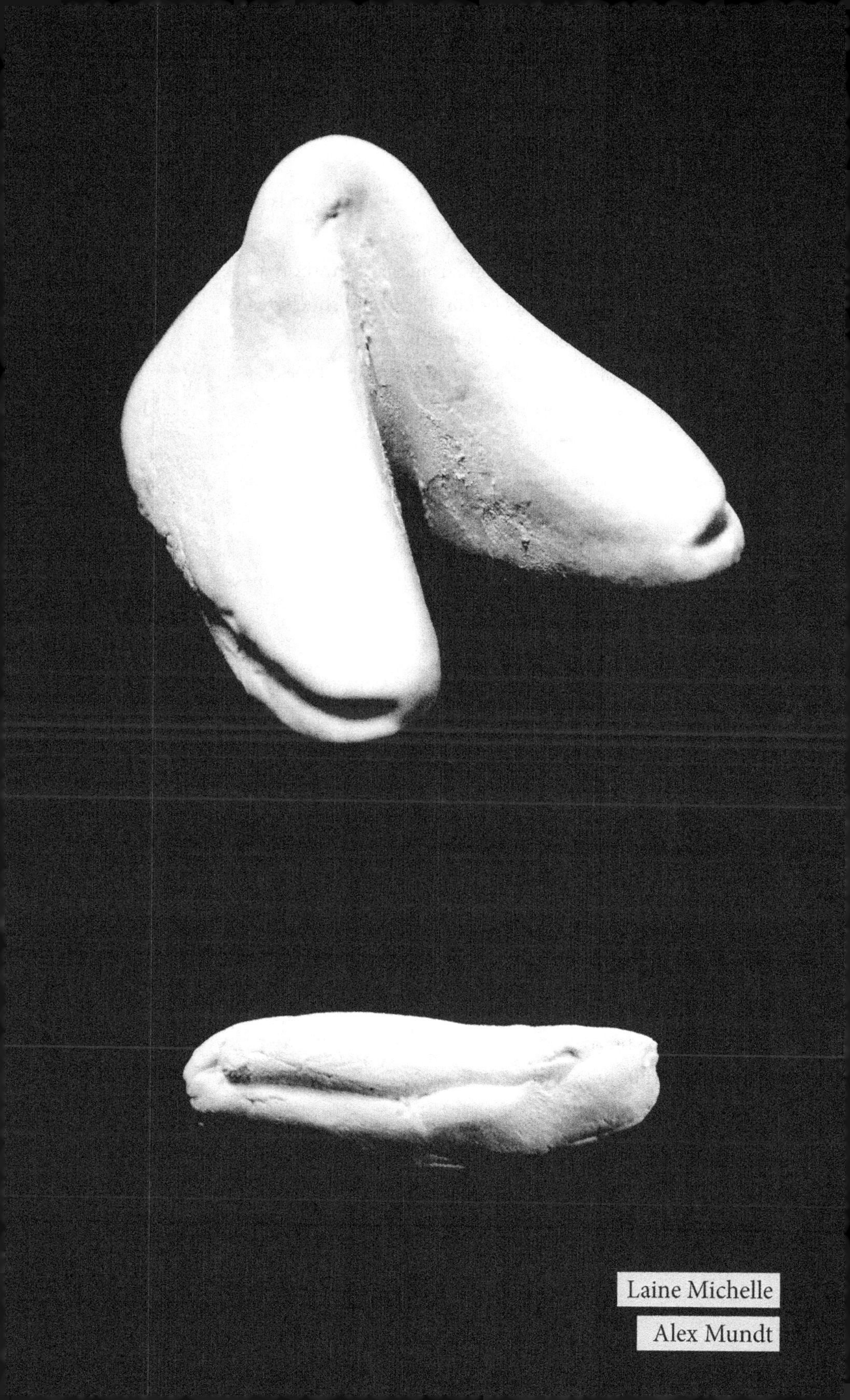

Laine Michelle

Alex Mundt

you might think it were made by the blackbirds
or that they plucked it from trees
the way they'd drop it on Jeromes and Anthonys.
if it were scarce, lines of families would shuck steam
in the cold streets, in tenements
for portions to break into fives or fours, threes,
as if it were aseptic, to be relished,

a twin to breath, though opposite in substance.

it's a field wrecked and condensed into scrap.
it's beaten, ground, and cursed into its preciousness.

-Christopher Jamie Johnson

Manna

Ravens returning,
Black arrows shot from the winged bow,
Bring bread:
Corpus lumen (the crust)
Corpus sanctum (the flesh)
Enough for one day in the desert.

-Stella Reed

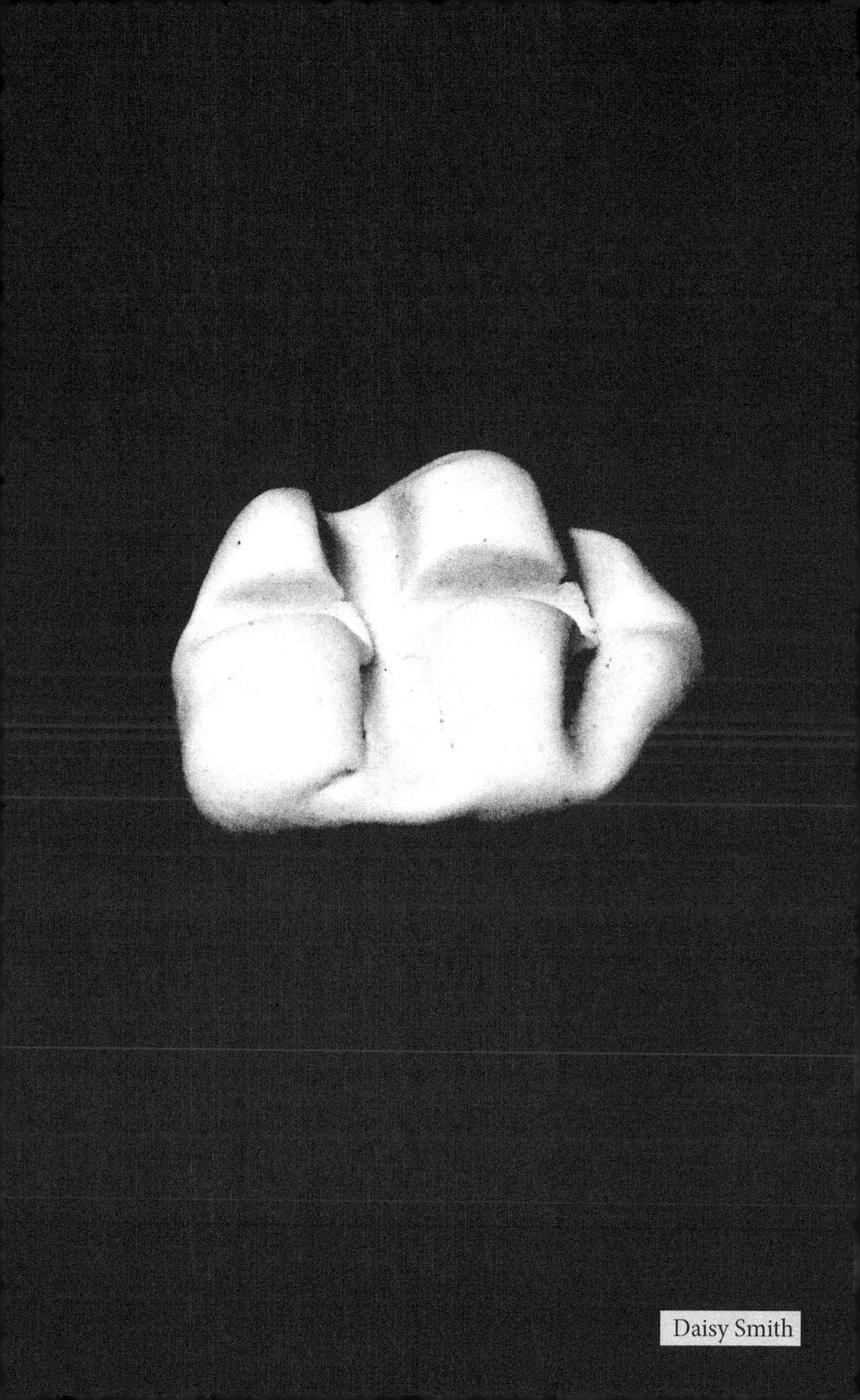

Daisy Smith

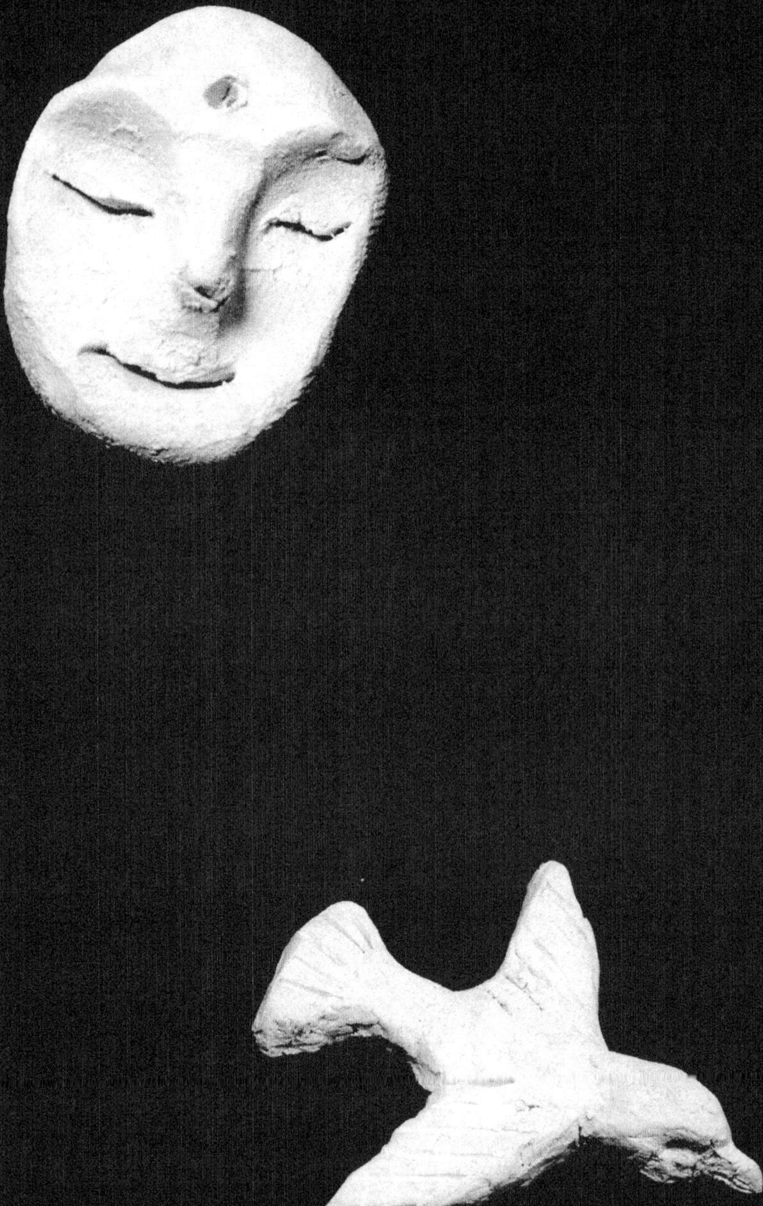

Marion Wasserman

Nancy Brandt

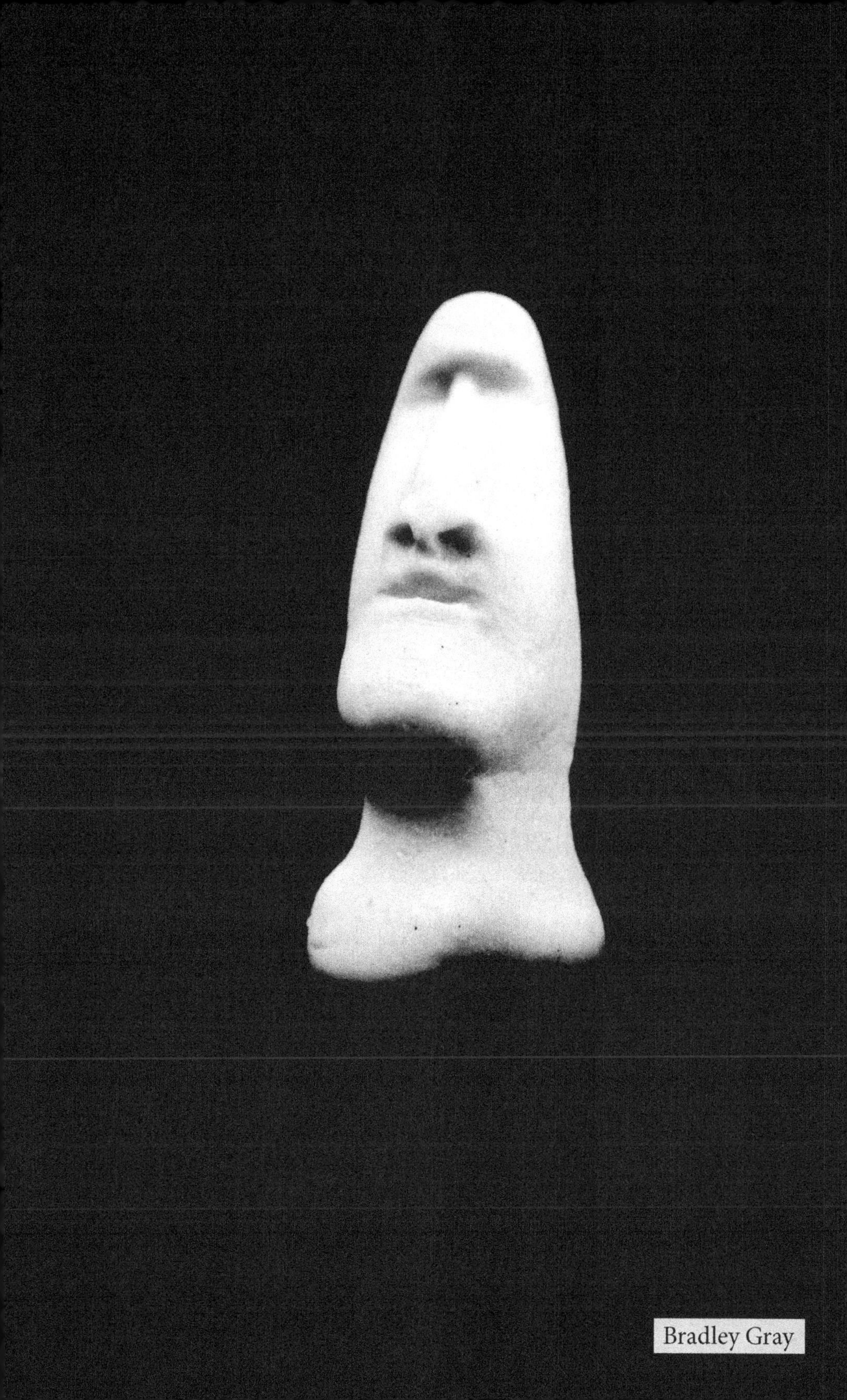

Bradley Gray

How To Make Bread

yeast flour water
a little salt
some sugar
your hands

-Cheri Ibes

To make bread is a ritual
Setting the time aside
Gathering the ingredients
Measuring the yeast
Adding the touch of sugar
And warm water.
Allowing to bubble
Mixing in the rest of the ingredients
Kneading the dough
Kneading the dough
Kneading the dough
Let Rest
Let Rise in Warm space
Punch down
Knead again, rise
Bake
SMELLS OF BAKING BREAD IS THE BEST

Bread is done
Slice, butter, eat & enjoy!

Bread Done the Traditional WAY

-Dana Simmons

How It's Done

Scrape.
Make.
Shape.
Bake.

Break.

Partake

-Dennis Goza

the journey of a particle of yeast

-Lauren Camp

Ode to bread

I love bread
Glutinous
Oil- drenched
Butter dripping honey soaked
The whole catastrophe of western civilization in every bite

Give me bread or give me wings
Liberated risen flour
I heart you

-Kathleen McCloud

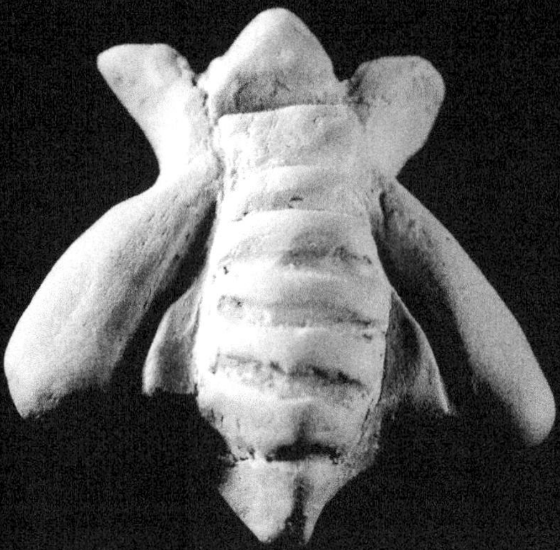

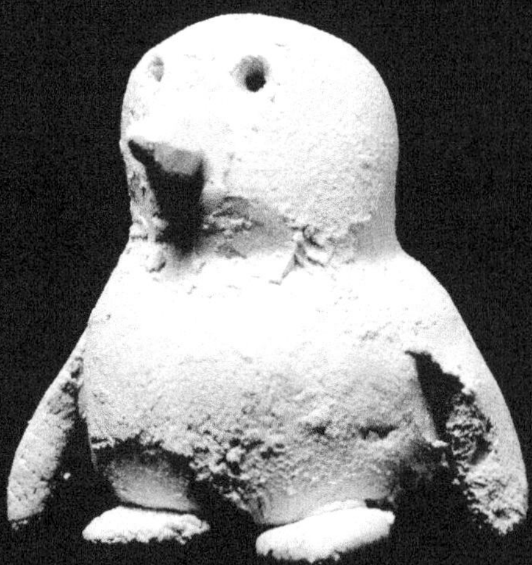

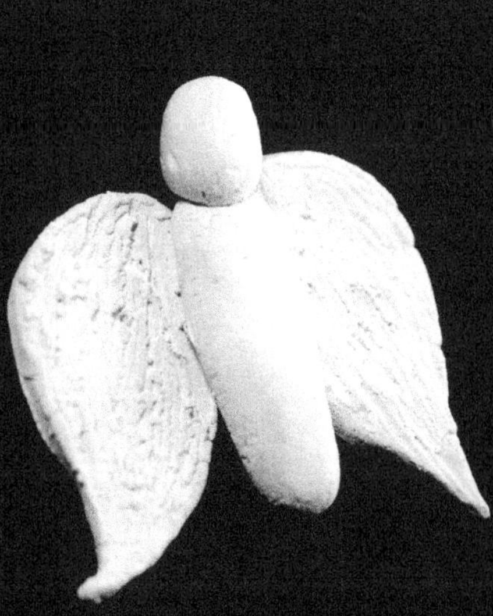

Sarah Bienvenue

Kimberly Palma

Anjali K.

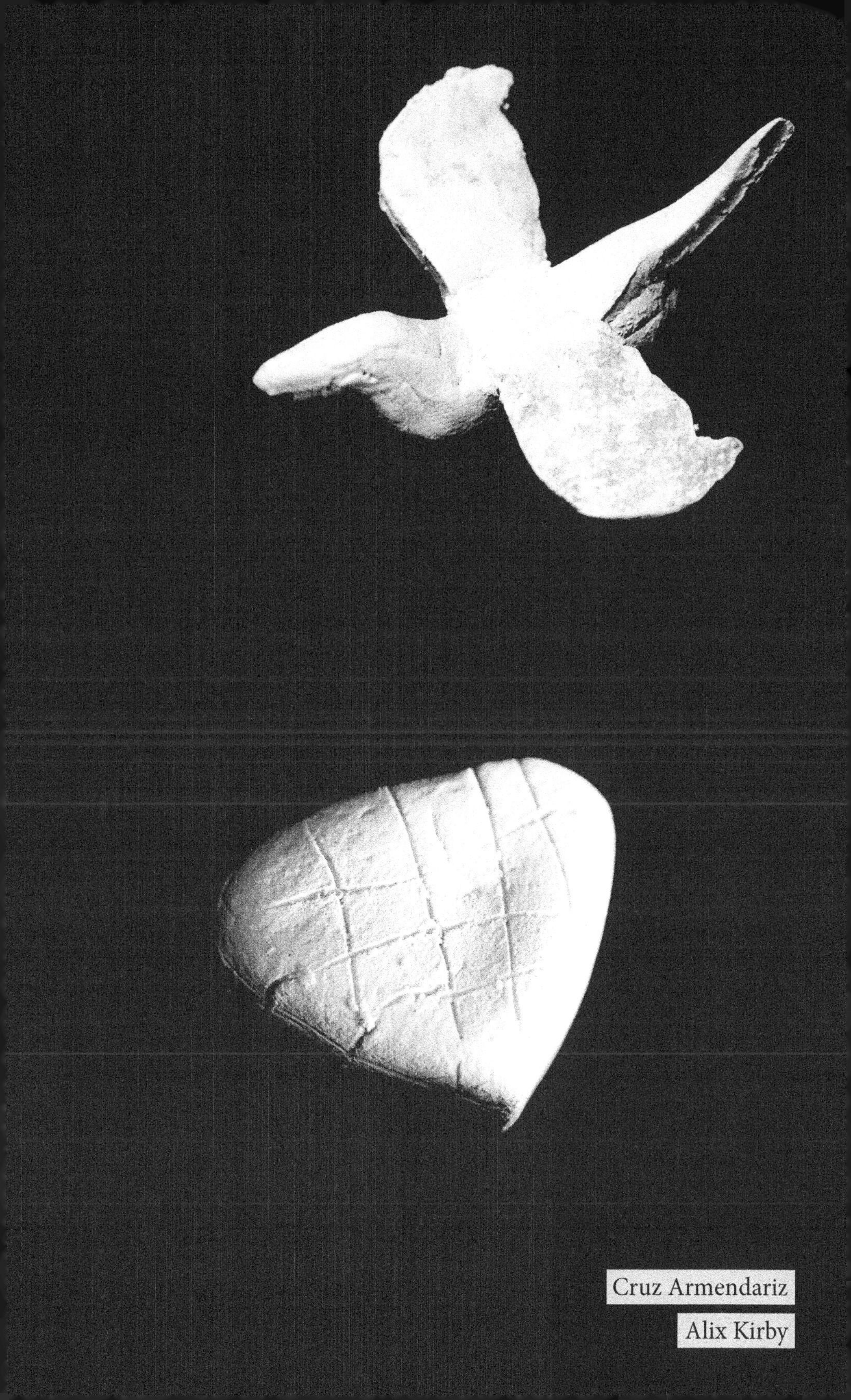

Cruz Armendariz

Alix Kirby

Bread

In memory of Ginny Wilson

1)
Cradle between the hands
large blue bowl, its rim
rose-purple sky at dusk.
Draw water
            from invisible springs.
Spoon honey
            sweet sacrifice of bees.
Sprinkle yeast
            for miracle of rising.
Add milk
            from cows with names.
Hold egg tenderly
before it breaks against
the bowl's bruised lip.
Spill hard, red winter wheat
            slowly from the cup.
2)
Leave to warm while you
            sip tea from a china cup.
Watch fledgling hummingbirds
            wobble at the feeder.
Sprinkle sea salt
            currency of kingdoms.
Whisk warm oil from sunflowers
            whose fertile faces
            turn with the sun.
Stir with wooden spoon
            stir with vigor, stir, stir, stir.

Savor your strength.
Knead, fold and push,
engage shoulders, wing bones, thoracic spine.
Let latent quarrels fall.
Anoint blue bowl with oil,
            its womb
of perfect roundness.

3)
Leave bread to rise
Walk the arroyo.
Allow the mind to roam
            like a coyote at night.
Lather loaf pans generously
with butter.
Punch down the dough.
Divide.
Knuckle each loaf flat.
Roll, knead, roll, massage,
stroke as if it were muscle and sinew, a lover's back.
Swath with a warm towel.
Leave to rise again.

-Linda Whittenberg

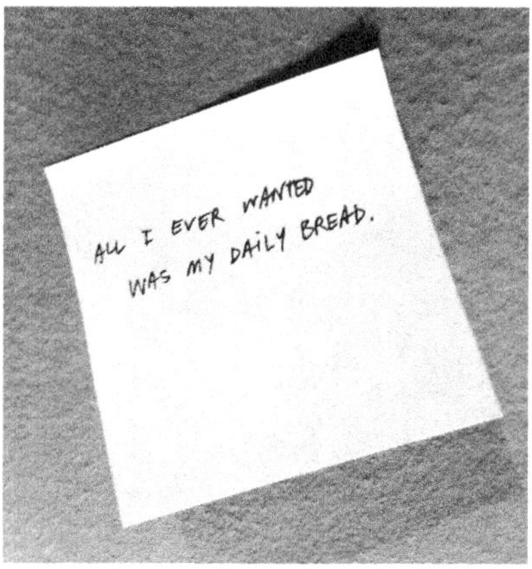

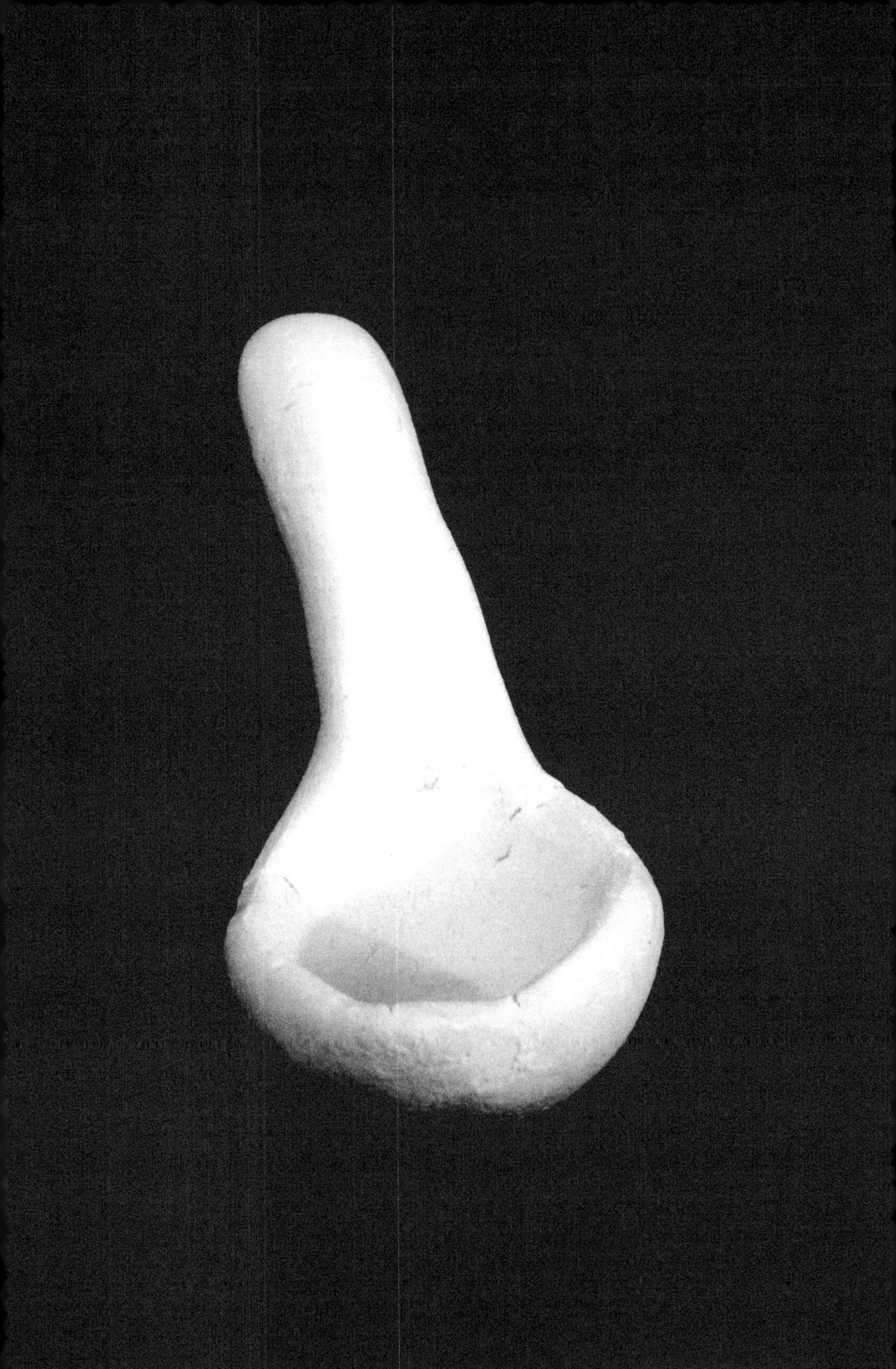

Kristen Martincic

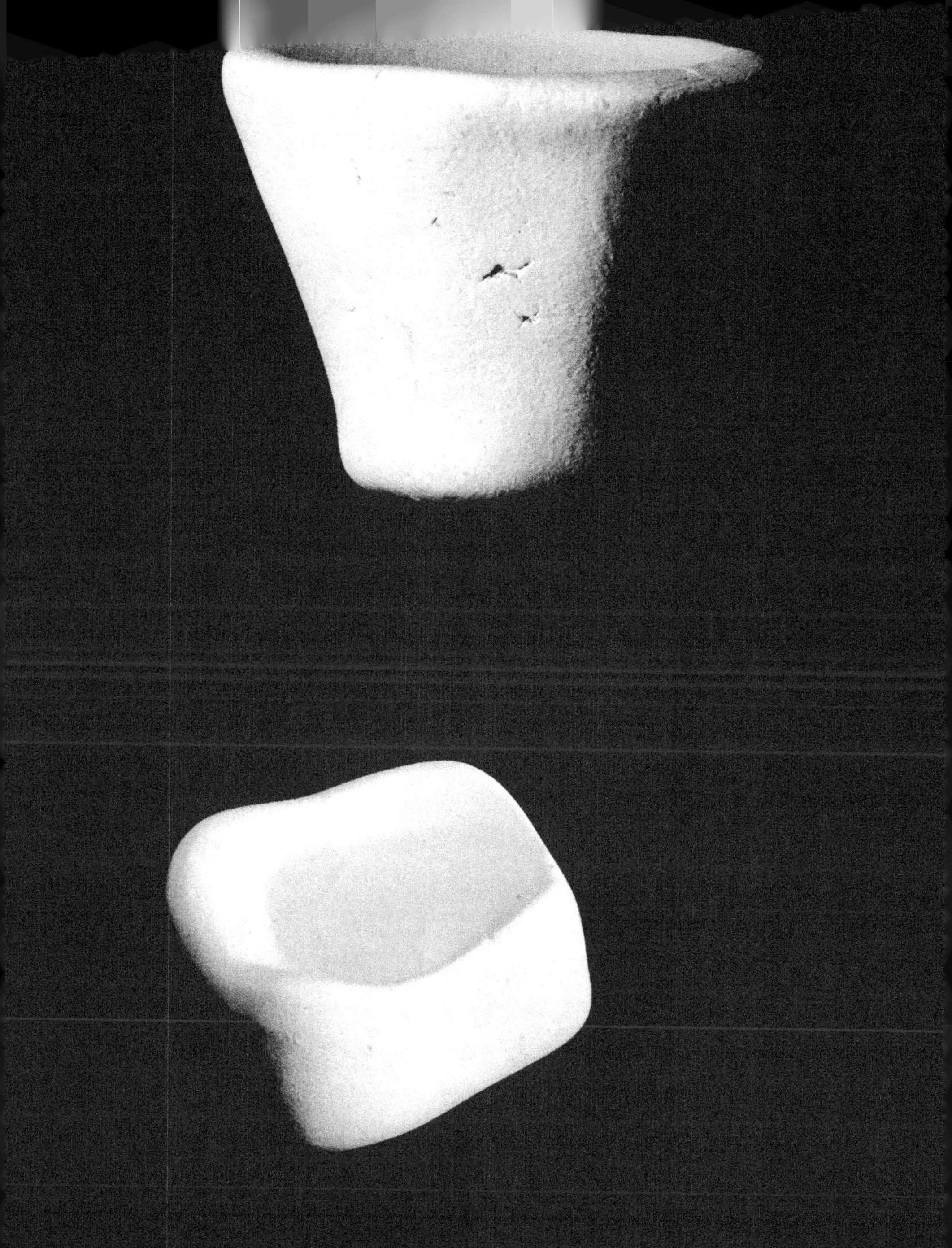

Santa Fe Youth Development Program

Craig Duncan

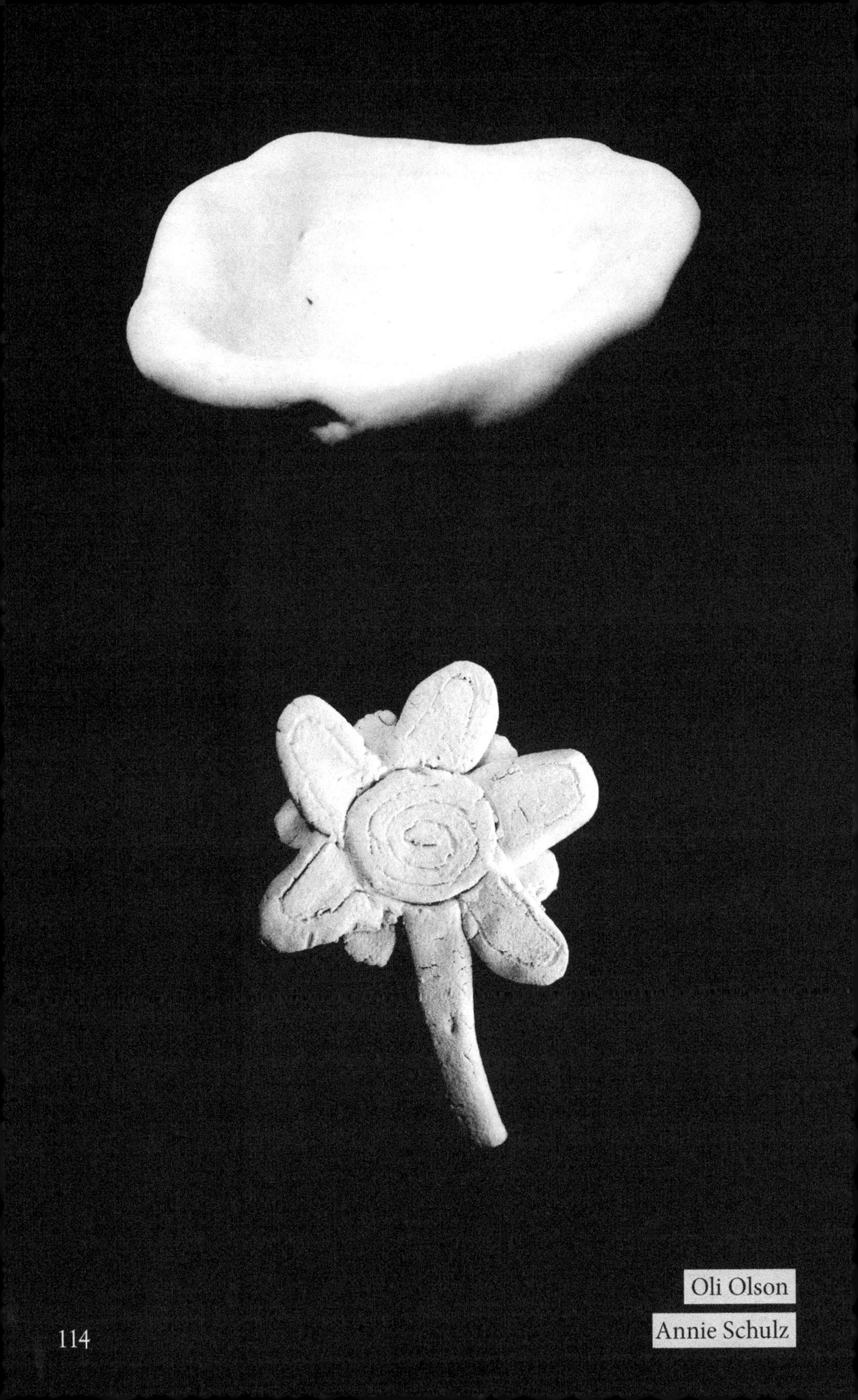

Oli Olson

Annie Schulz

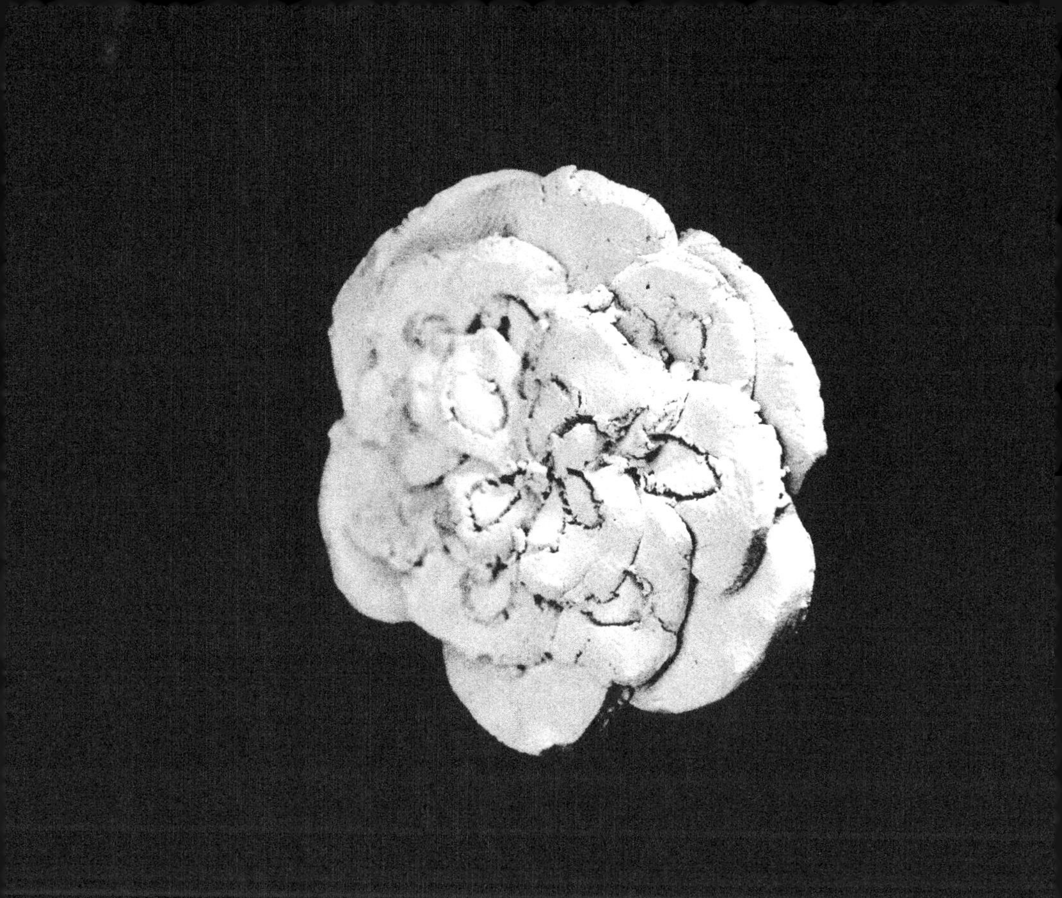

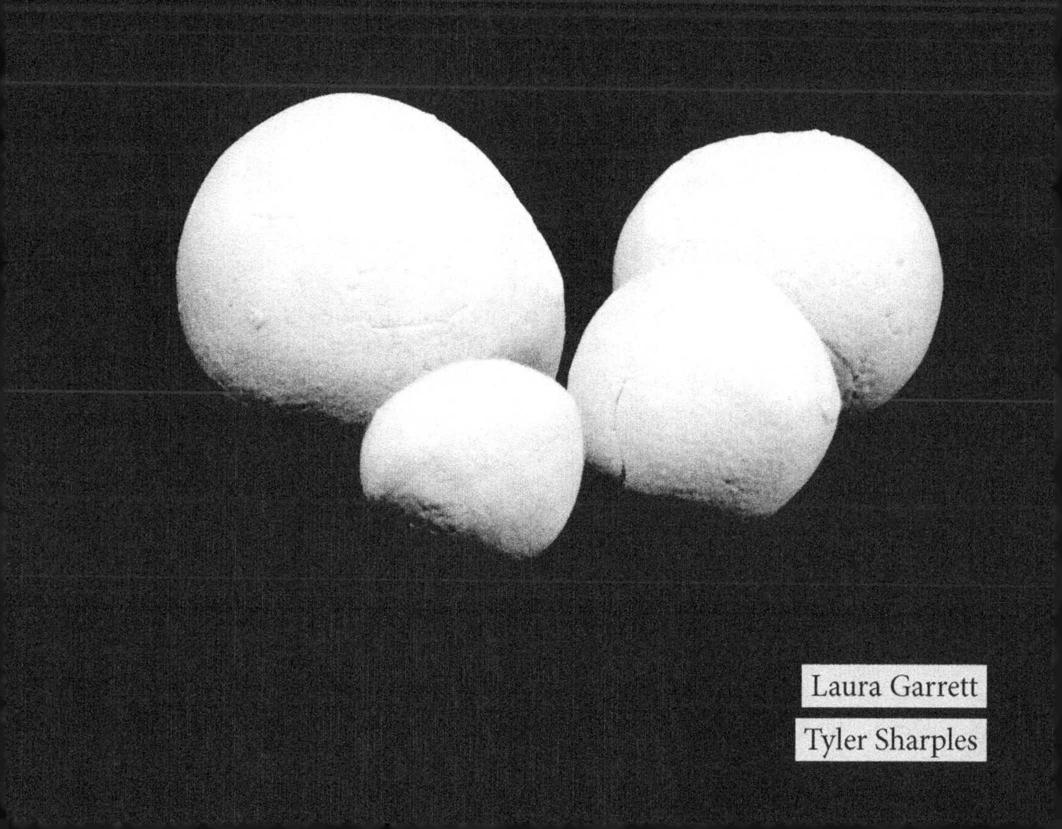

Laura Garrett

Tyler Sharples

You Can Eat it Plain

A true communion, this
it starts with nearly a kiss
lips whisper against smooth, warm form
firm circularity
in curving finger links
eternity embodied in wheat
transfigured by heat
fire and water both required
for this alchemist's feat:
(drum roll, please)
a bagel...
no hard-crusted, soft-bellied loaf compares
with its brawny tone
in that moment
before the bite
that spirited rebound so like
the spring of flesh
without fear of causing pain
to this pain not-so-ordinaire
teeth plunge,
meet again and again,
their hidden frottage
grinding through
bread that is more than bread
more than substance
repository of regrets and afflictions
comforts and affections
host of desires met and unmet
memories of meals, moments,
interlinked lives,
bloodless sacrificial sacrament
for man does not live by bread alone,
that much is plain;
this holy, holey, wholeness
contains more than itself
reminds us
that we, too,
are grain, fire and water
and contain more than ourselves
we, too,
remain more than ordinary
when we are plain

-Tamara Lichtenstein

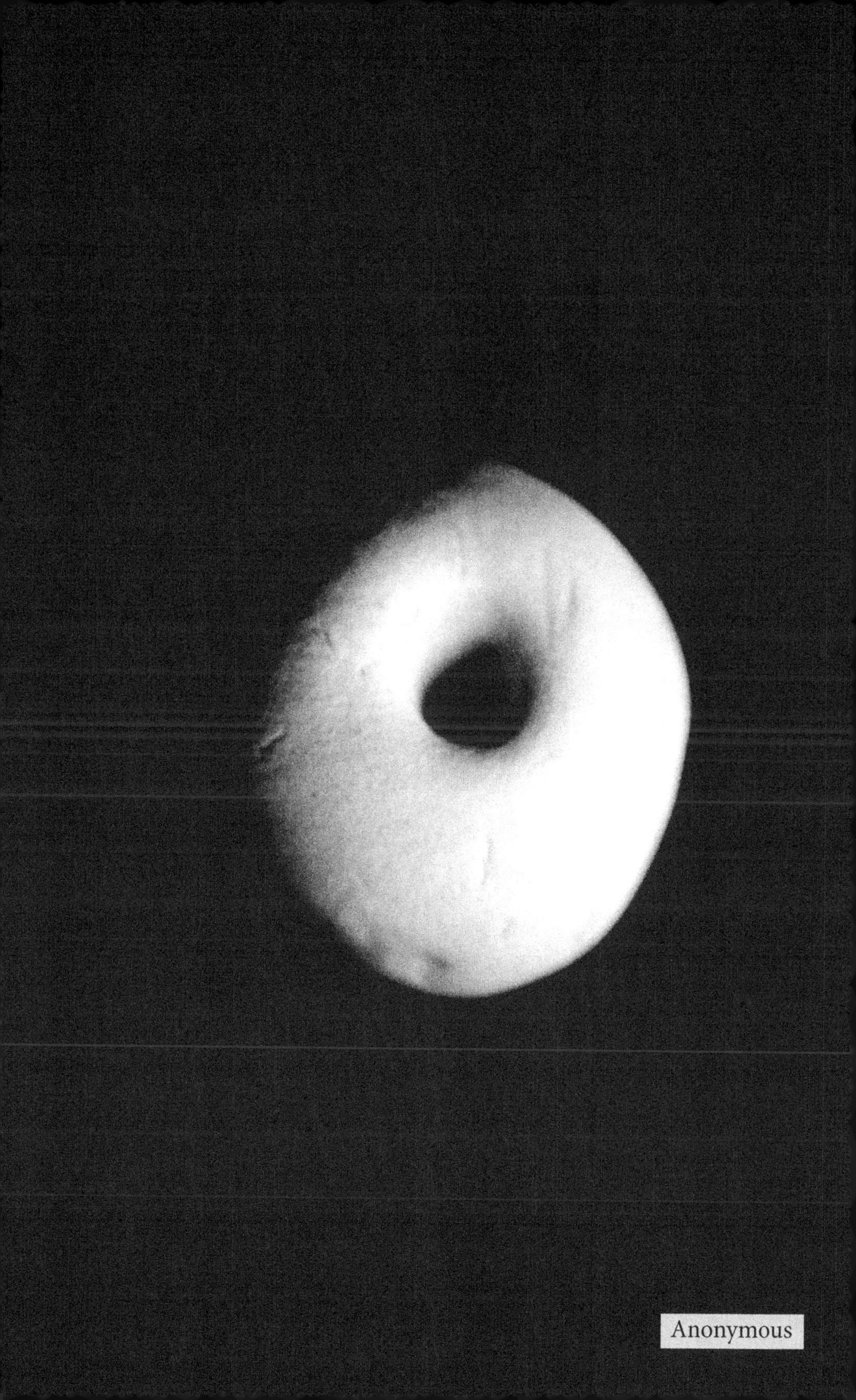

Anonymous

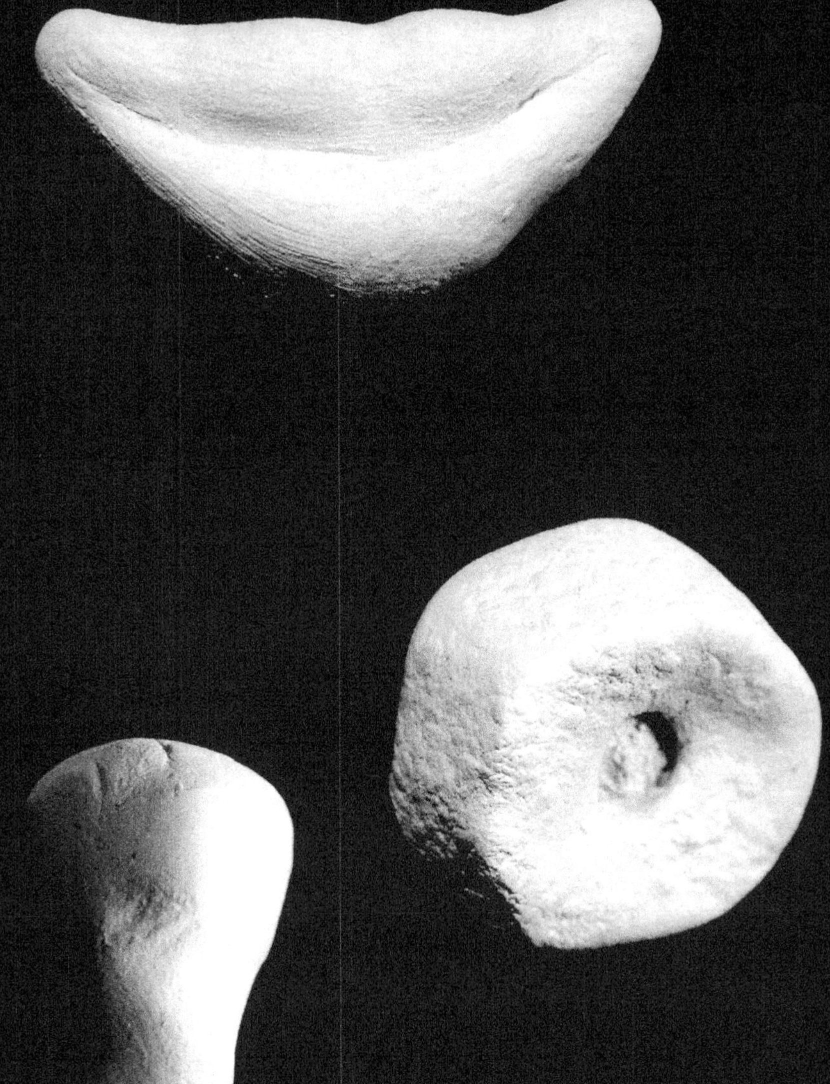

Suzanne Greenwood

Bruce Wilson

Anonymous

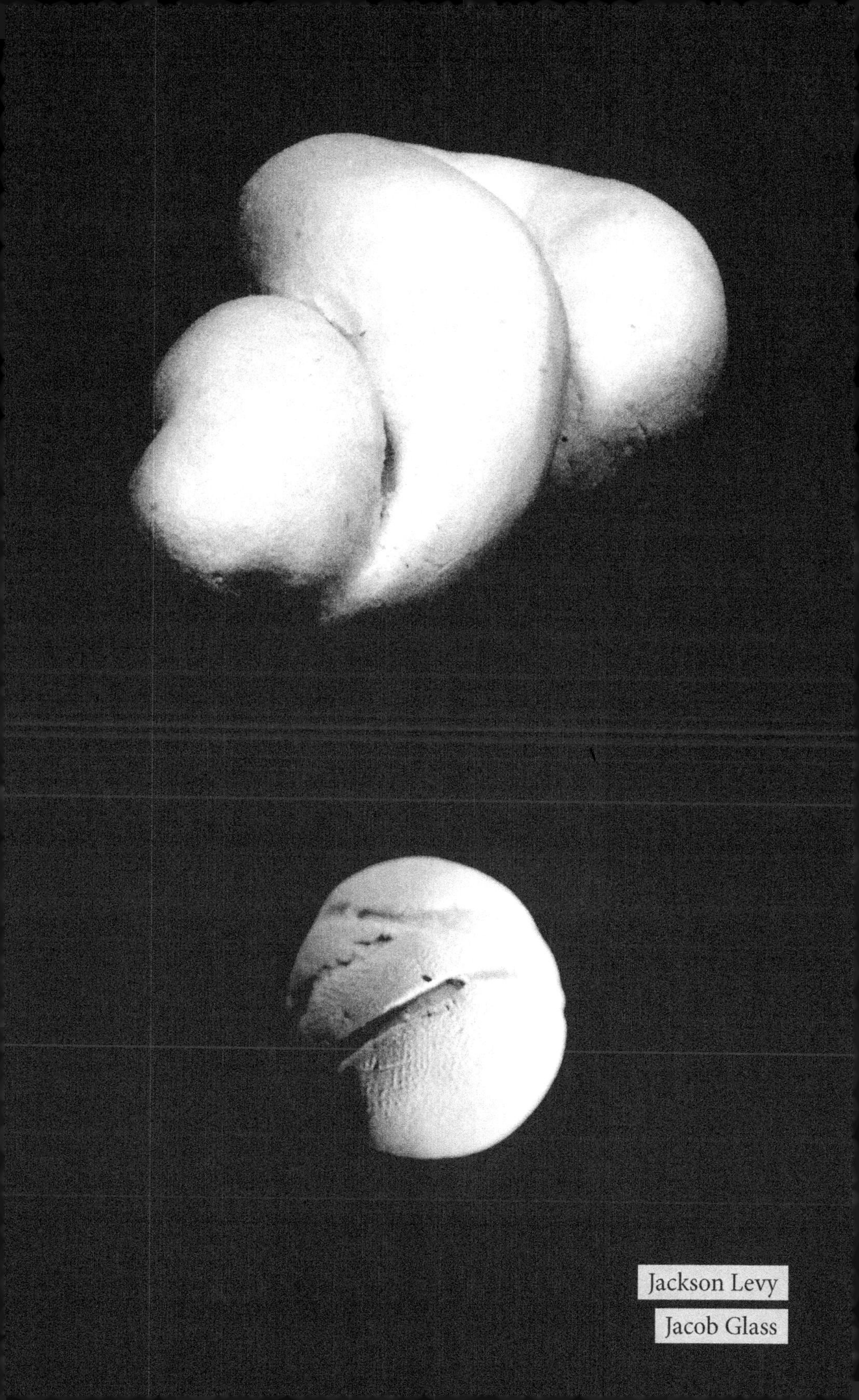

Jackson Levy
Jacob Glass

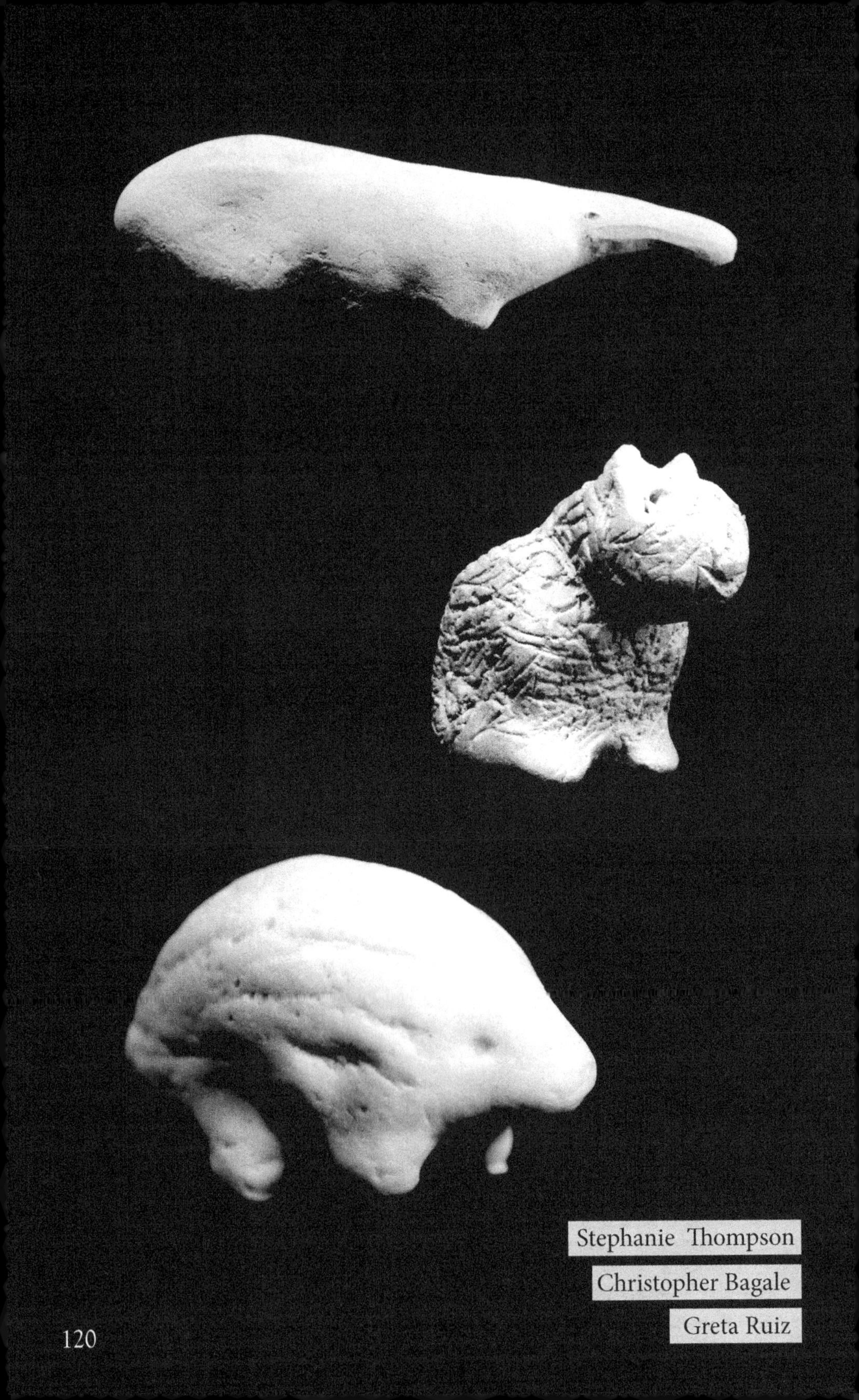
Stephanie Thompson
Christopher Bagale
Greta Ruiz

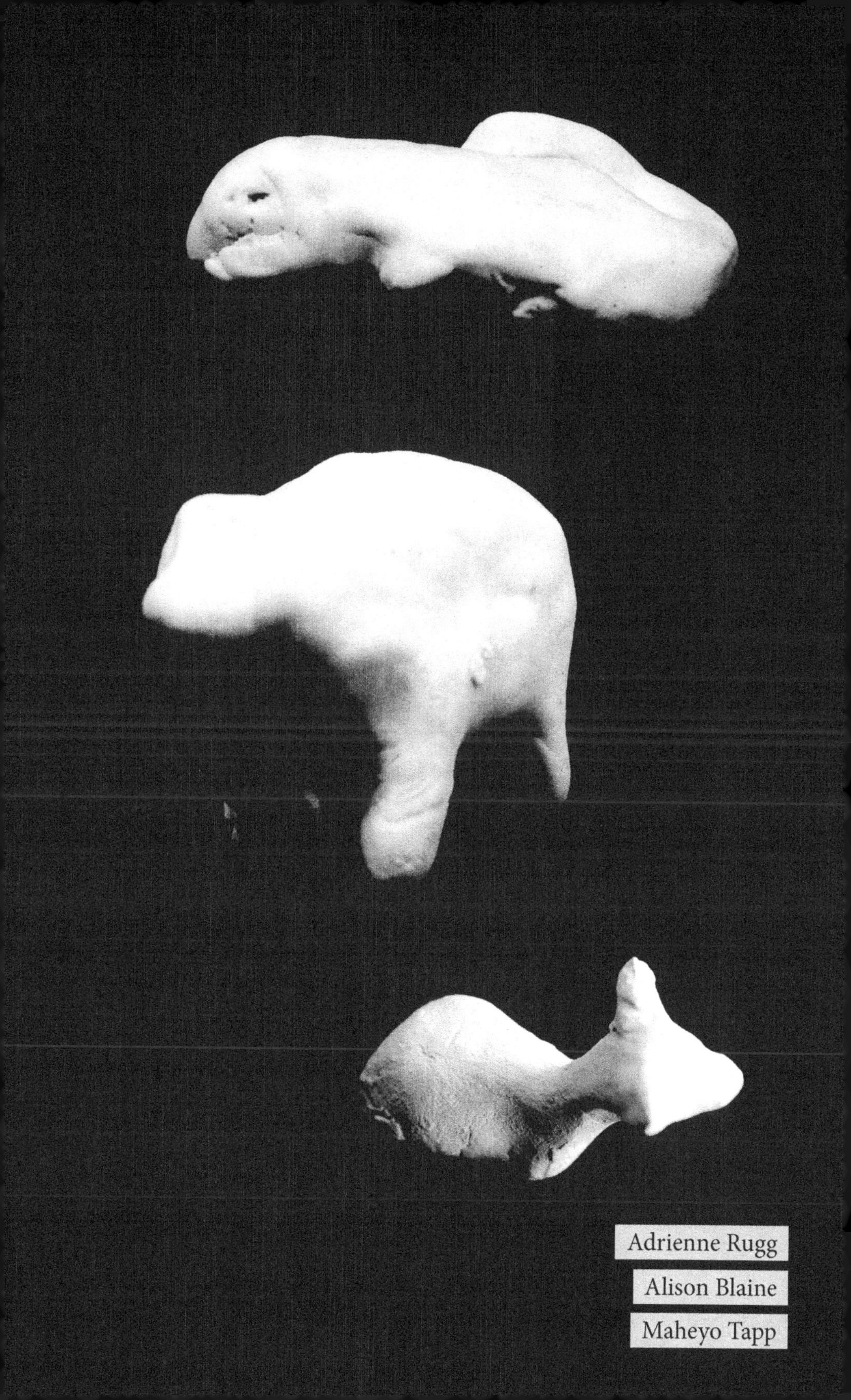
Adrienne Rugg
Alison Blaine
Maheyo Tapp

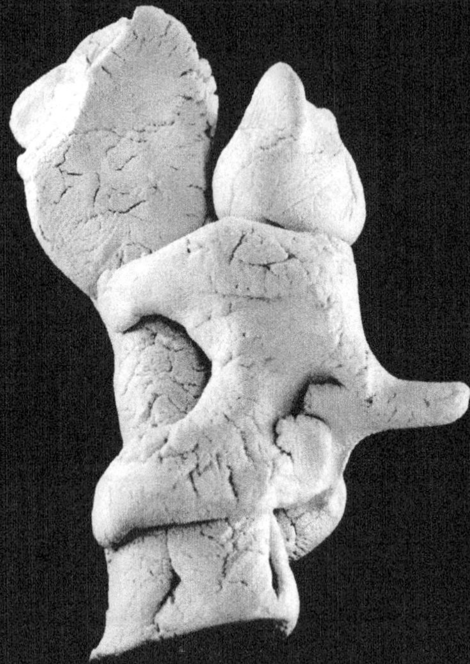

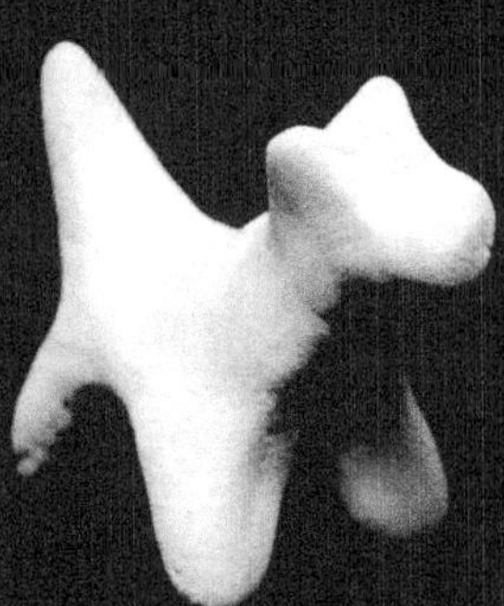

Lola Kark

Kristen Steffgen

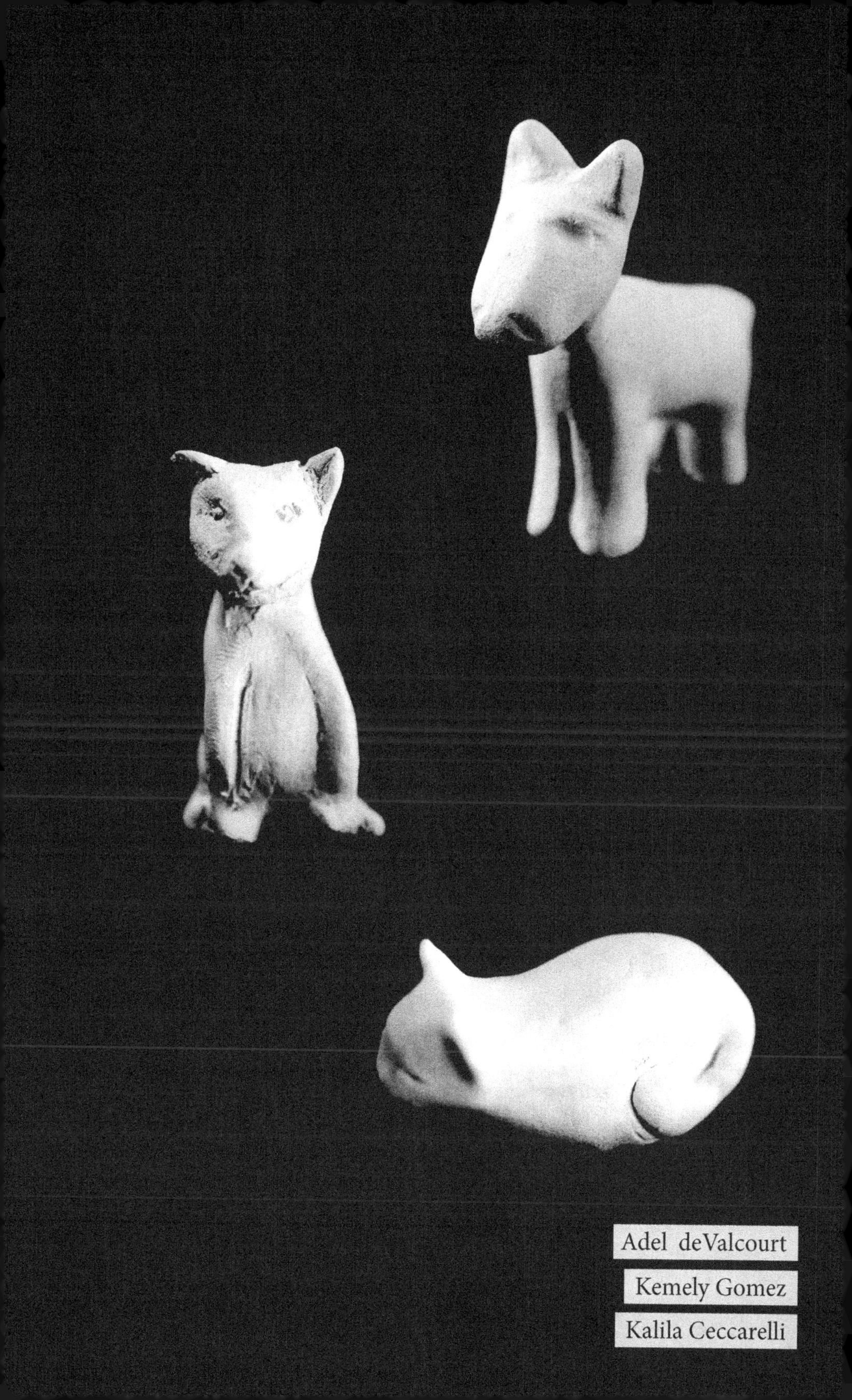

Adel deValcourt
Kemely Gomez
Kalila Ceccarelli

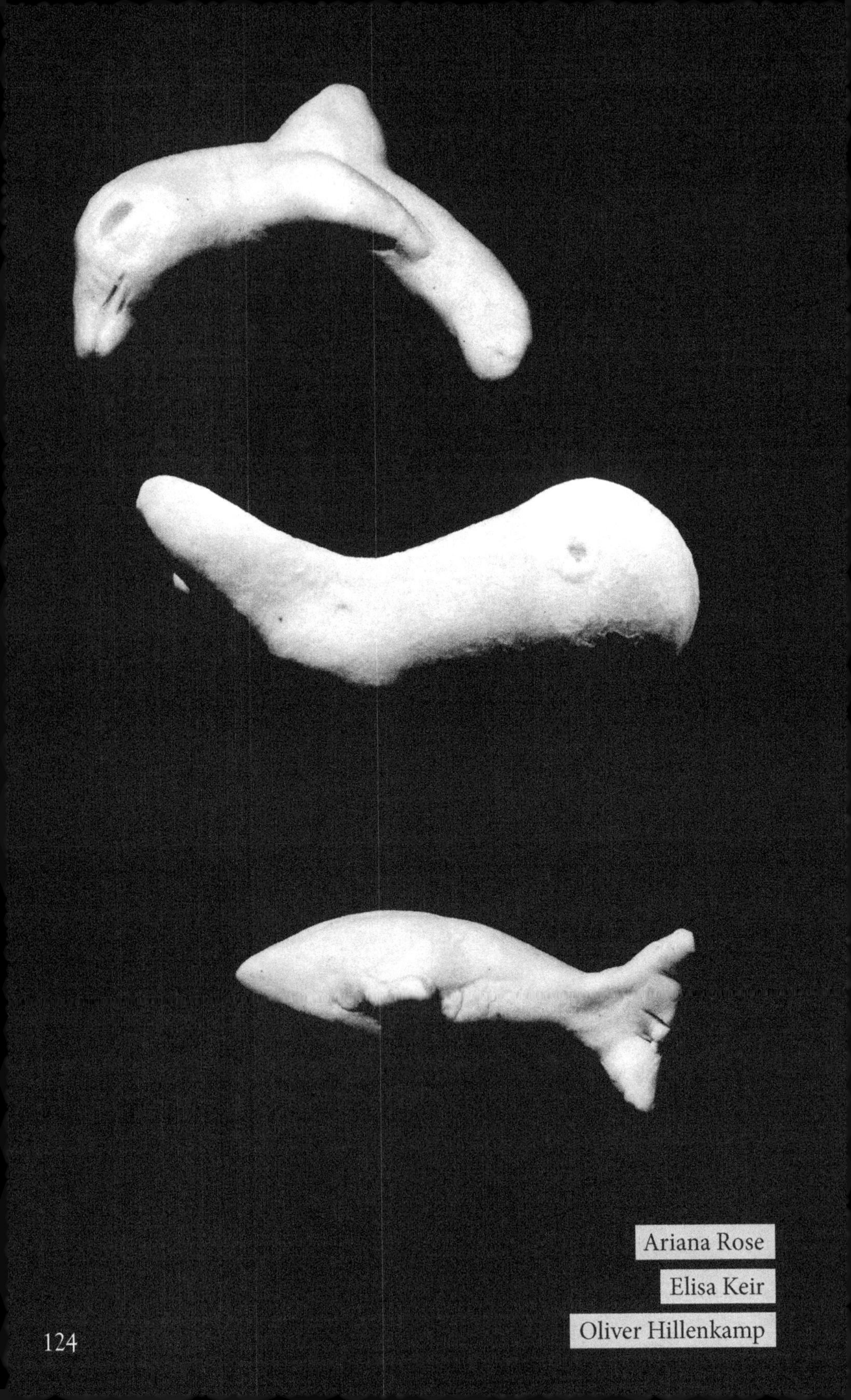

Ariana Rose

Elisa Keir

Oliver Hillenkamp

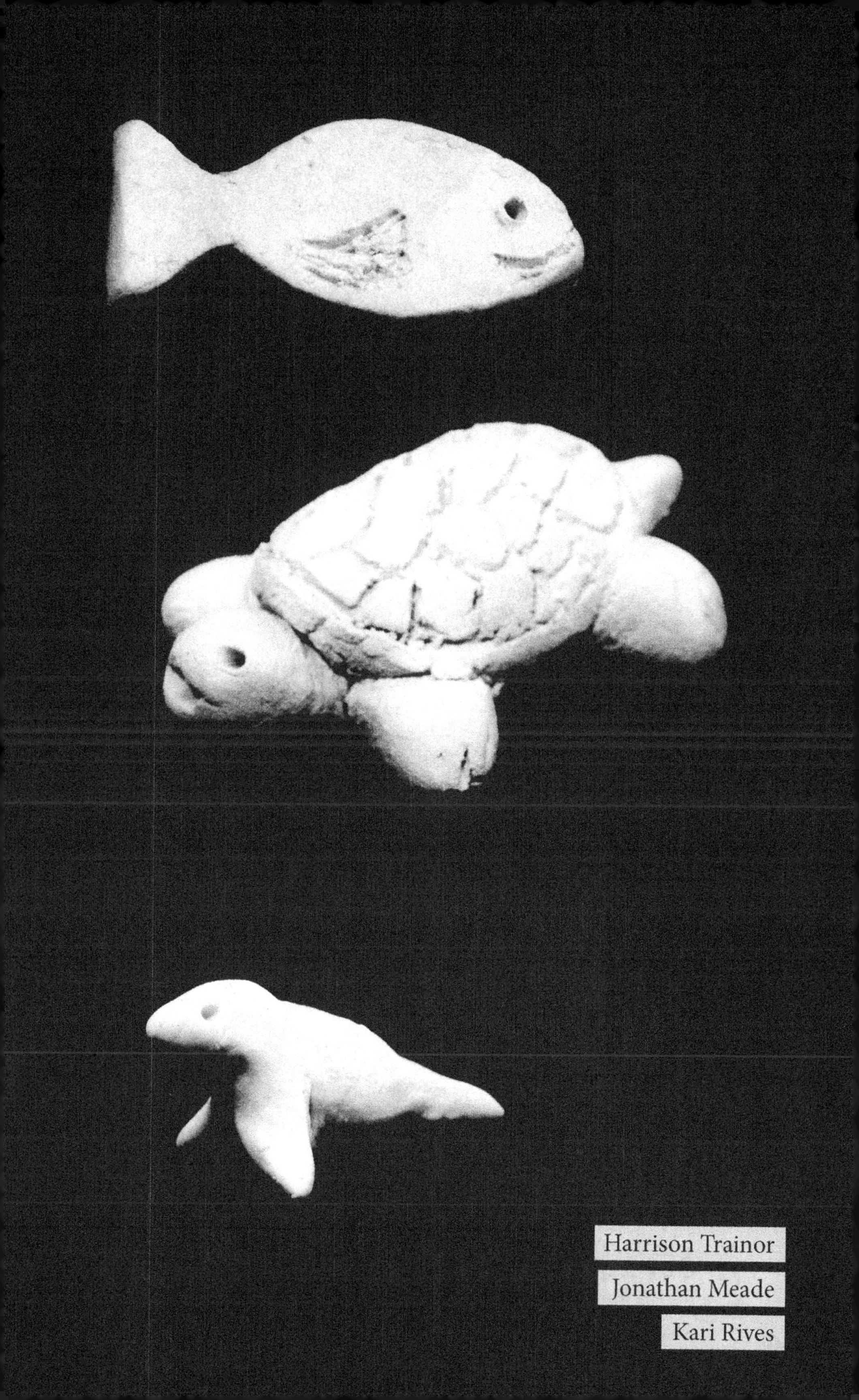
Harrison Trainor
Jonathan Meade
Kari Rives

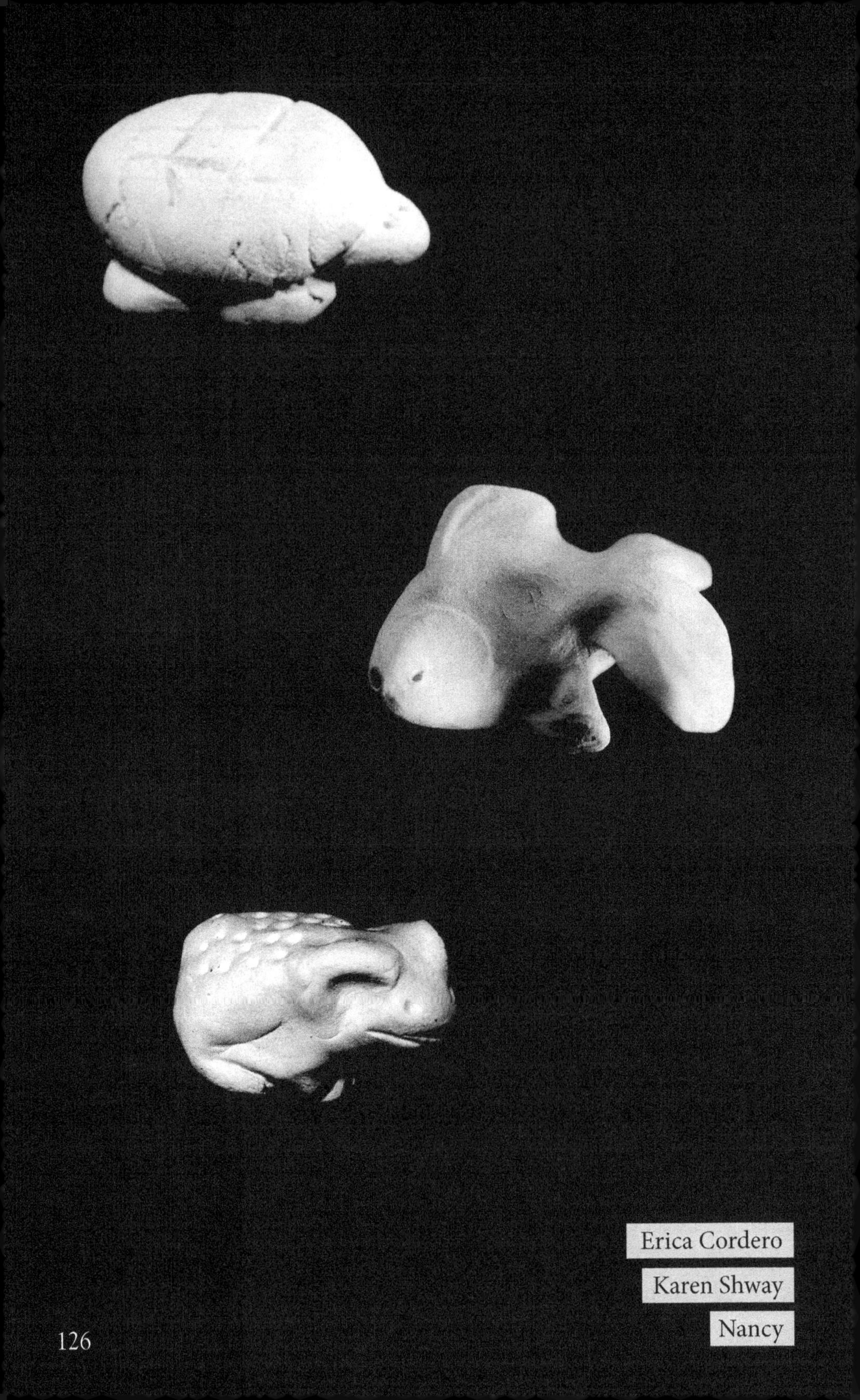

Erica Cordero

Karen Shway

Nancy

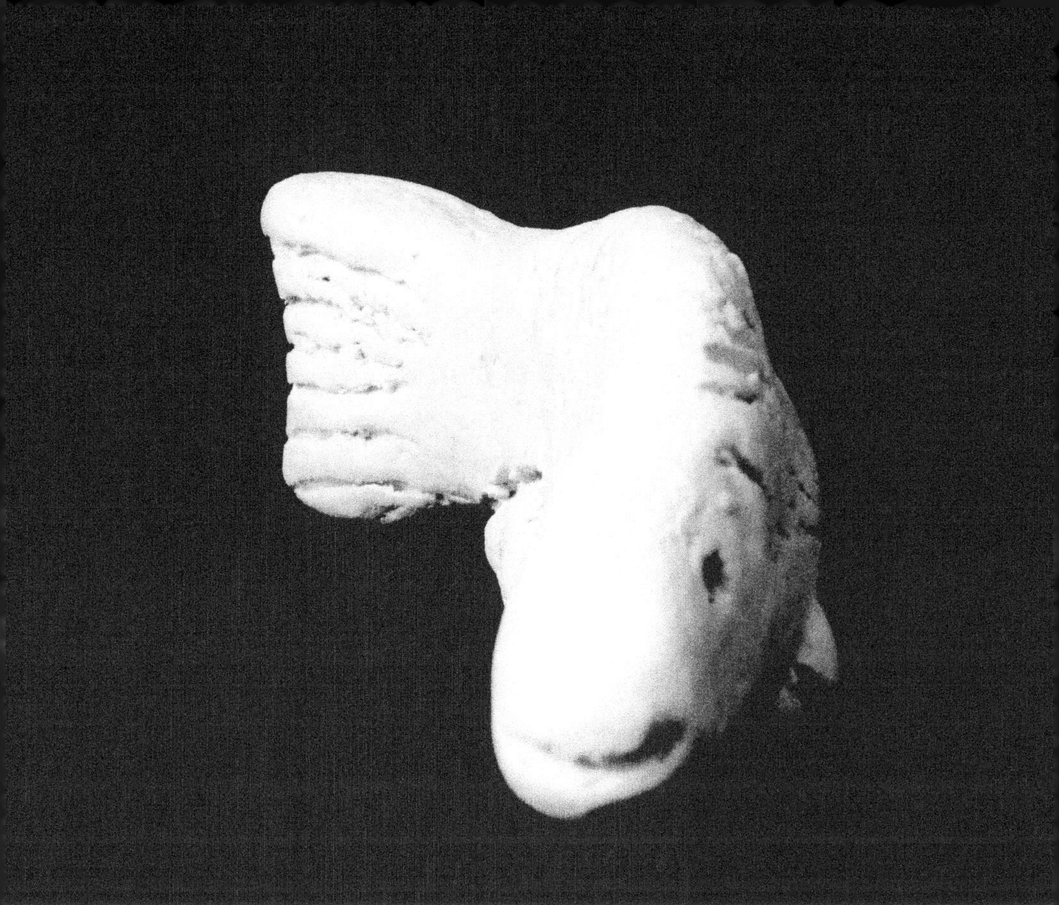

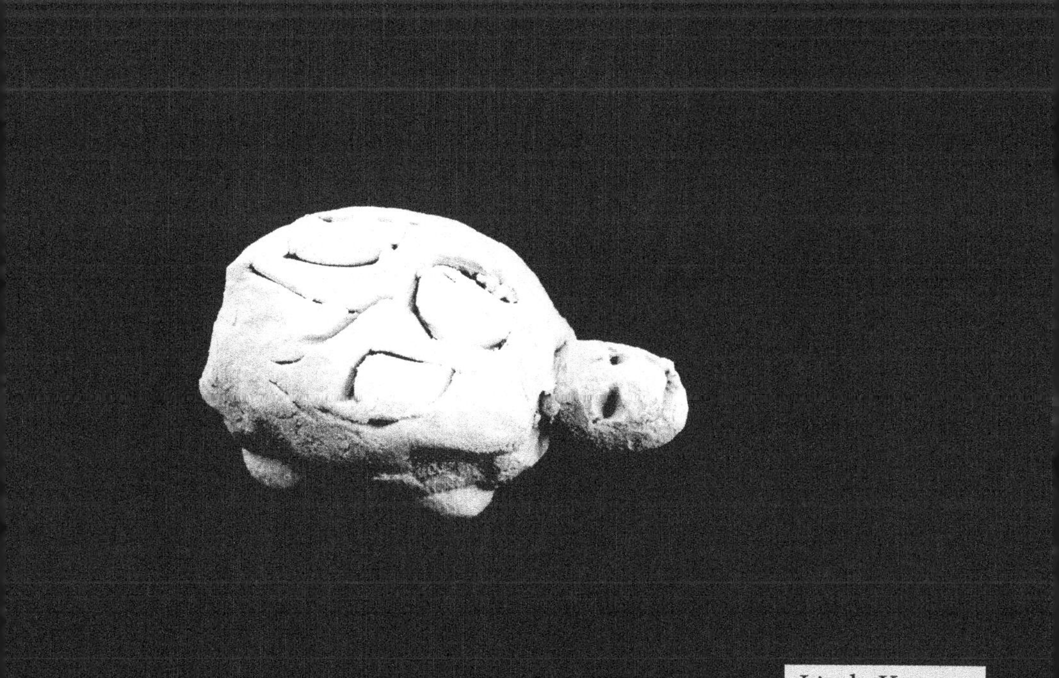

Linda Kastner

Molly LeBron & friends

Ode to Wheat

It begins with grace,
a rain of golden kernels
on the ground, ploughed field
upon which goddesses
are born, or descend
into earth,
eat of some seed
or other.

Demeter
held Persephone
for nine months.
Hades holds her
for three.
Either is
a mother's joy
and sorrow.

Yet, out of darkness
comes the golden light,
sheaves
stamped on pennies –
for aren't they abundance too?
or held aloft in hands
like staffs
as if to say see, see
what we can do.
Without you there is
no communion,
no Cain to murder Abel –

what if he had kept
his brother?
no resurrection,
no food to accompany
the wine at any supper
and certainly not the last.
No body
for the blood.
No gift from
the Father.
No miracle
by the Son.

All this and more
in one simple grain
that gives us
our daily bread,
that with its
fruity yeast
leavens or
unleavens
our lives.

For how can we look away,
how can we not bear witness,
when you bow your golden heads
in prayer
when you are ripe
and ready to be taken.

-Jenice Gharib

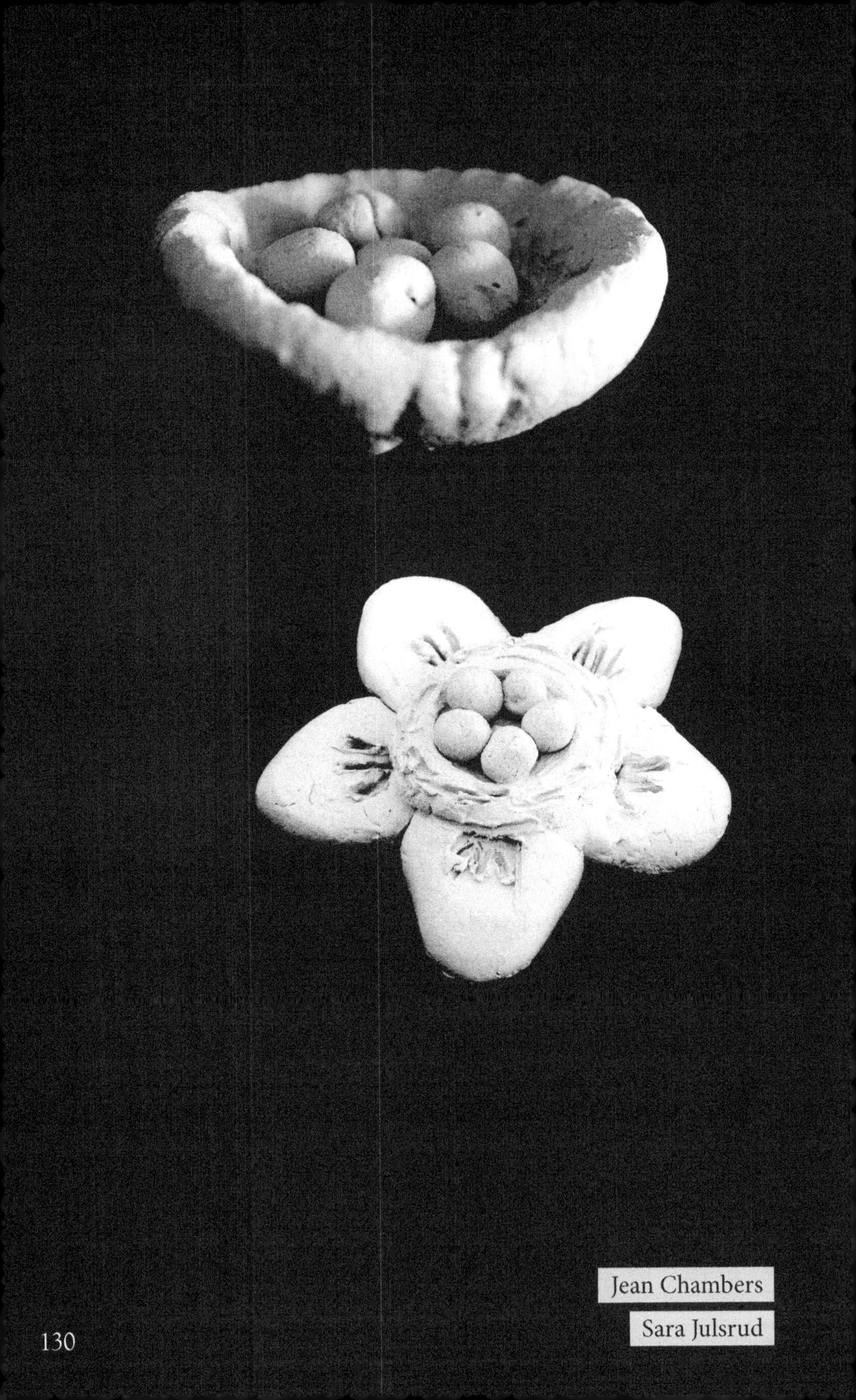

Jean Chambers

Sara Julsrud

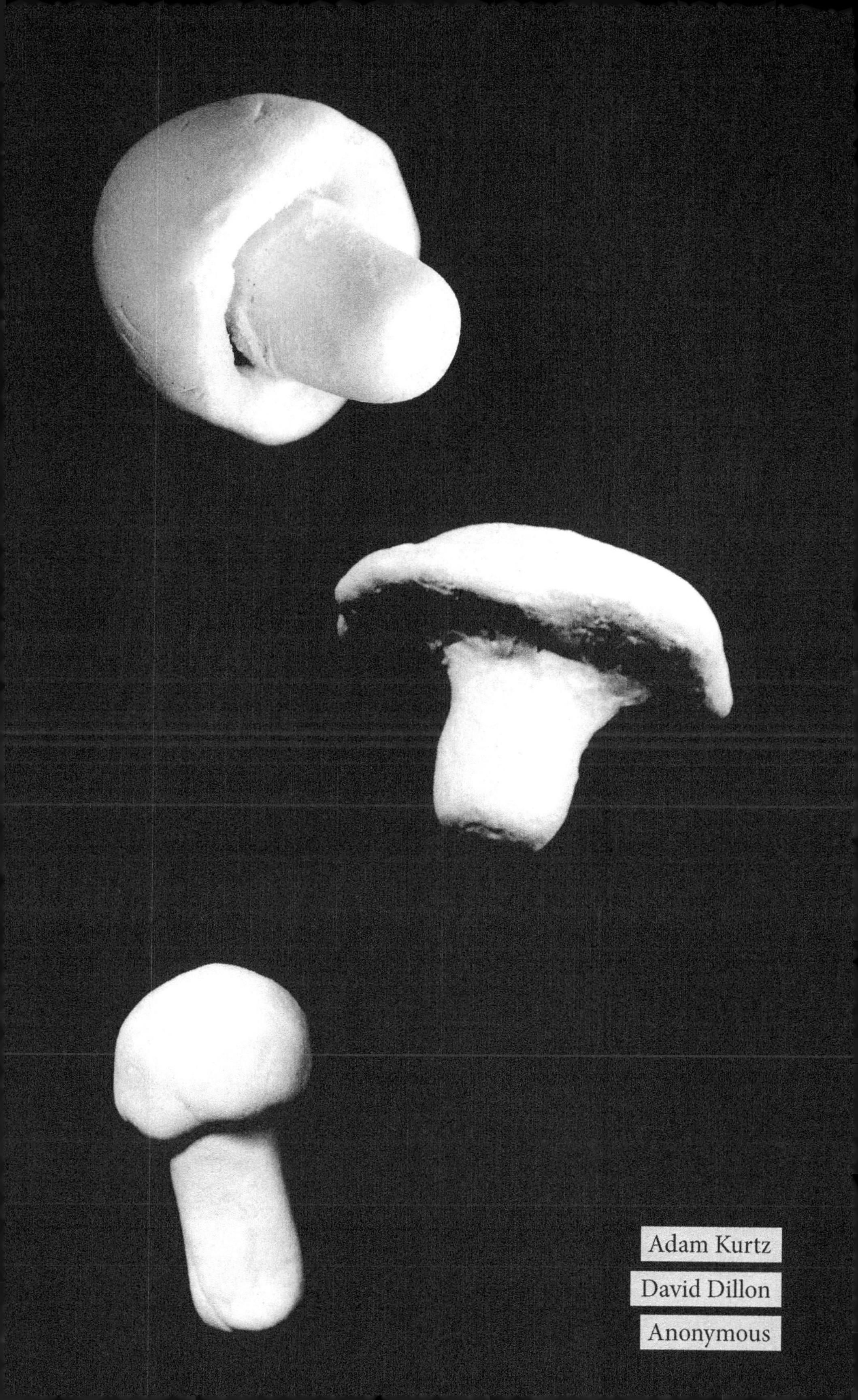
Adam Kurtz
David Dillon
Anonymous

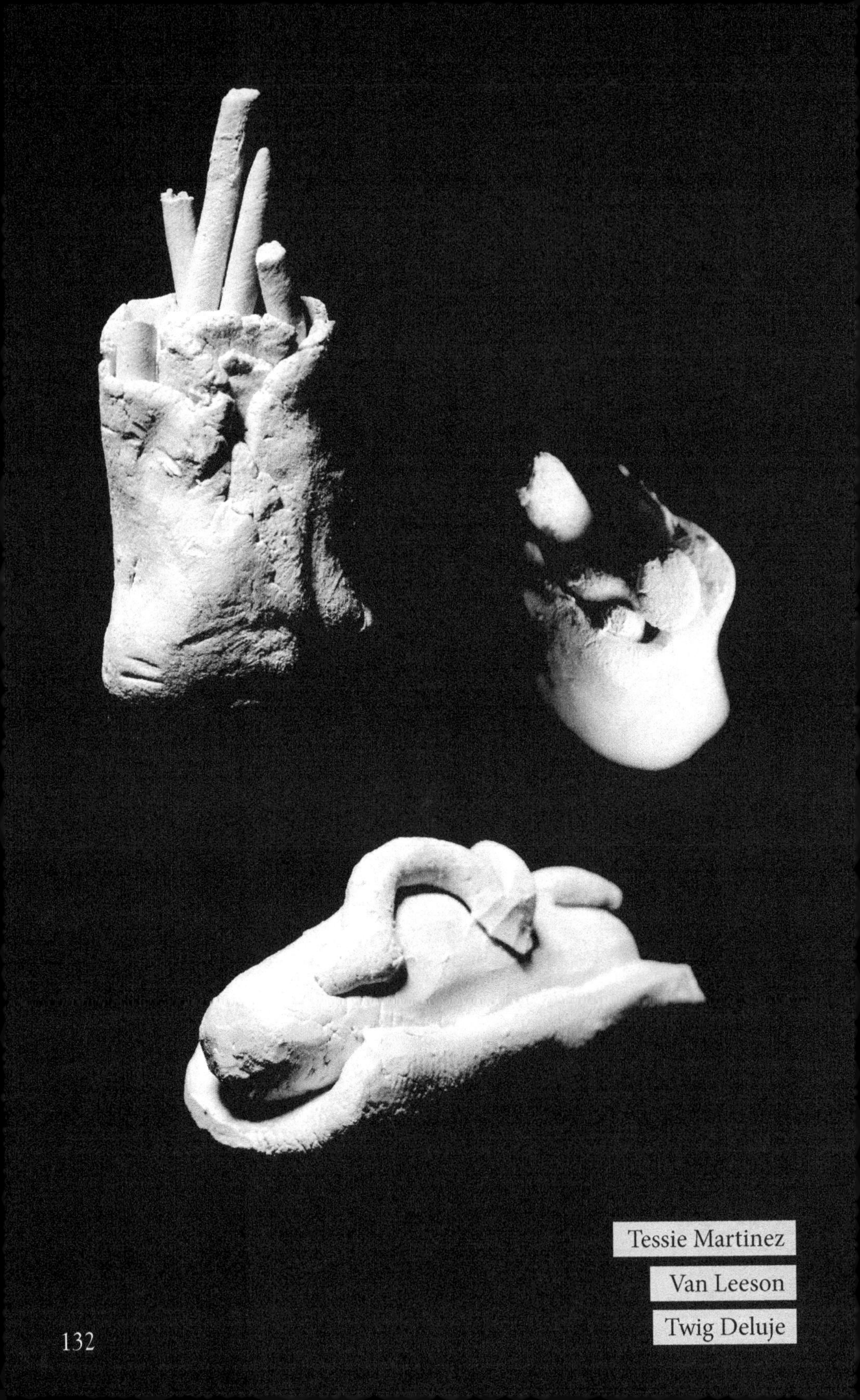

Tessie Martinez

Van Leeson

Twig Deluje

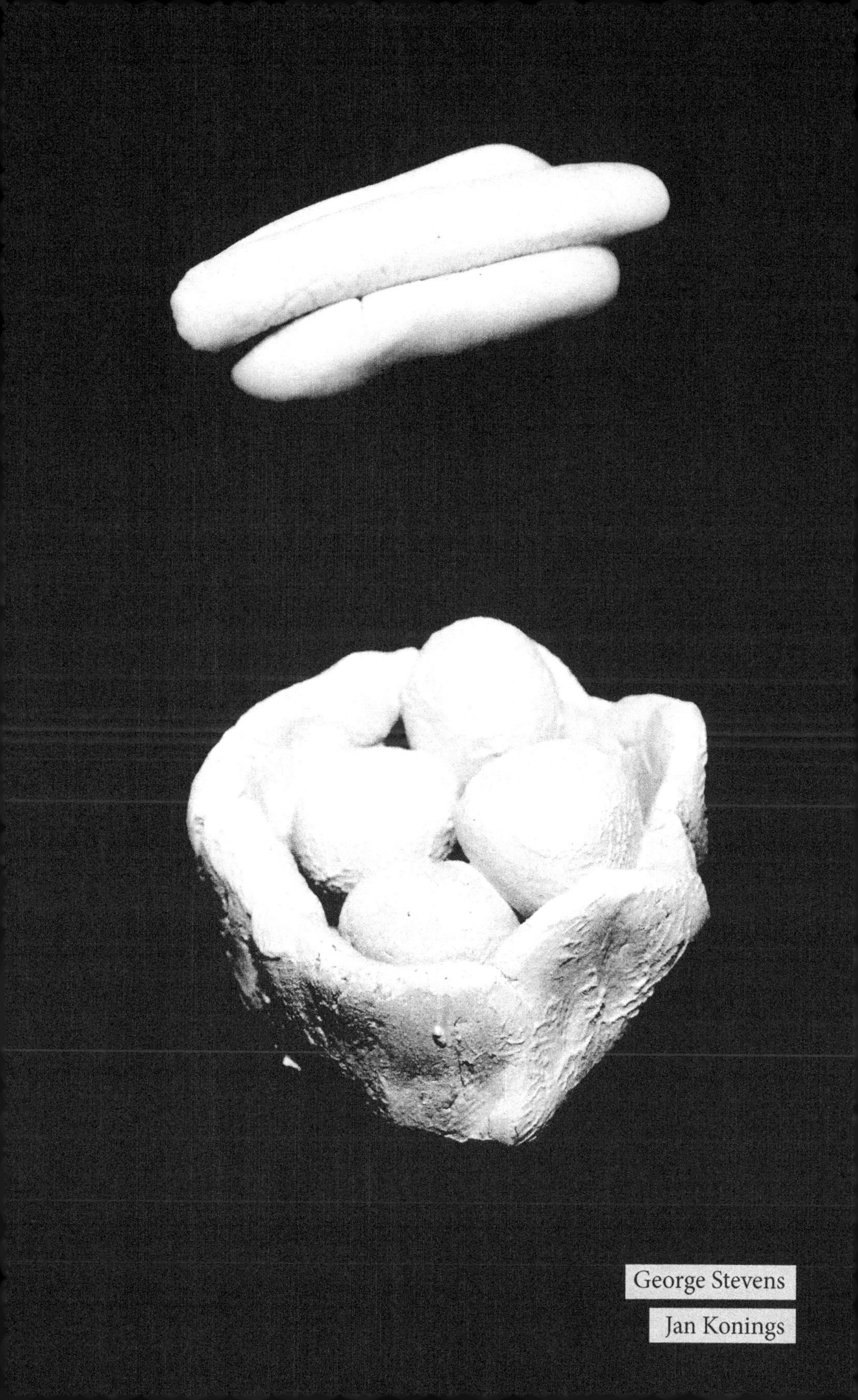

George Stevens

Jan Konings

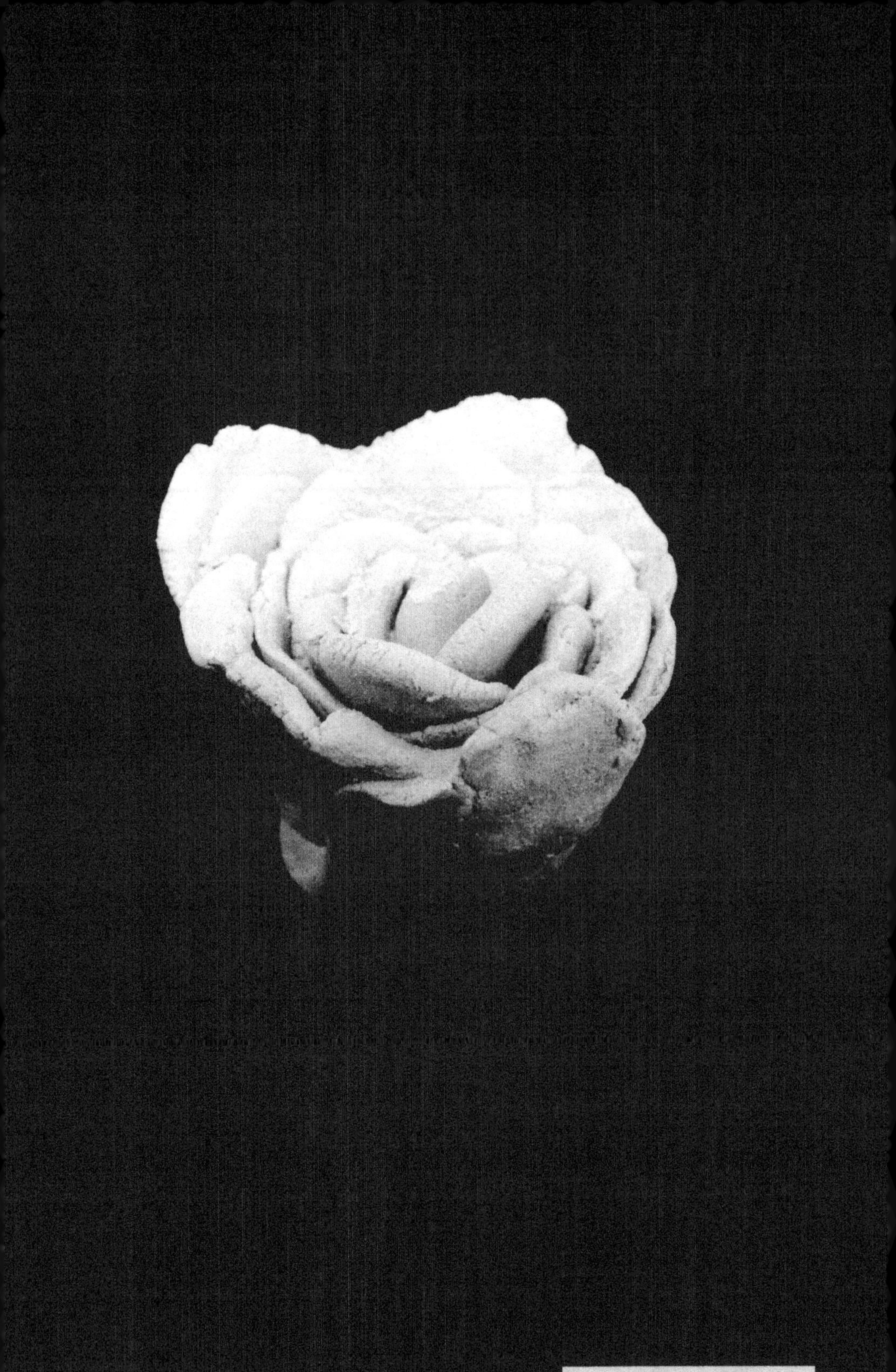

Lucio Cooper Da Silva

I loved watching the French walk or ride down the street with their fresh baguette tucked under their arm- ready for anything.

-Anonymous

Benjamin Franklin walks down the street
A loaf of bread under each arm
Lightening smiles

-Anonymous

Just Past Watertown

Bread in one hand
Steering wheel in the other
Road opens
Through fields of soy and grain
997 miles of culture
to Wheat Ridge

-Jerry Wellman

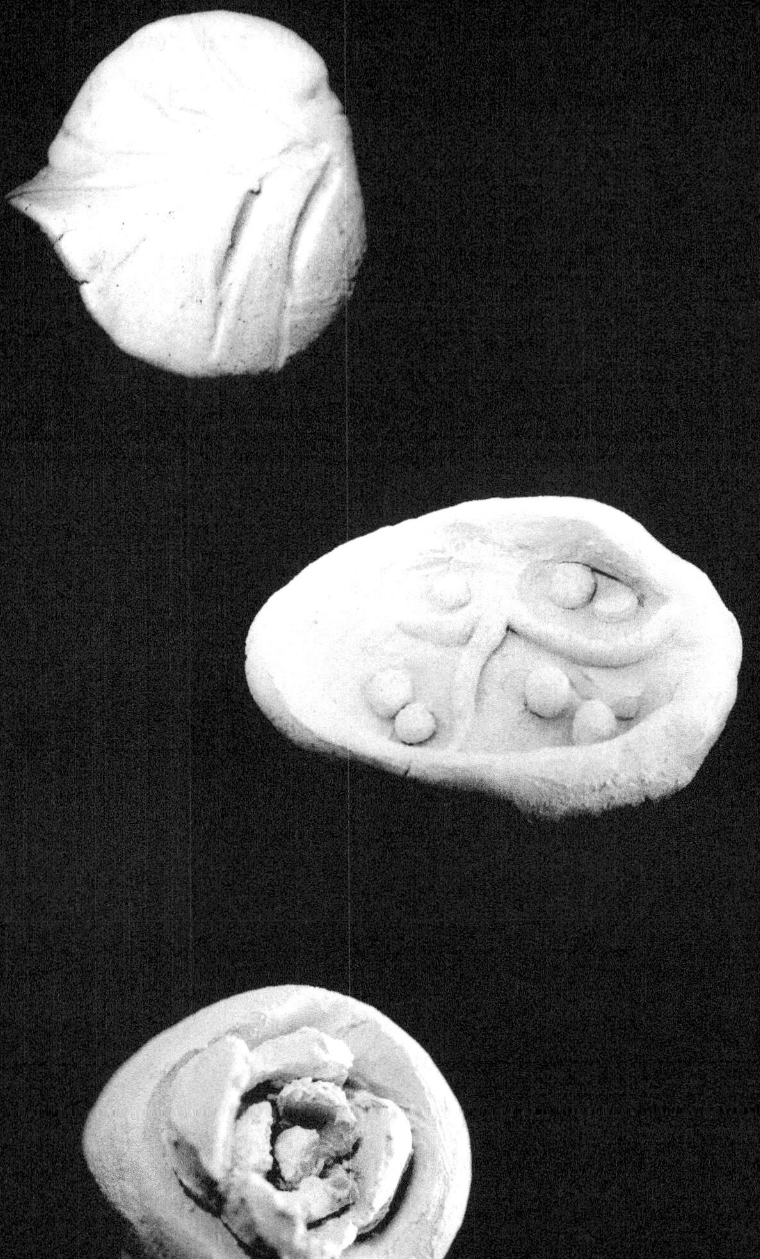

Lura Brookins

Ellen Shapiro

Melissa Connally

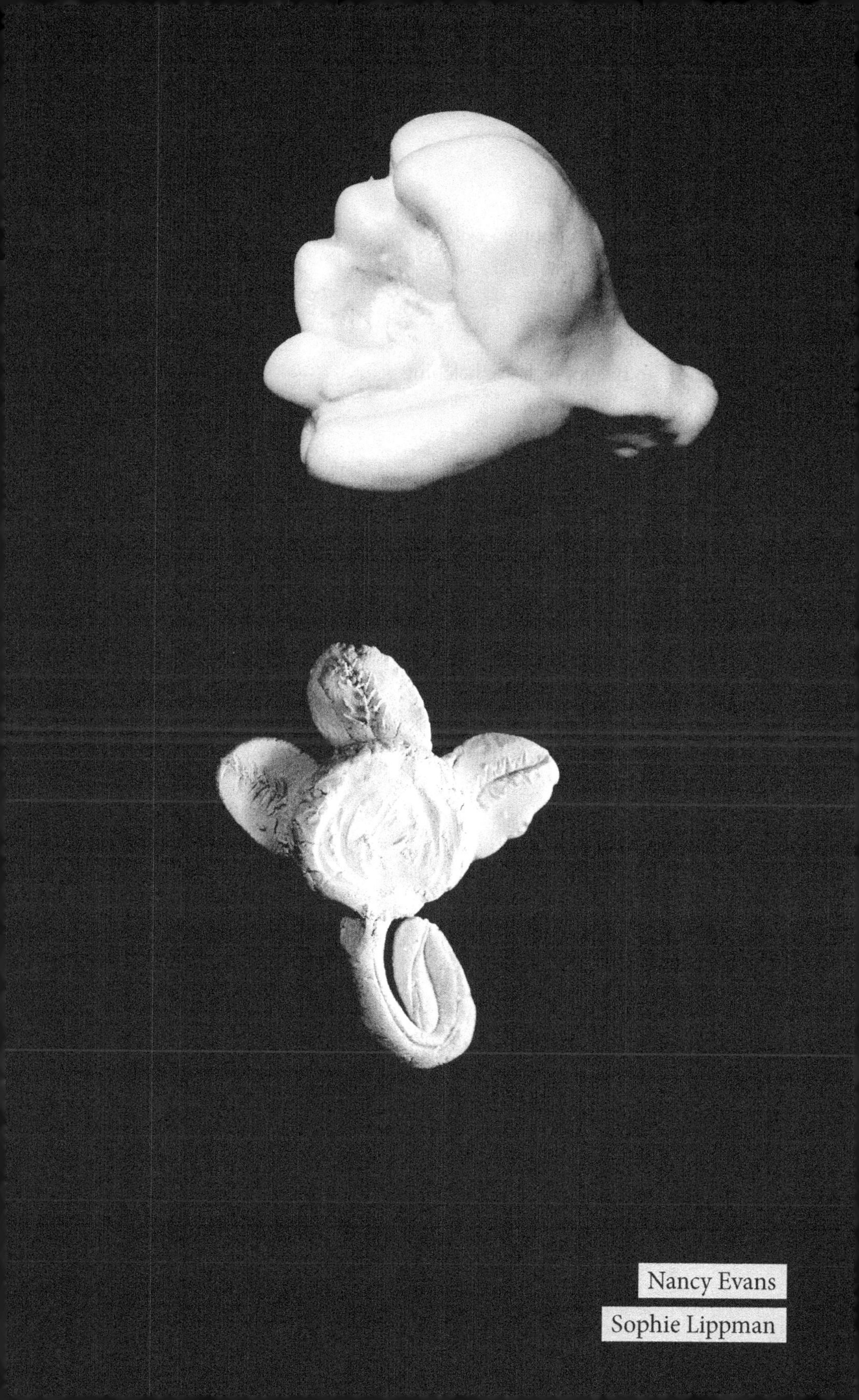

Nancy Evans

Sophie Lippman

Proof of Life

Please know–
that each bubble
beneath this crust
is owed
(in part)
to the appreciative belching
of well-fed yeast

-Hope Cahill

Bread for the poor
Bread for the rich
Bread for the cop
Bread for the snitch

-Anonymous

Wess Brot ich ess, dess Lied ich sing.

-German proverd via K. Stritzl

When you read a story about a poor thief, or when you hear a tale of a miracle performed for a slum and even an account of a fond memory of home... it's always about the bread.

-Anonymous

My mind always wanders to thoughts of steaks and soups but the bread always takes my hunger away before my craving is met.

-Anonymous

Slices of Bread

Cut with sharp little knives,
Falls off like snow,
And tastes like "the grass is greener on the other side."

Makes the lonely feel comfort,
Helps the bitter be better,
And gives joy to all the little girls and boys.

You can mix it with anything
But even just left plain,
It still fills every desire

-Marlena Chapman

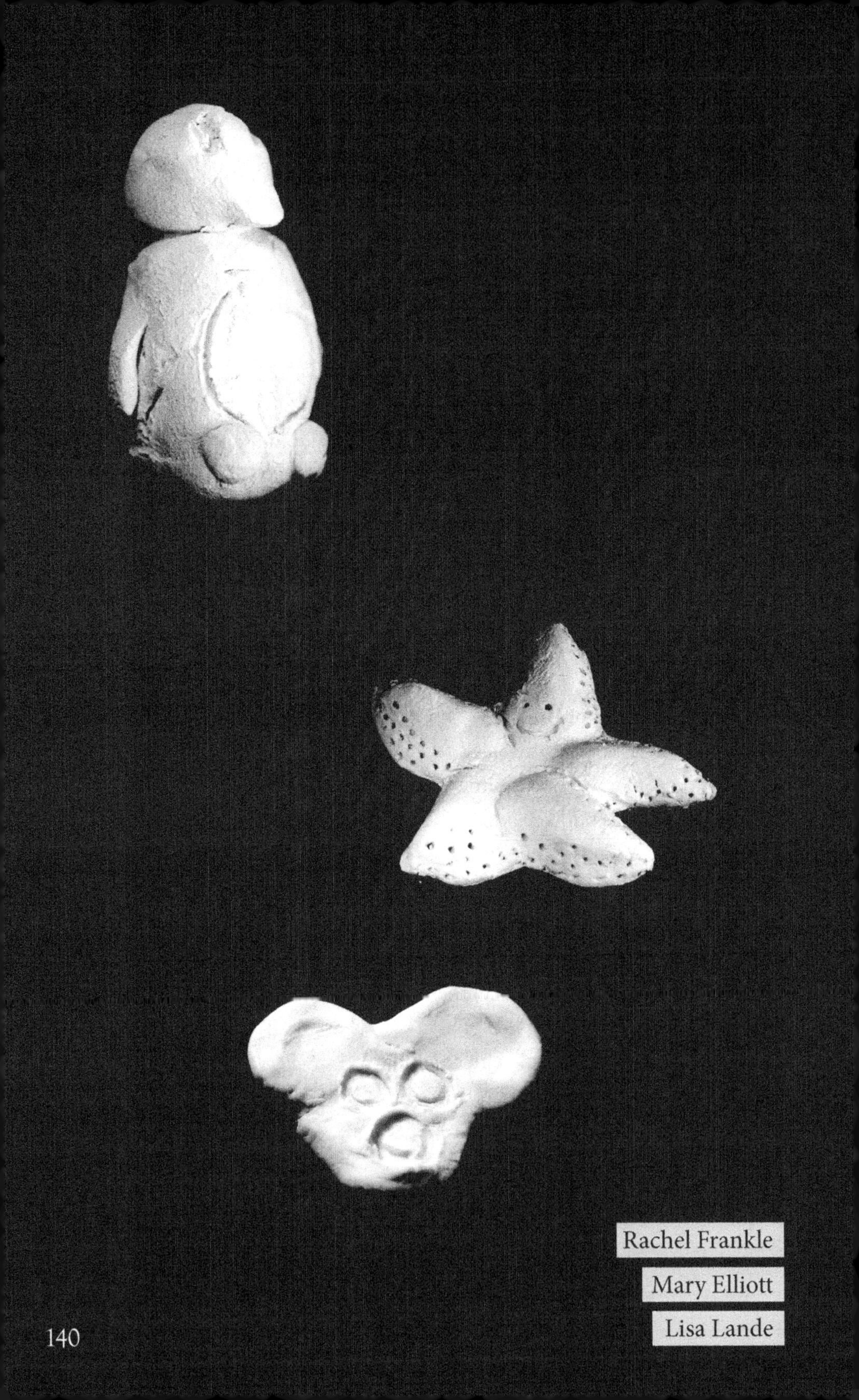

Rachel Frankle

Mary Elliott

Lisa Lande

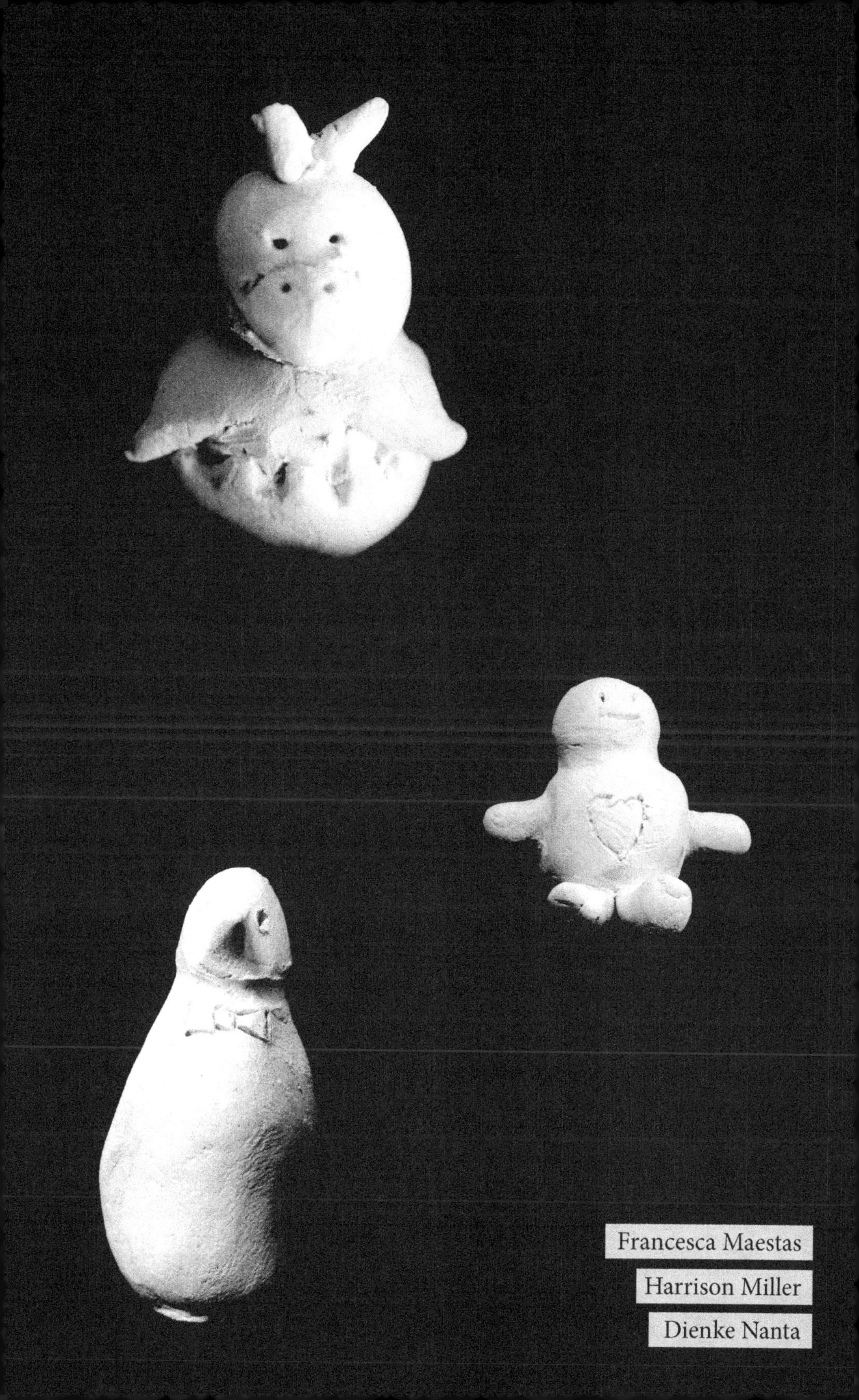

Francesca Maestas

Harrison Miller

Dienke Nanta

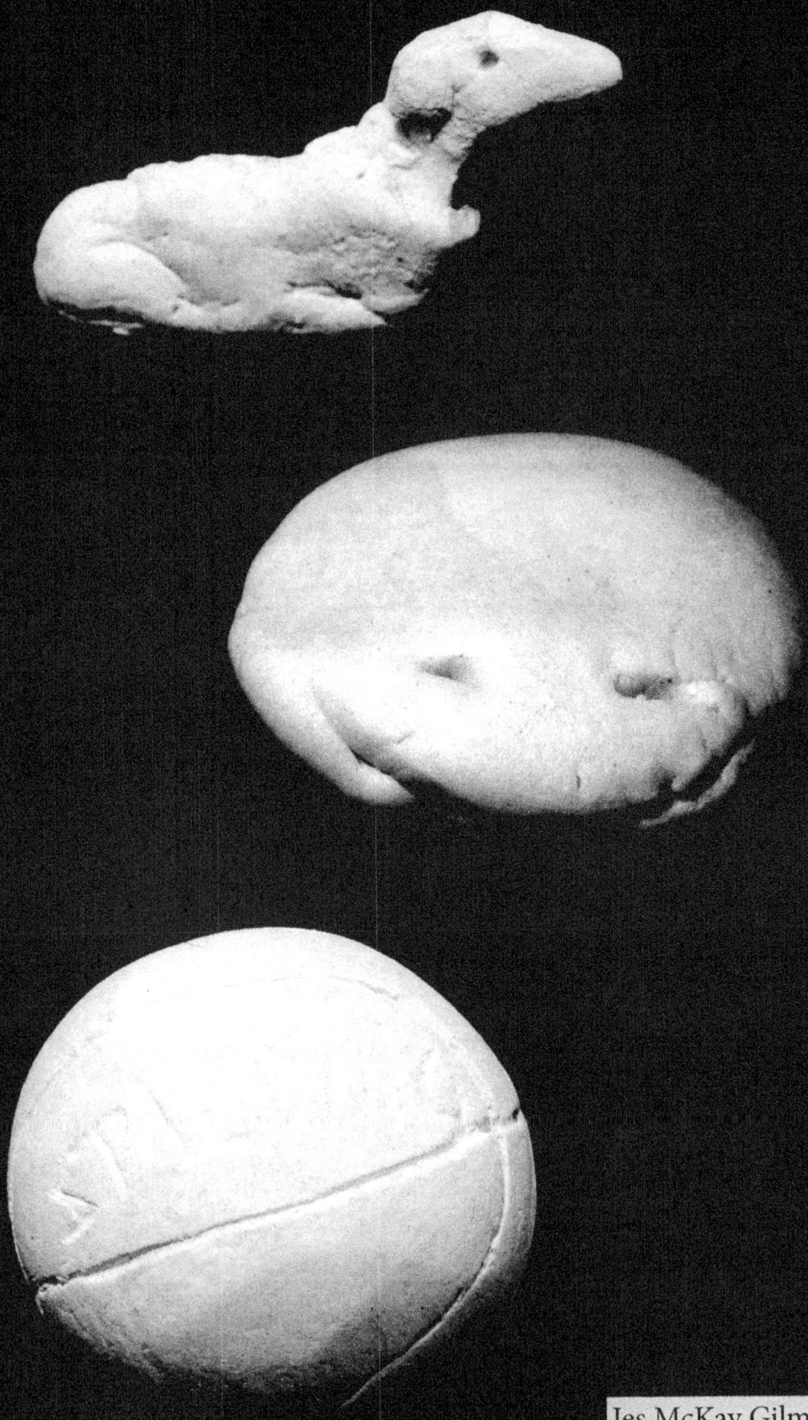

Jes McKay Gilmore

Connor Woods

Reed Gustafson

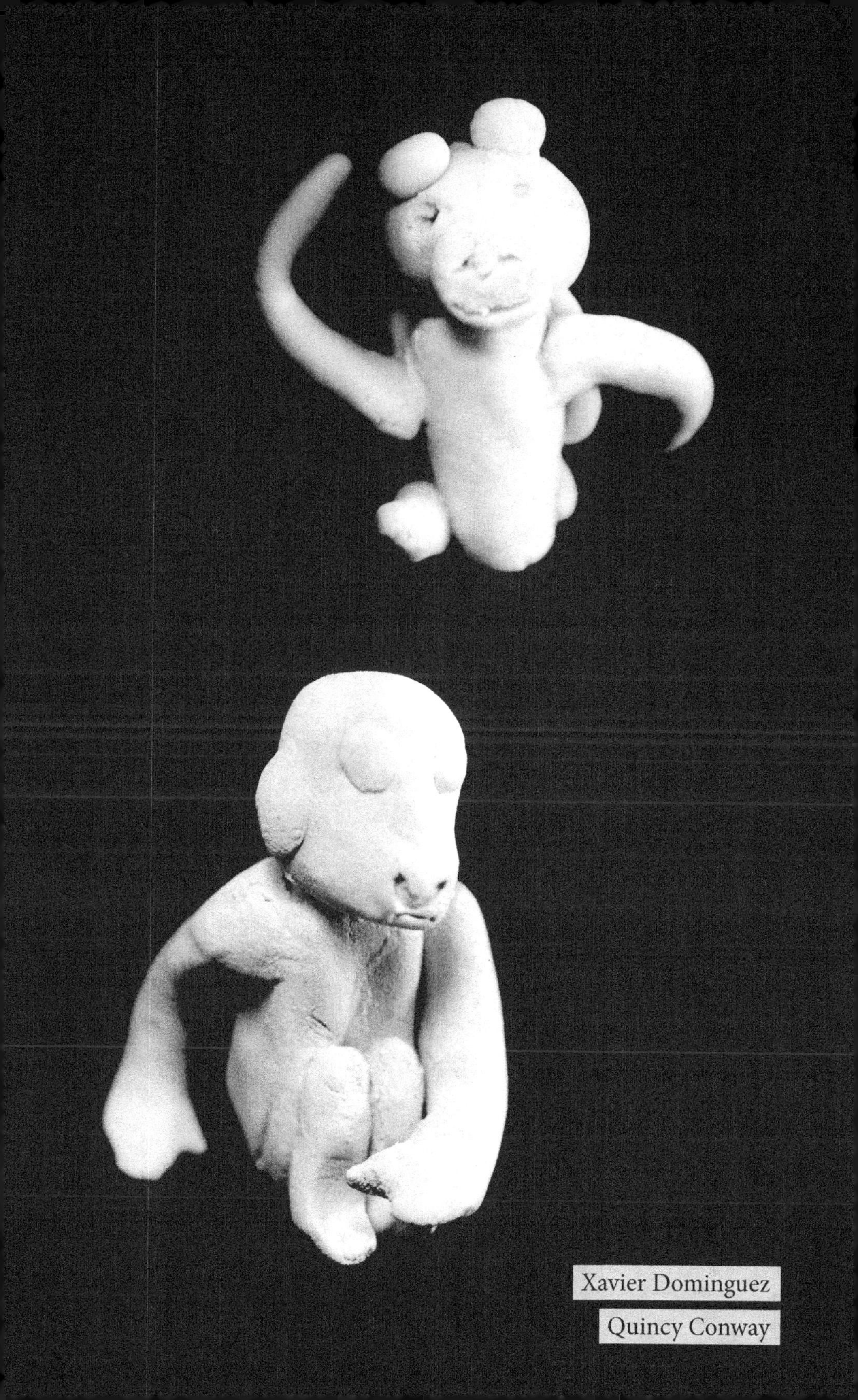

Xavier Dominguez

Quincy Conway

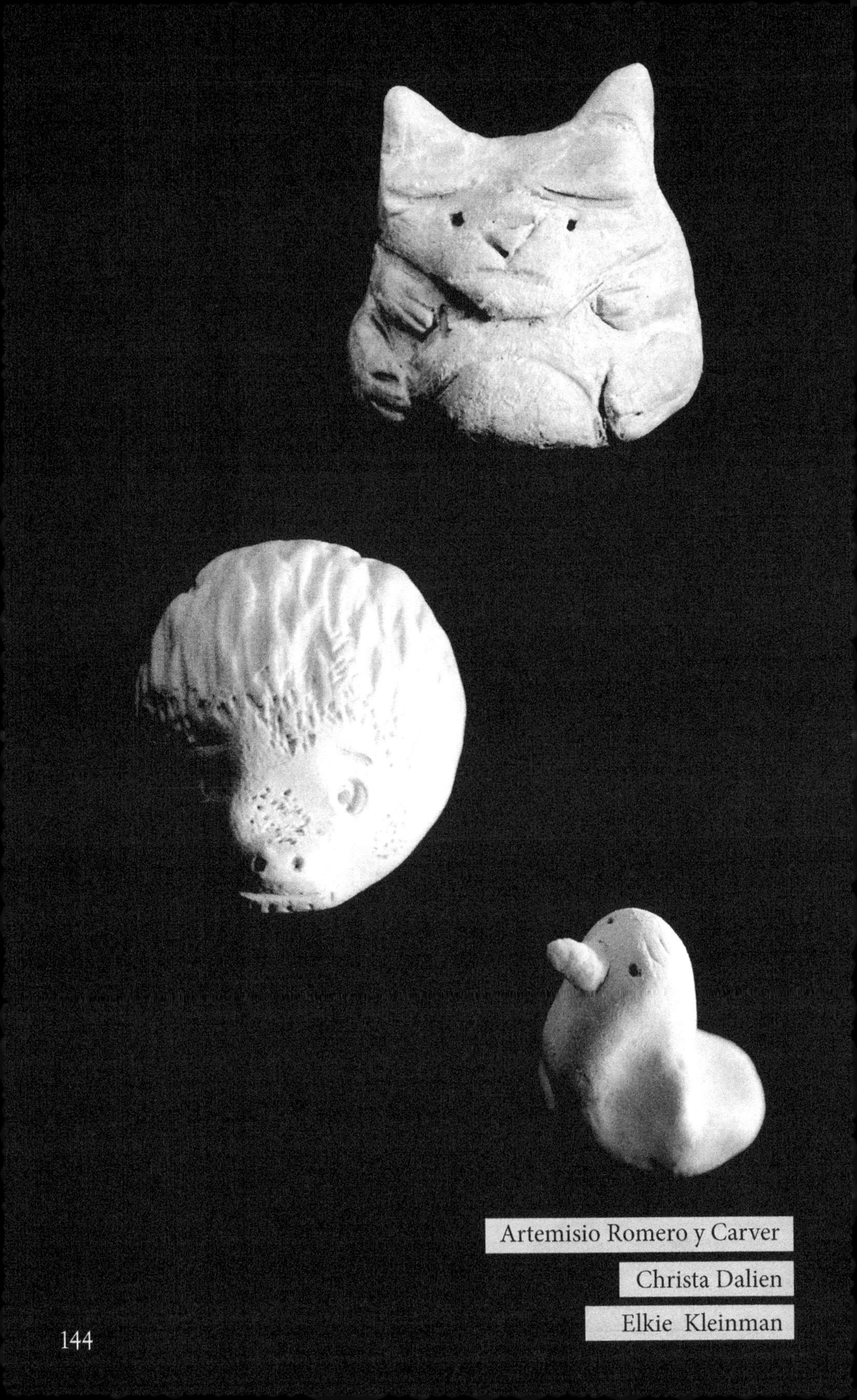

Artemisio Romero y Carver

Christa Dalien

Elkie Kleinman

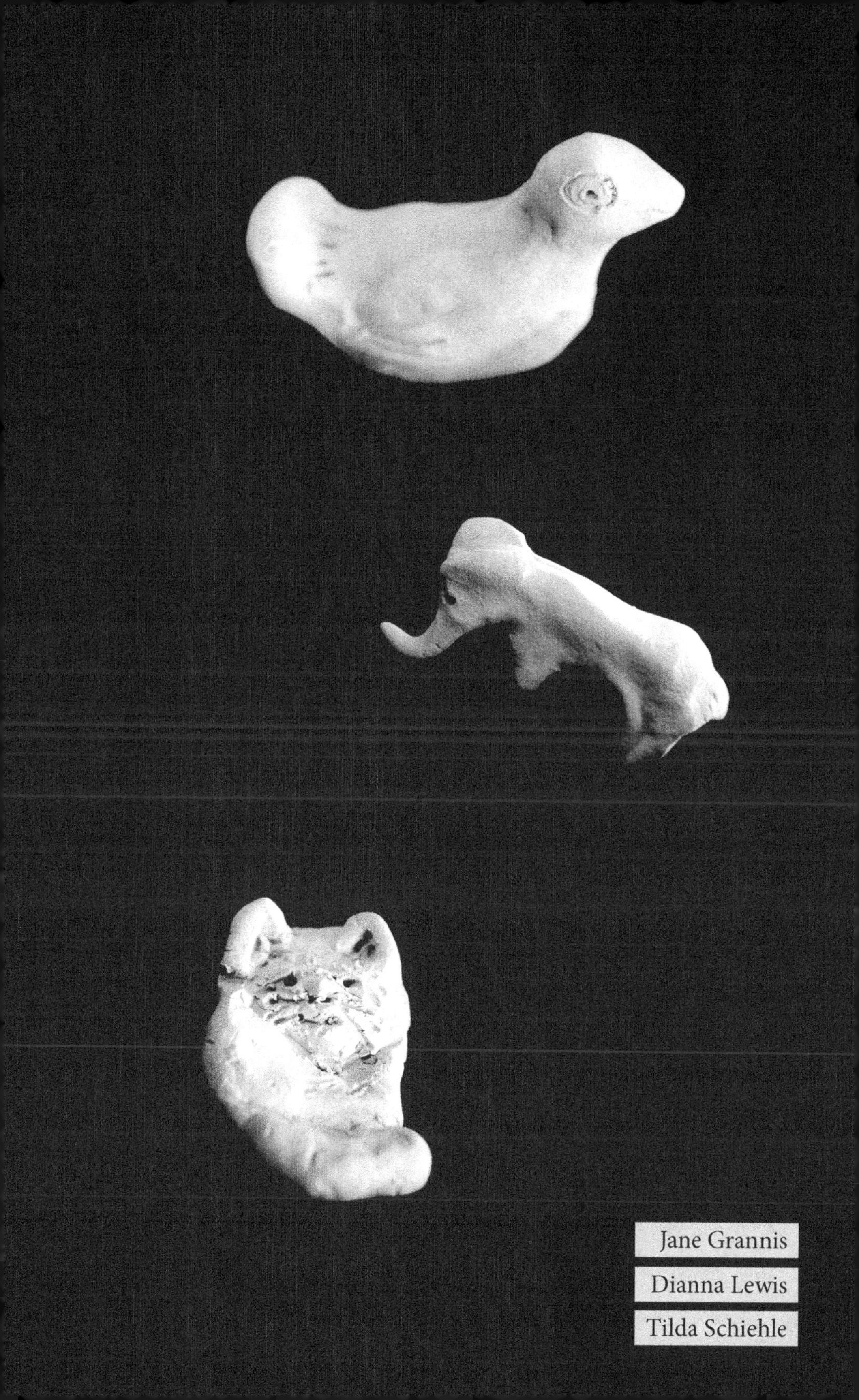

Jane Grannis
Dianna Lewis
Tilda Schiehle

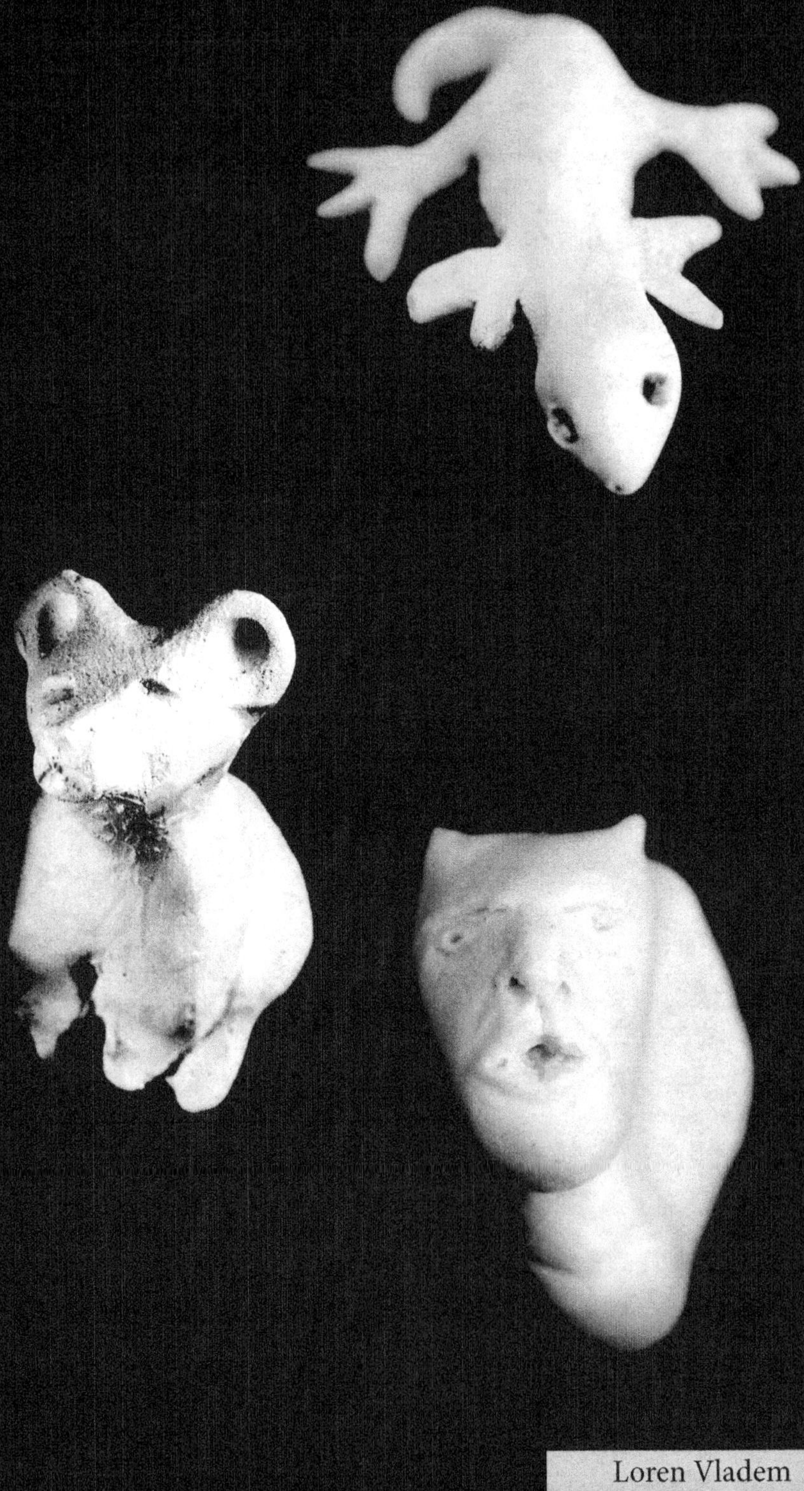

Loren Vladem

Leslie Wizner

Mira Engel

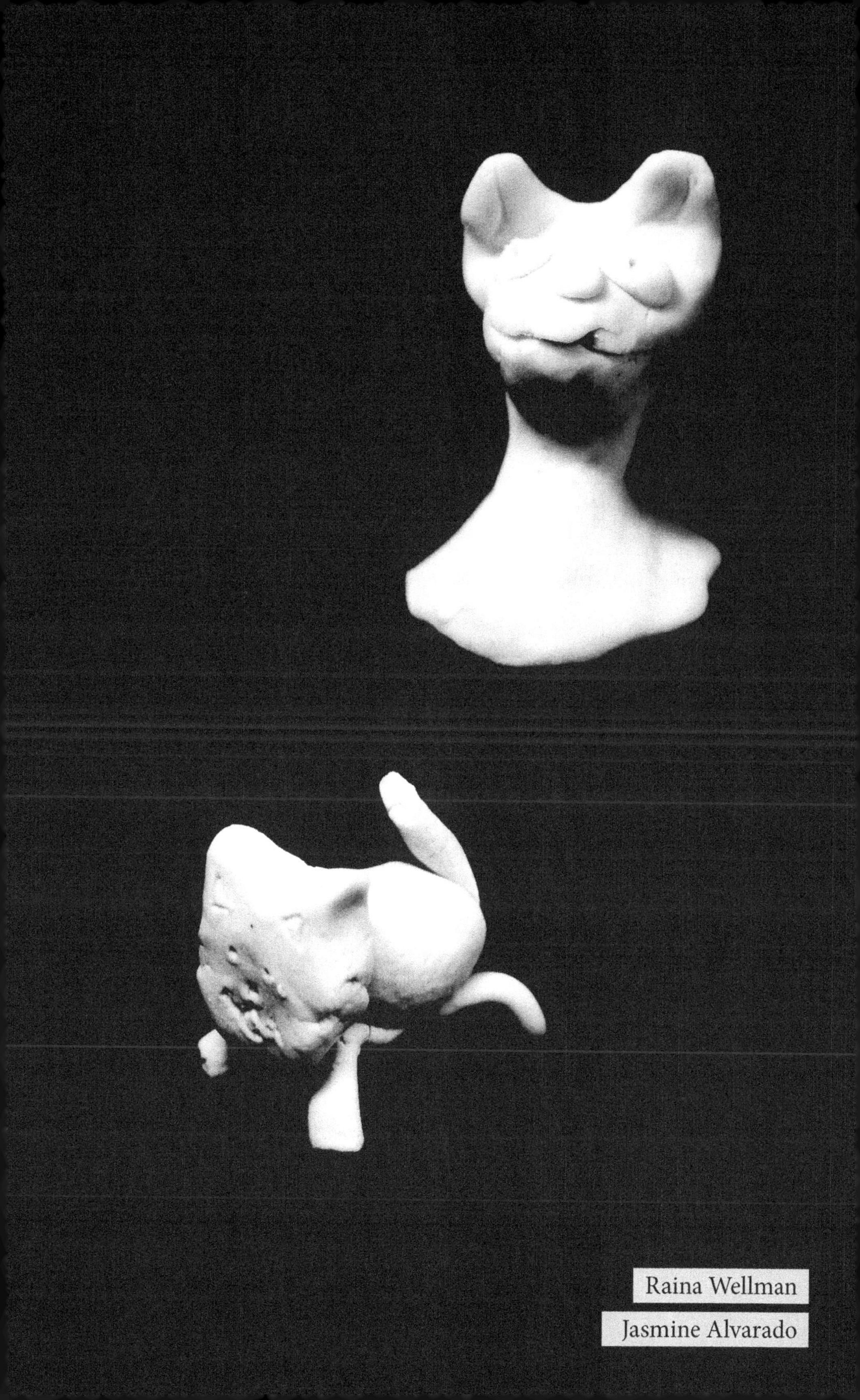

Raina Wellman

Jasmine Alvarado

Bread is tasty but its really just the way I savor the butter.

-Melanie West

My Grandmother's yeast is still alive even though she has been dead for 22 years.

-Anonymous

The smell of baking bread is the most welcoming aroma ever!

-Anonymous

The bread in my hand leaves crumbs in the sand.

-Anonymous

You are the butter to my bread.

-Anonymous

How do you know if it's surrealist dough?
There's no flour or water, just the body of a fish and the head of a crow

And what do you spread on that postmodern bread?
Some kind of content from something you read?
And how do you know if you've eaten post modern surreal?
You'll never know as one's undefined and one you can't feel

-Anonymous

Well, you already know my thoughts about bread. Rarely do we find such an amazing, no- ordinary, way of expressing ourselves. It's with our hands, it's with our brains, it's with our he arts . I didn't mean to say art, Ha. Freudian slip! The truth always comes out!

-Anonymous

Bread is a sponge for soup, tomato sauce, butter, salad dressing, olive oil, sweat from under your breasts.

-Anonymous

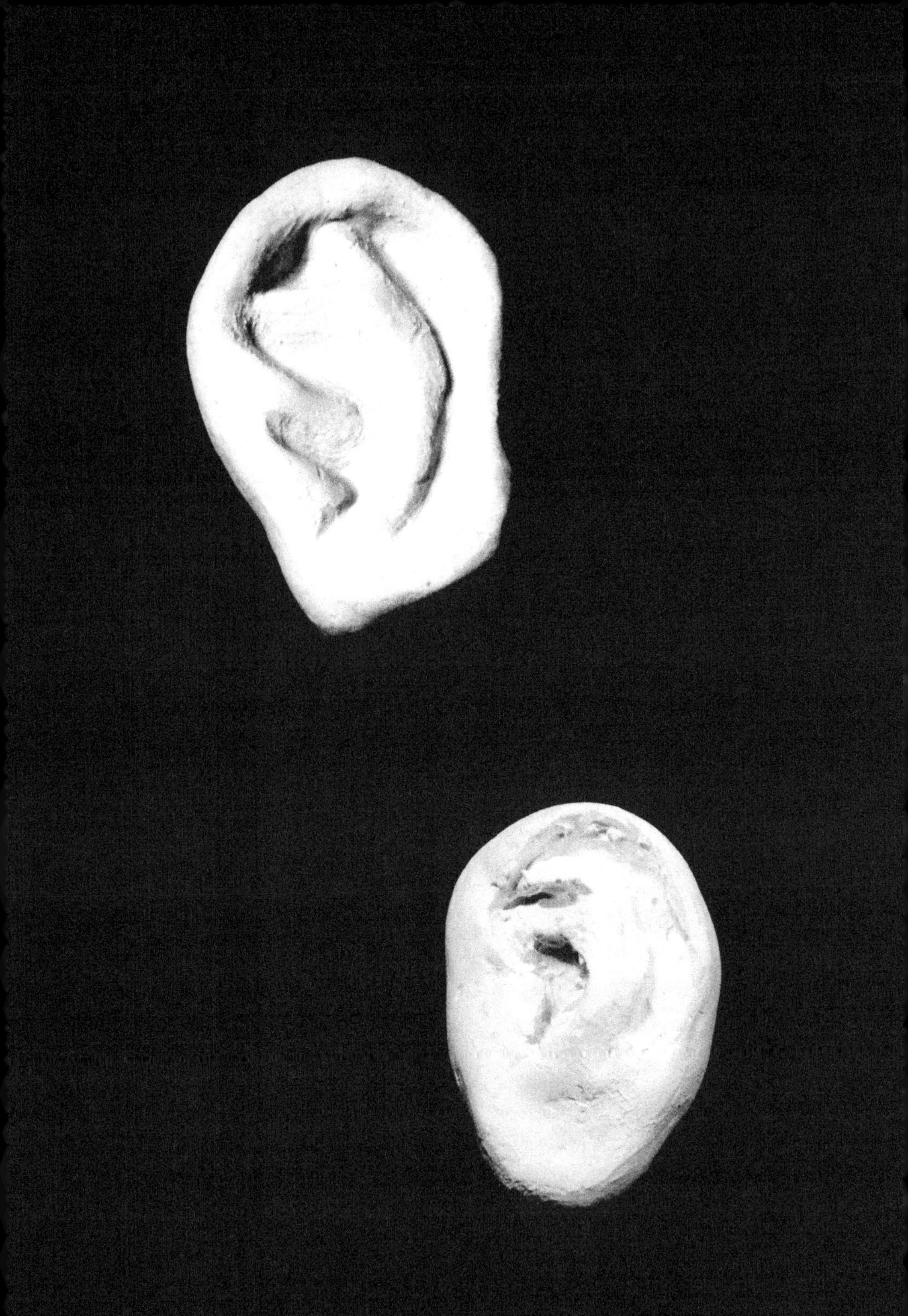

Jon Carver

Thelma Mathias

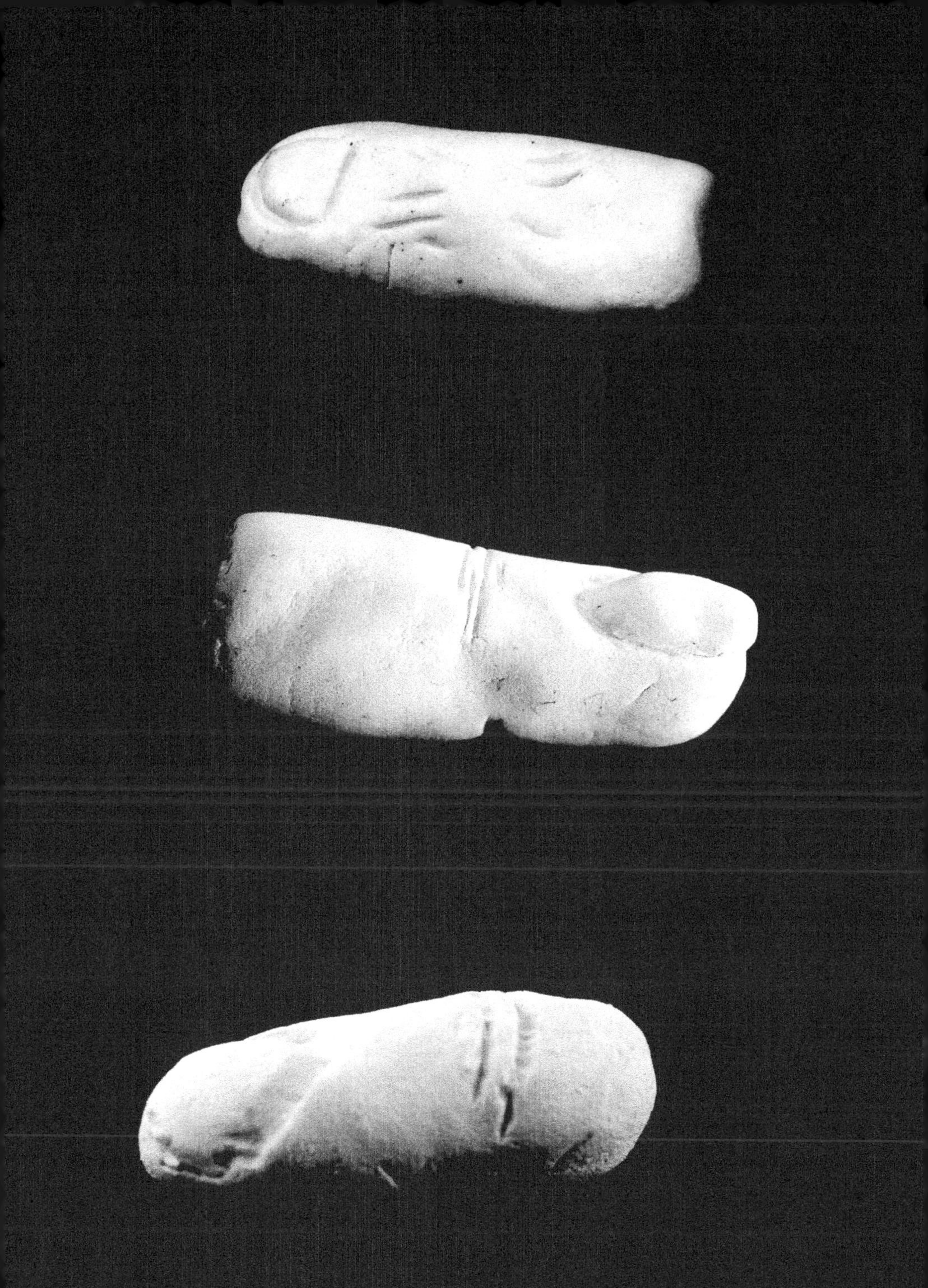

Hunter Merriman

Sondra Goodwin

Shirley Ormond

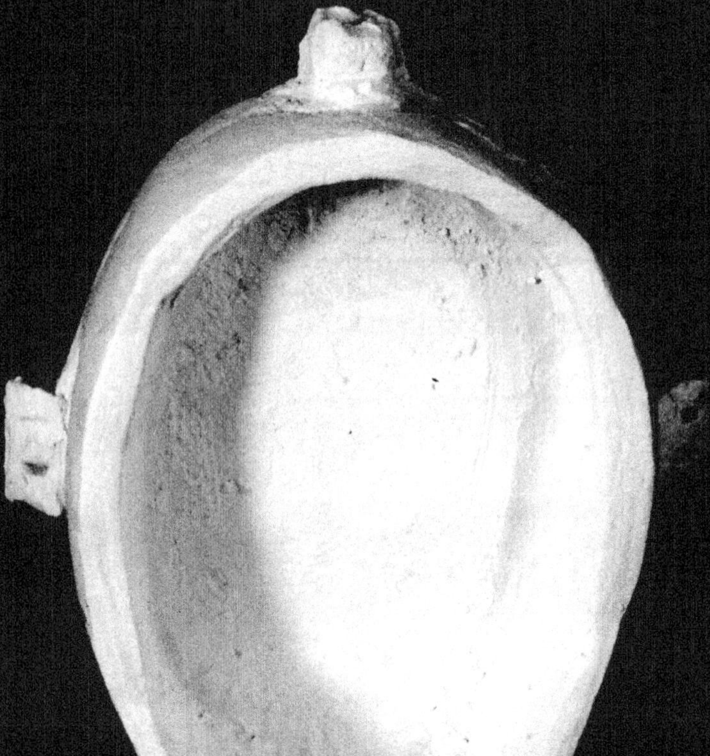

Eric Pino

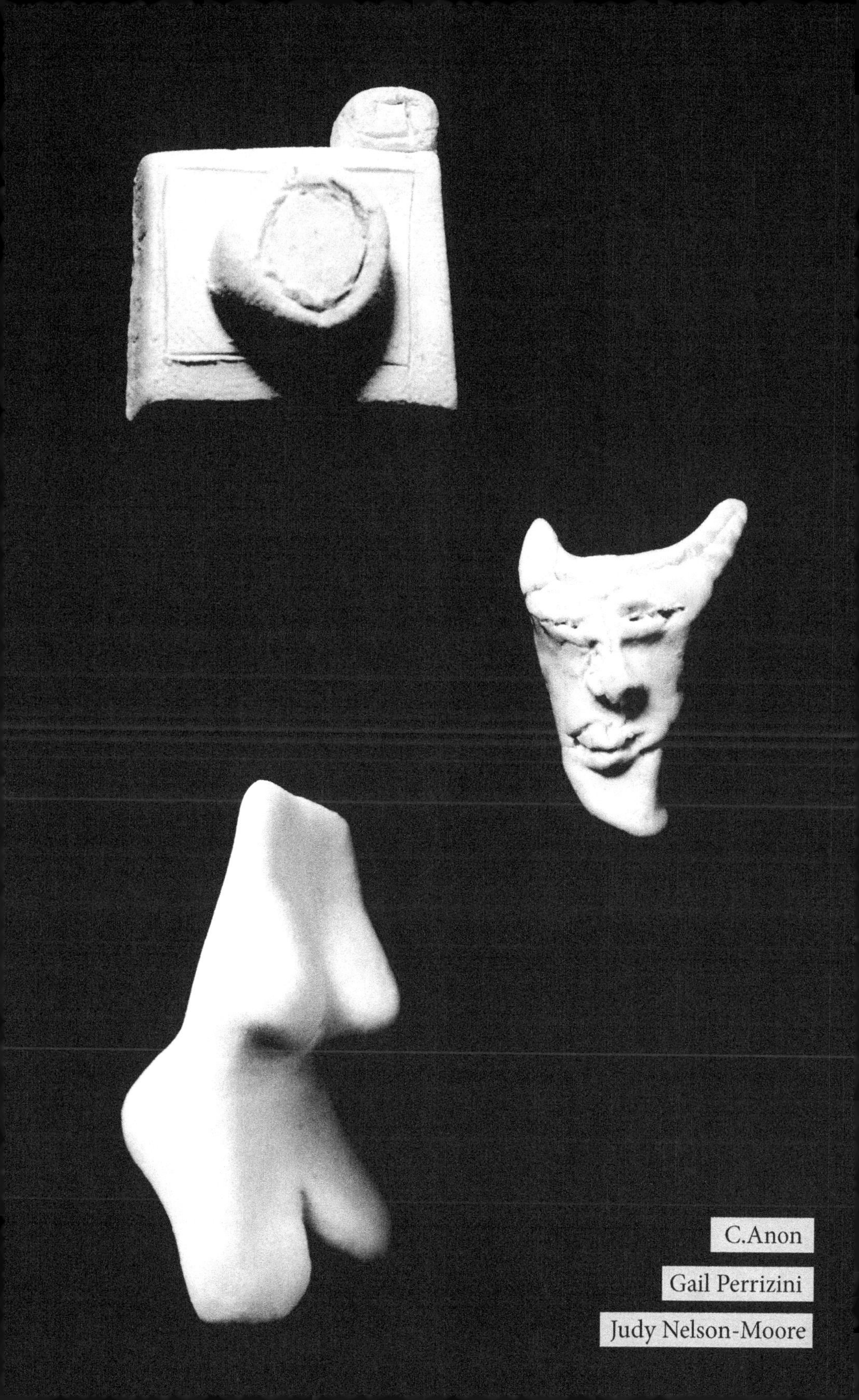
C.Anon
Gail Perrizini
Judy Nelson-Moore

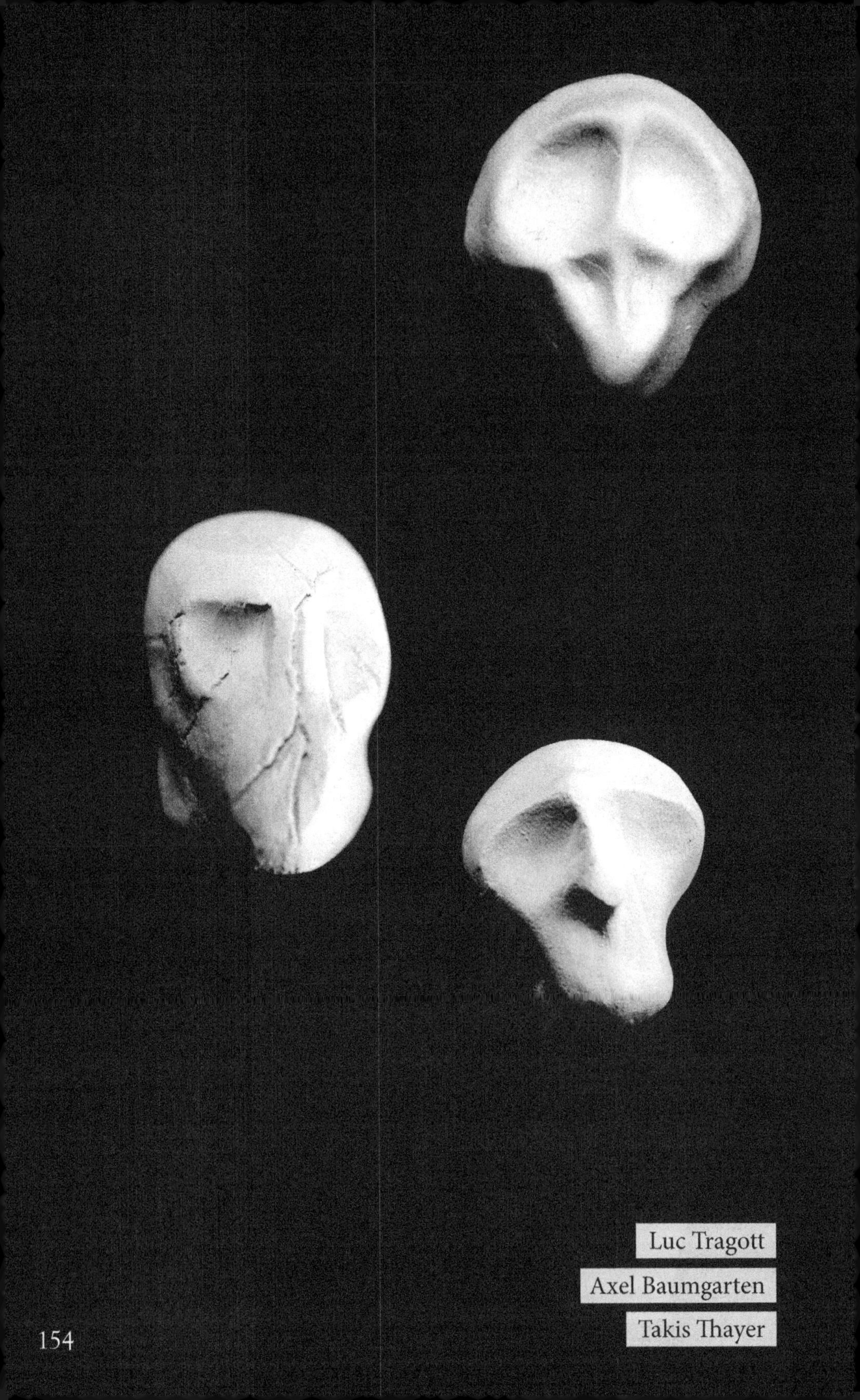

Luc Tragott
Axel Baumgarten
Takis Thayer

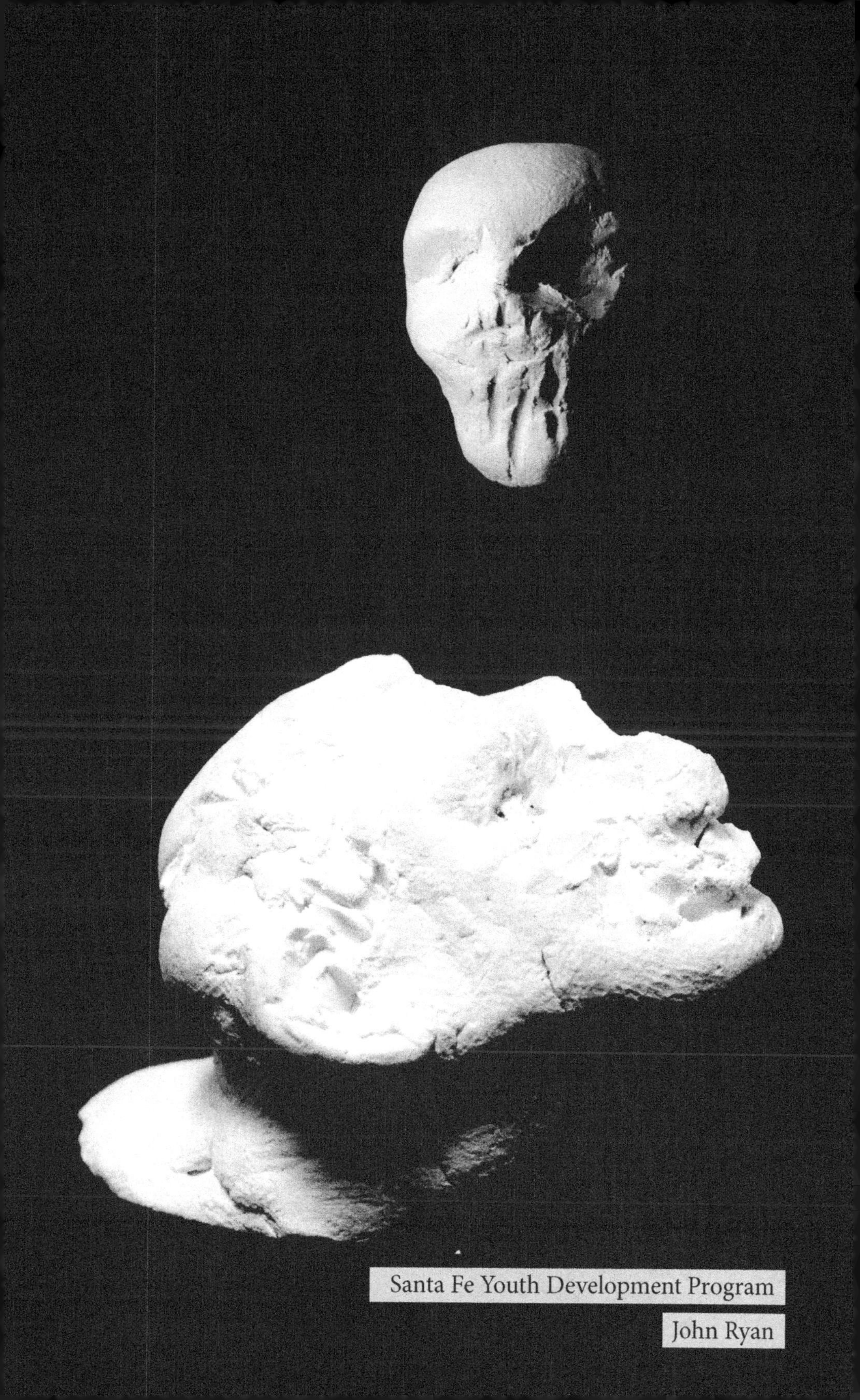

Santa Fe Youth Development Program

John Ryan

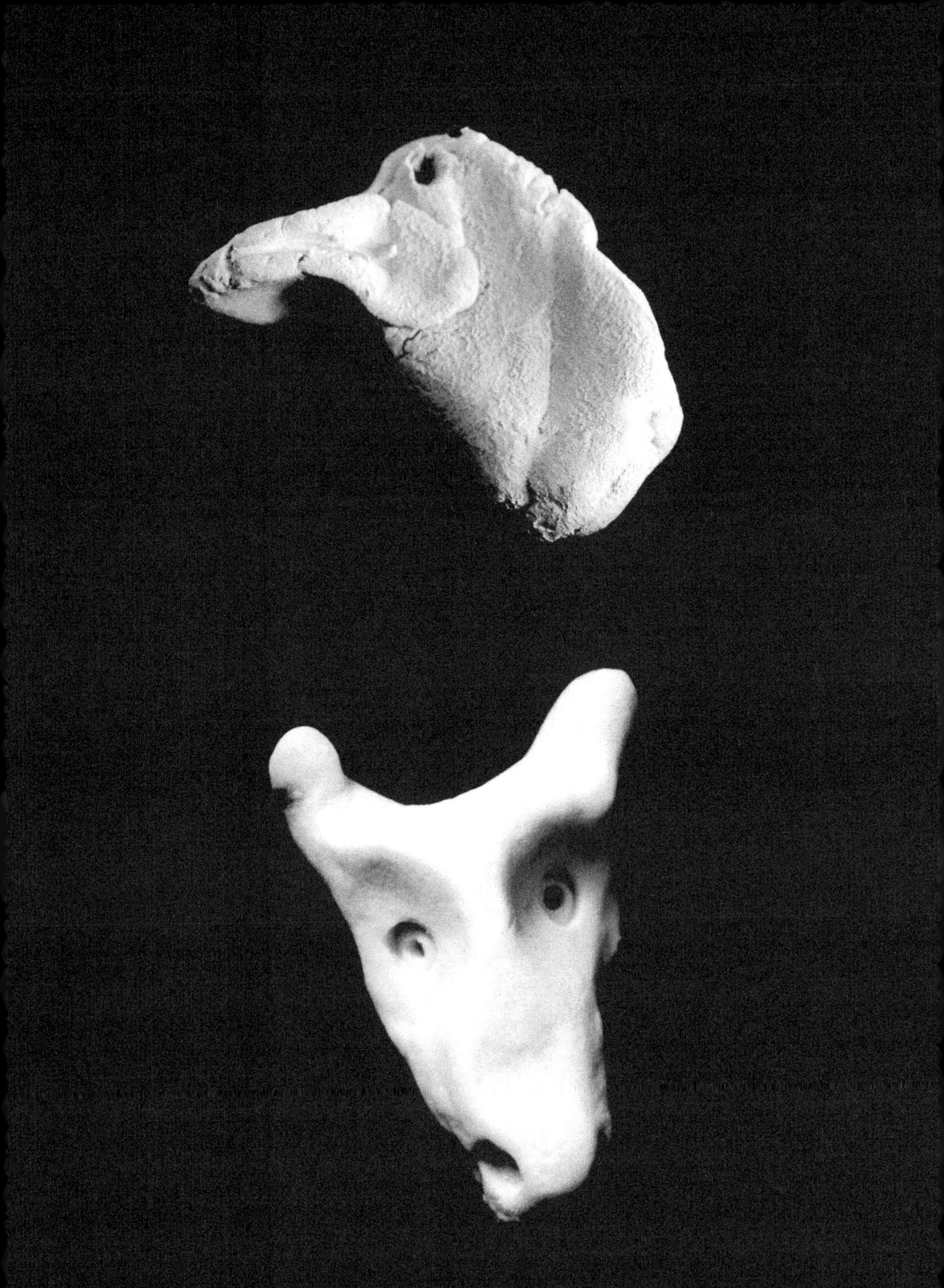

Conchita Lopez

Nina Mastrangelo

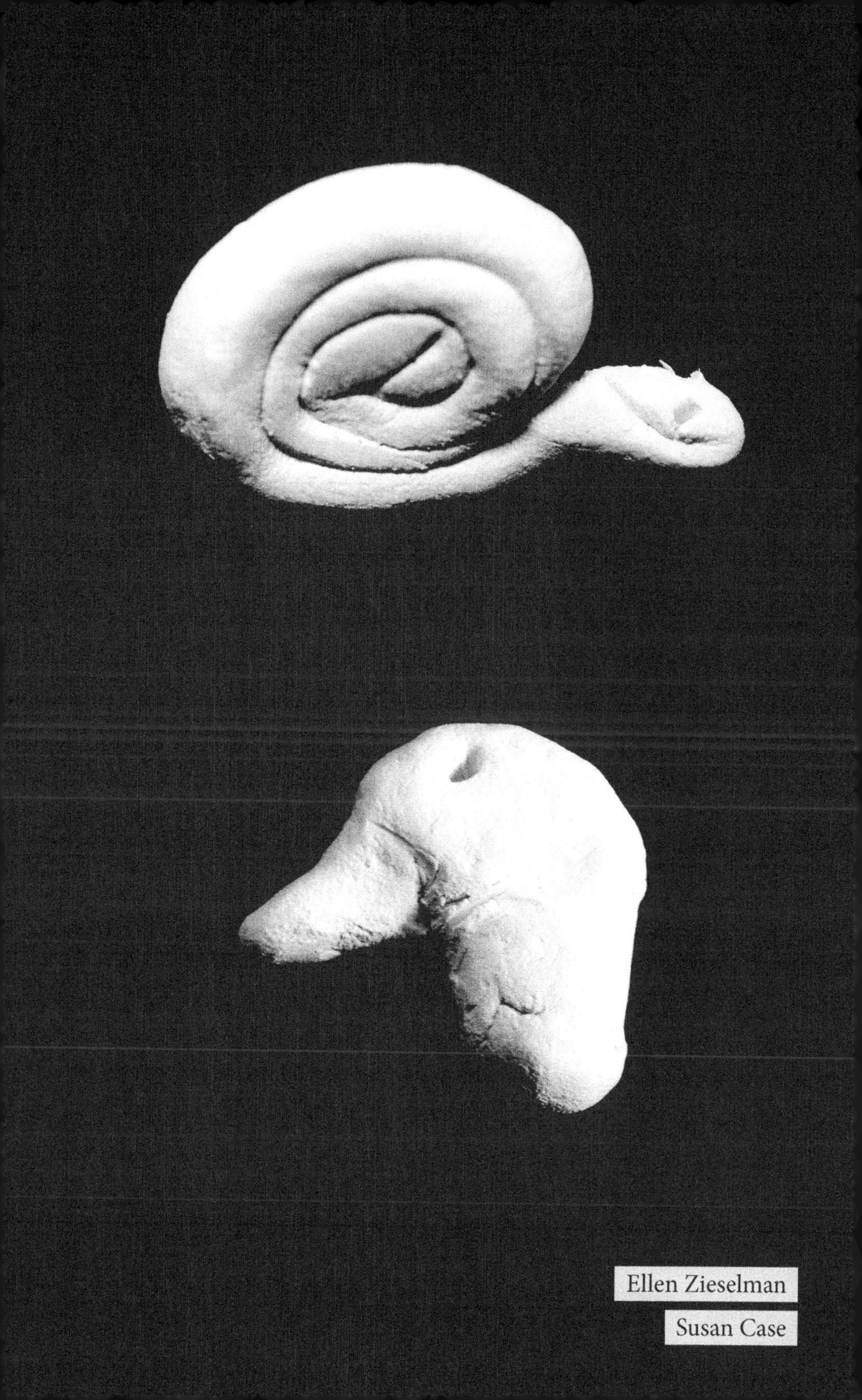

Ellen Zieselman

Susan Case

Seedy, grainy, gluten-free
Nutty, chewy, served with tea
Fried with egg or in a sandwich
Broke in crumbs or on a Manwich
Round or oval, even oblong
Brown or black or white – can't go wrong
Toasted, plain, whole or cubed
Buttered, jellied, dry or lubed
Dipped in oil is such a treat
Unless you drop it on your feet
Warmed, battered, soft with leaven
With each bite I go to heaven
Crunchy, fattening, satisfying
I'd say, "No more," but I'd be lying
Give me this day my daily bread
Without it I don't feel quite fed
Sweet with jam, don't hold the mayo
A delicious start – it makes my day-o

-Mindy Littman Holland

People complain that baking bread is time consuming, but the dough does not asked to be watched. Futhermore, it can be trusted in the house alone.

-Hannah Glasse

Crust Lust

It isn't the dough but the crust
that propels me to unbidden lust.
The dough submits willingly
to my bites so well filling me,
but I'm driven to do what I must:

I challenge that crust to some crumbling
as its firmness resists my weak bumbling -
to sink in my teeth
through to dough underneath
and spray copious crumbs nimbly tumbling.

-Nancy Ziegler Nodelman

Most grandmothers like to tinker with bread.

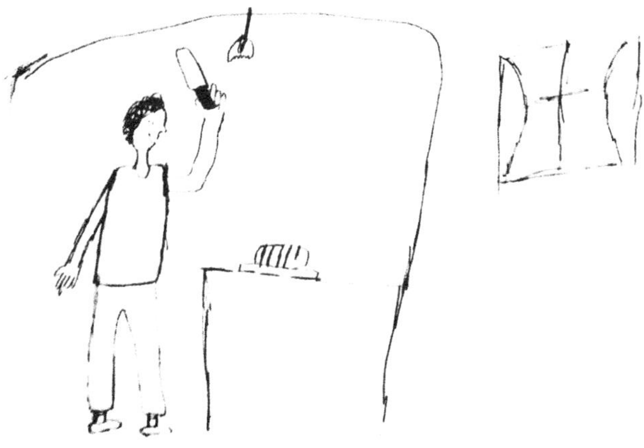

Cloud Cliff Bakery

I'm hanging on by a danish,
caught by tart, cherry skins,
skins like soaked feet
blissful and shriveled

in their cornstarch puddled pink.
I'm hanging on by a danish,
buoyed by its cheesy heart,
sweetened mortar of cottage cheese,

substantial as a solid cottage -
flour, water, sugar,
dough kneaded as the knot in my gut
needs to be softened, is softened,
poached through instinct -
mouth to the husband's puckered lips -

spooned with the Polish Jew in my bed.
Don't ask me to do another *think.*
I'm hanging on by a danish.

No, by a Pole

-Janet Eigner

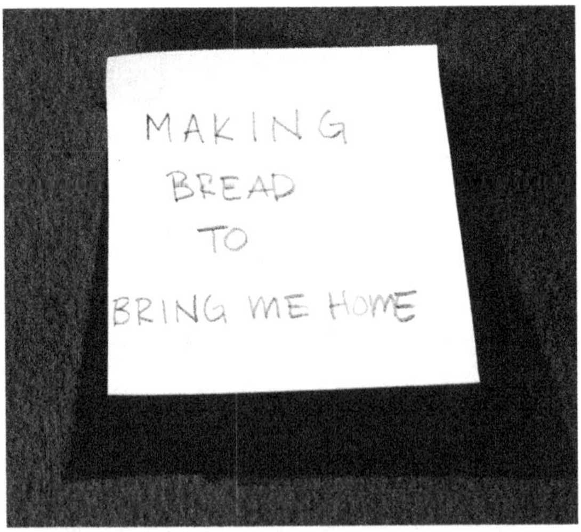

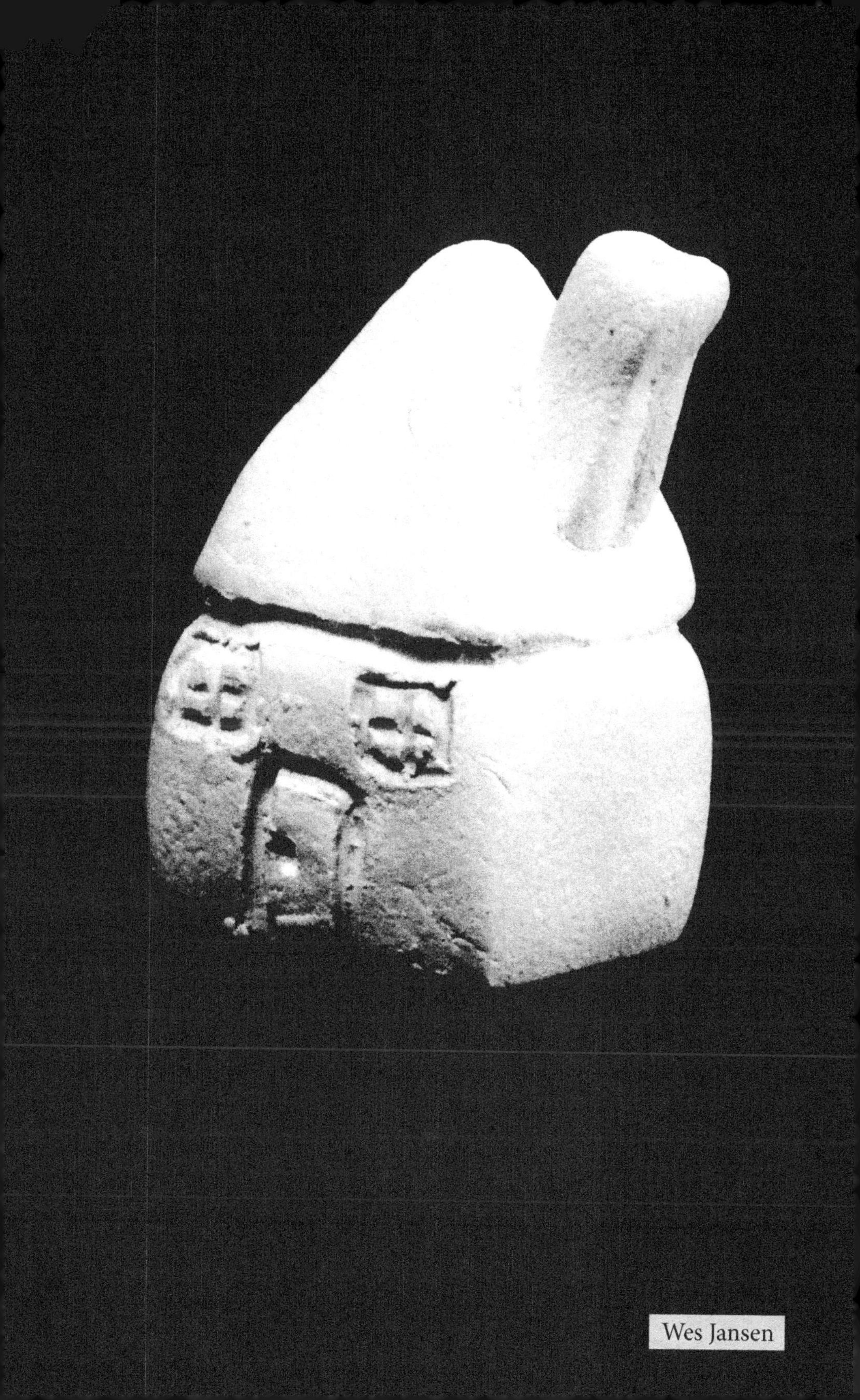

Wes Jansen

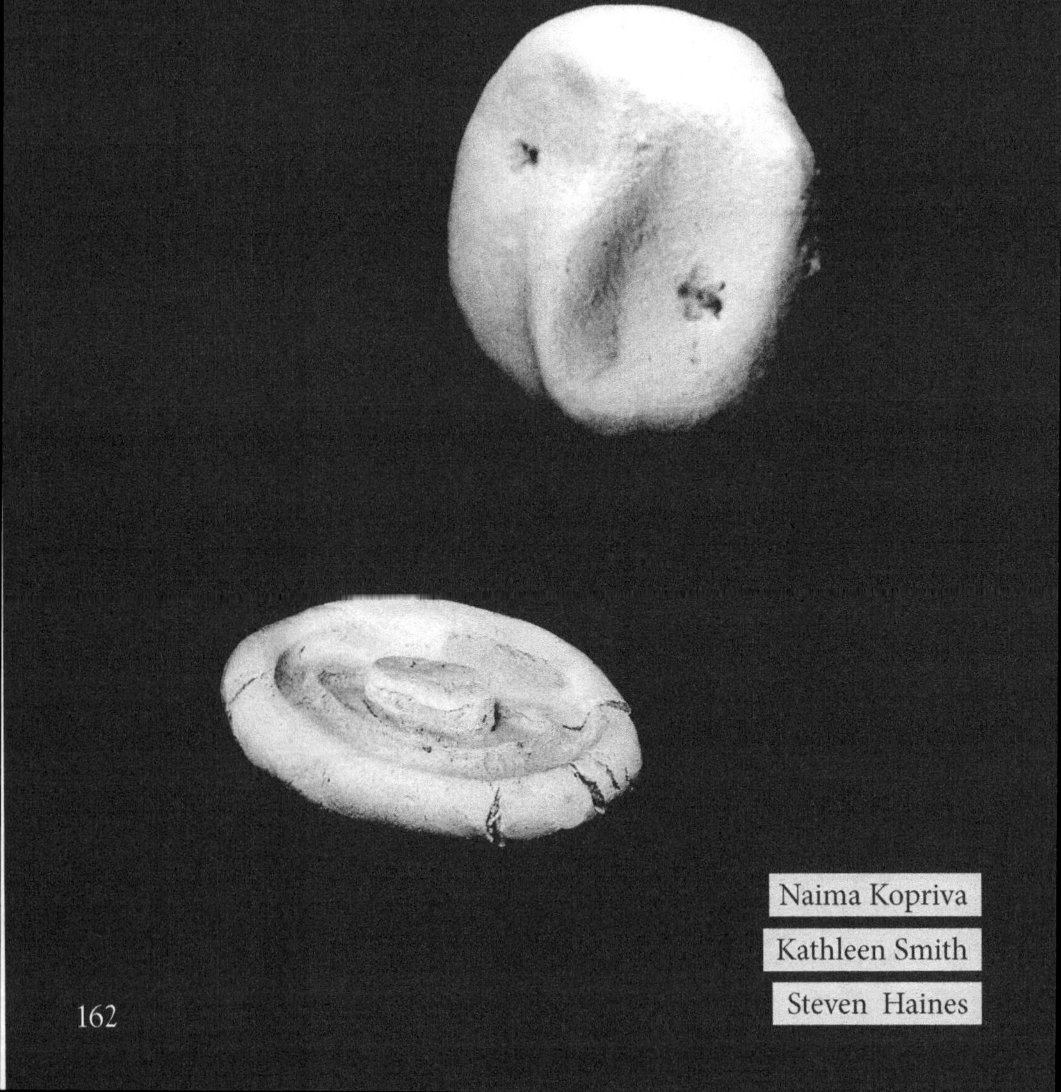

Naima Kopriva

Kathleen Smith

Steven Haines

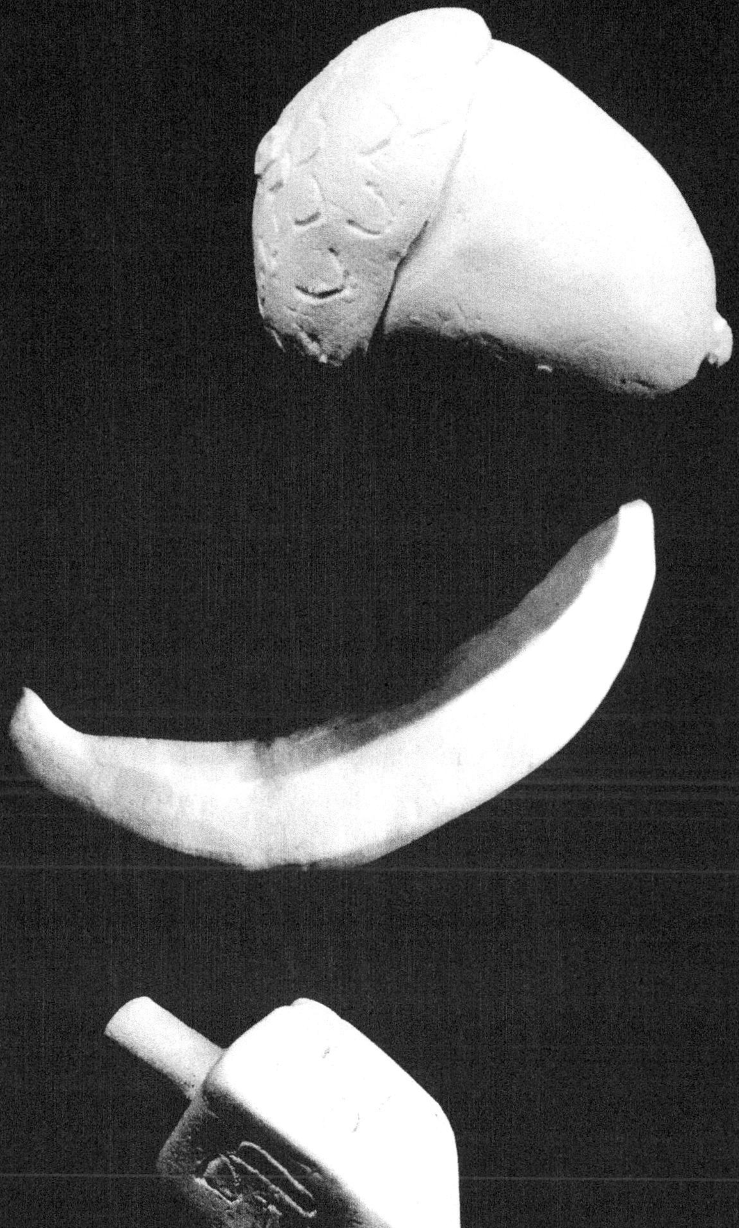

Jeremy Brooks

Jan Petry

Benton Lehman

Broken Bread

"I used to make fresh bread, all the time." He has said this many times before to her. She knows this, like she knows so much about him.

"Yes, you've said."

"Every week."

"Yes."

"I was good at it. Everyone liked my bread." By everyone he meant all the women he'd had before.

"Nothing is better than fresh bread with real butter," she says.

"I should make it again. I should." She puts her hand out, across the table. "I would love for you to make bread."

"Yes, I should make bread this weekend." He's said this before too. Often. The weekend comes. It goes. They have dinner with friends.

"This is good bread," he says to them, flicking a glance at the other woman at the table, Junie. "I used to make bread. Every week. Everyone loved my bread." Junie leans forward, eyes sparkling.

"I bet. I bet it was good." The bread is a tease, she thinks. The bread is a promise. The bread is sex. He leans toward Junie. The next day she gets out yeast, flour, salt, butter. She makes bread dough. She kneads until the smell fills her, until the dough is soft enough to sleep on, soft enough to dream on.

"This is for you," she begins by saying. She thinks about what he has said, so often. She thinks about how he's never made bread for her. She kneads more and more, harder and harder. She kneads until her knuckles are bloody.

"This is for me," she ends by saying. When the bread is baked, she takes it to the bedroom. She grinds the bread between her palms, into fine crumbs that fall onto the bed, their perfectly made desert of a bed.

"For you," she says, and leaves.

-Deb Auten

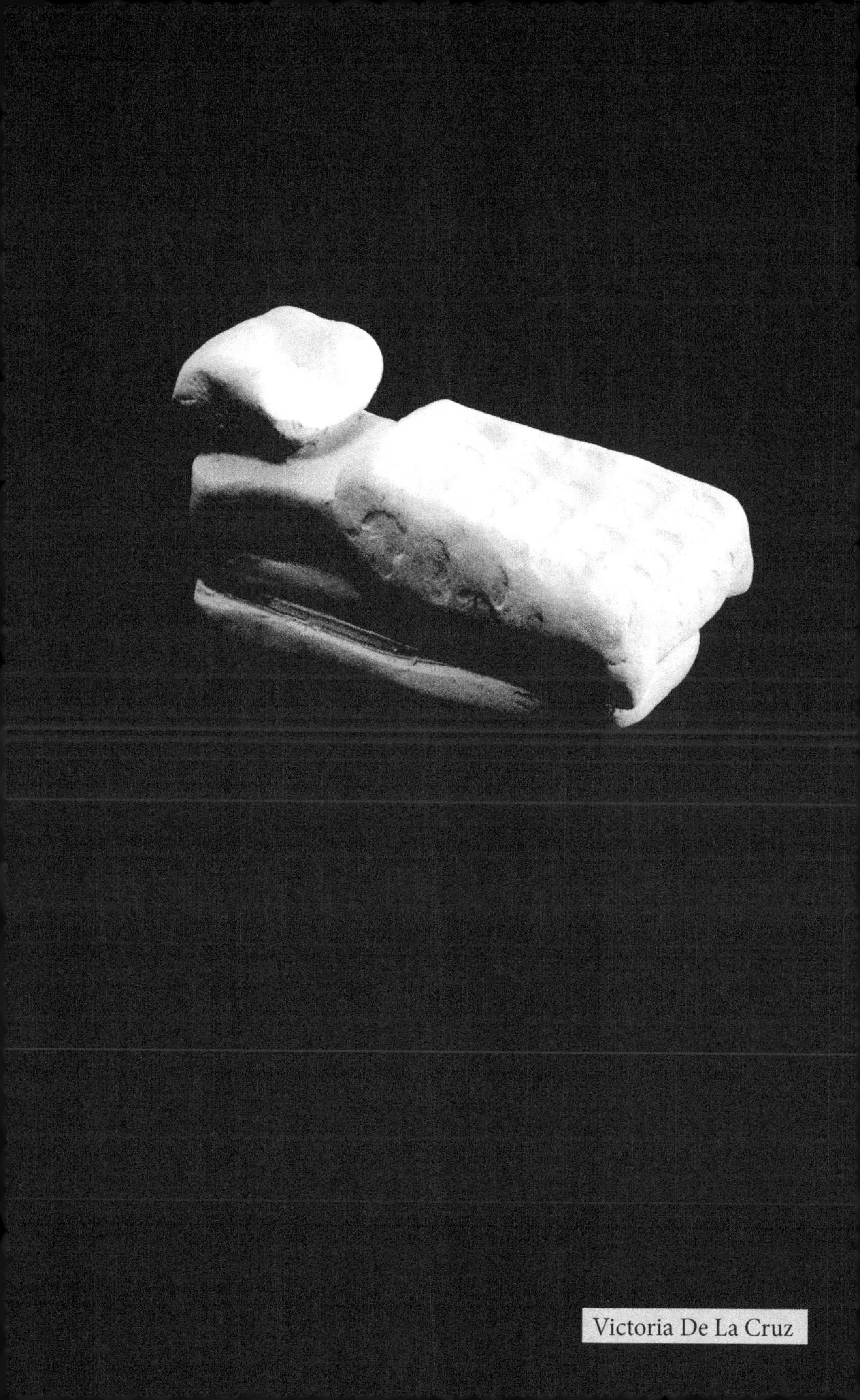

Victoria De La Cruz

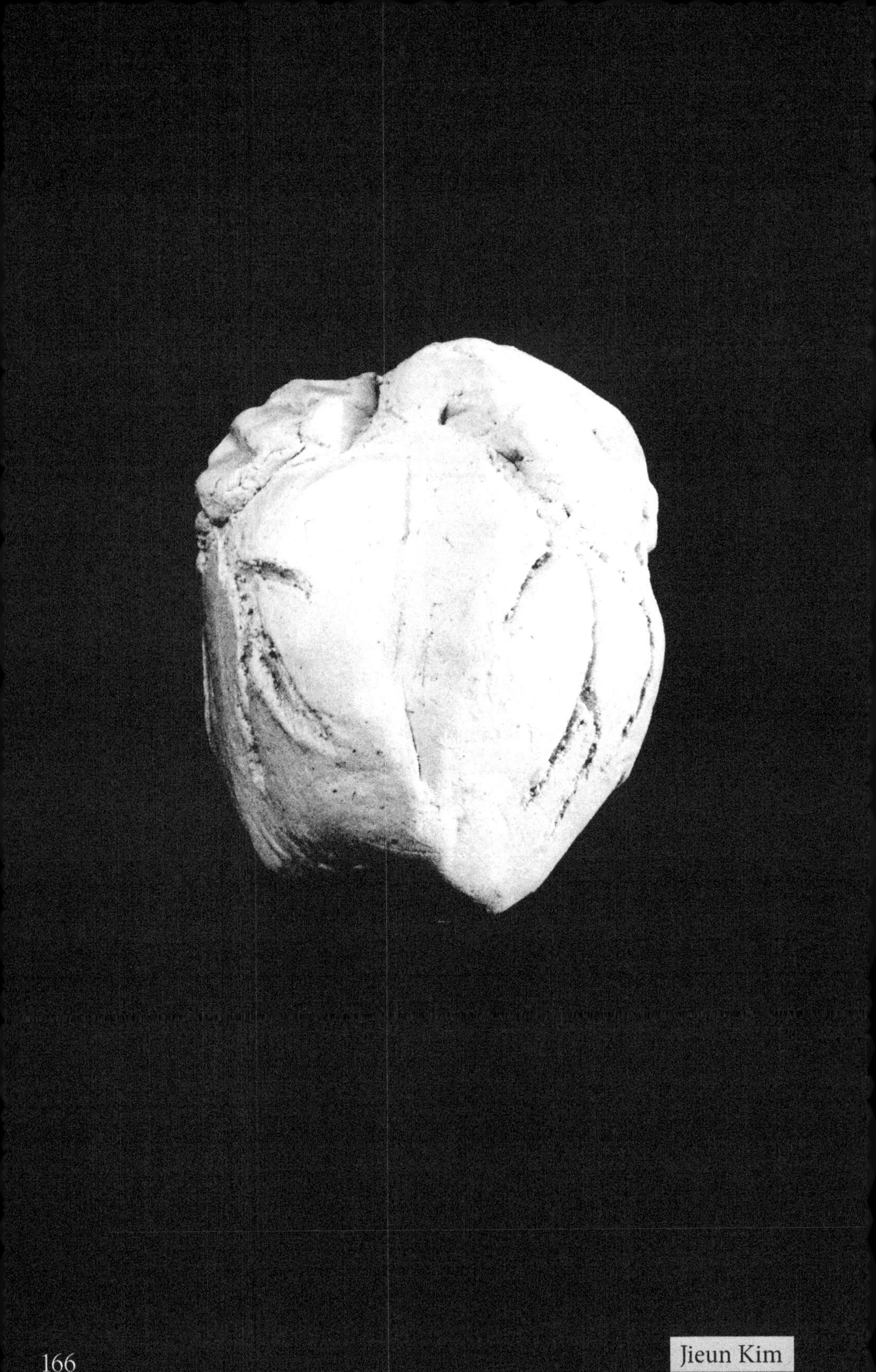

Jieun Kim

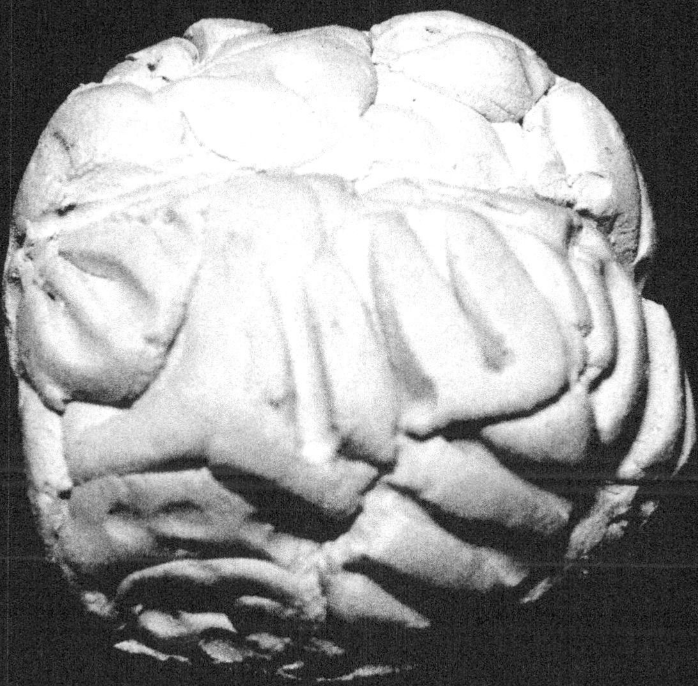

Sydney Cooper

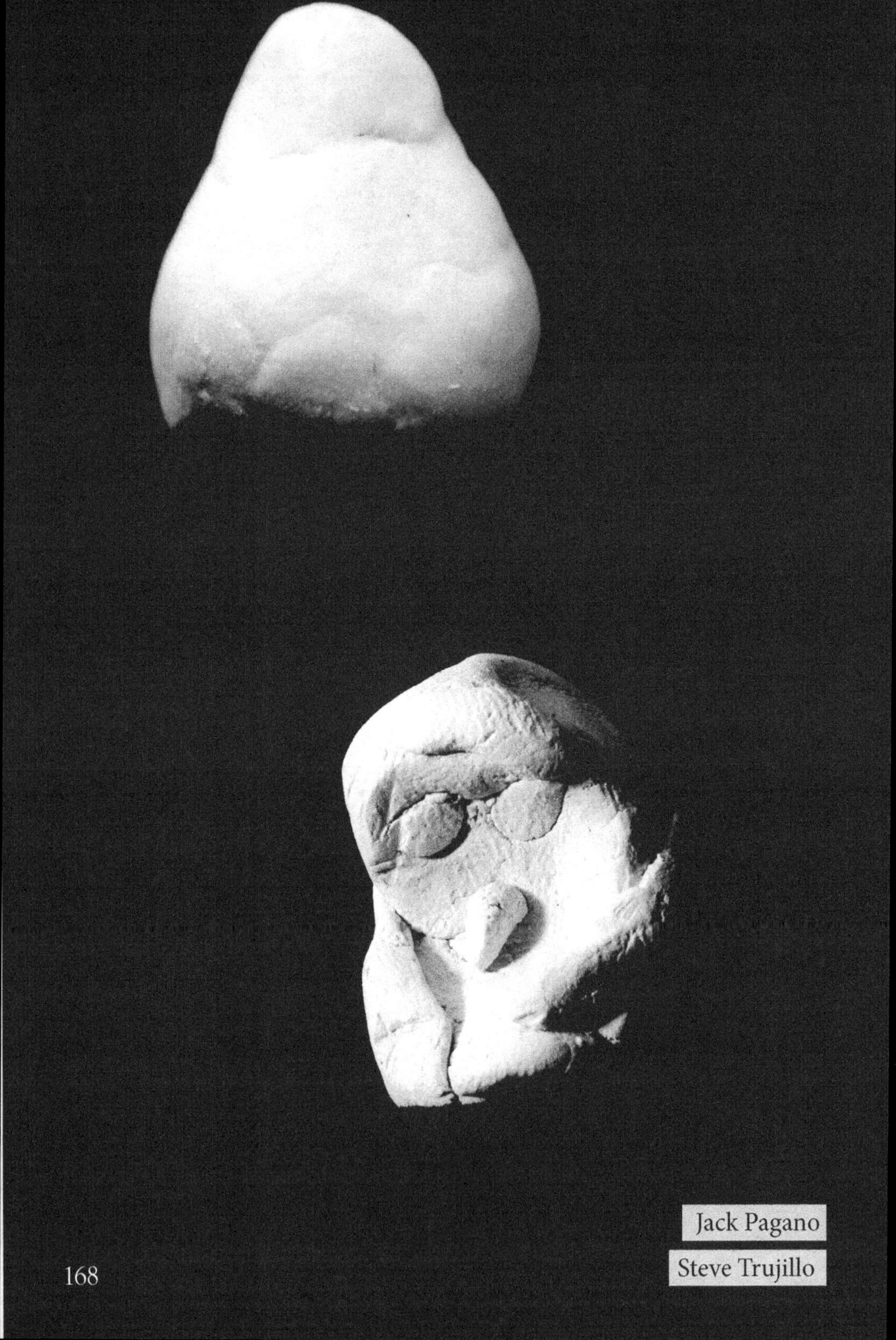

Jack Pagano

Steve Trujillo

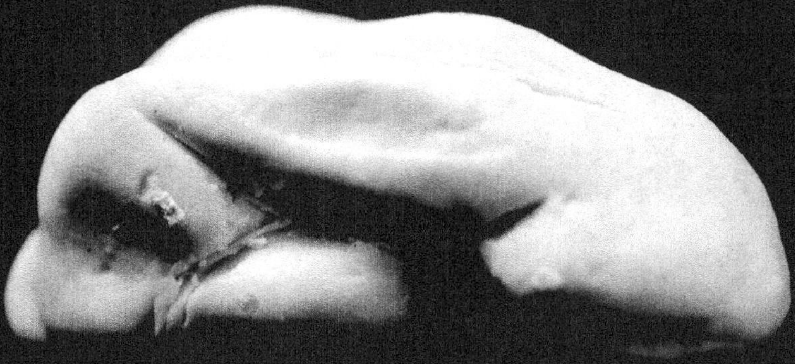

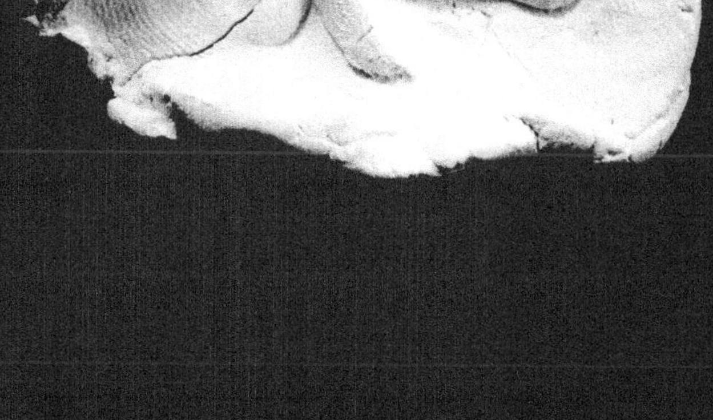

Natalie Buckner

Cole Gartner

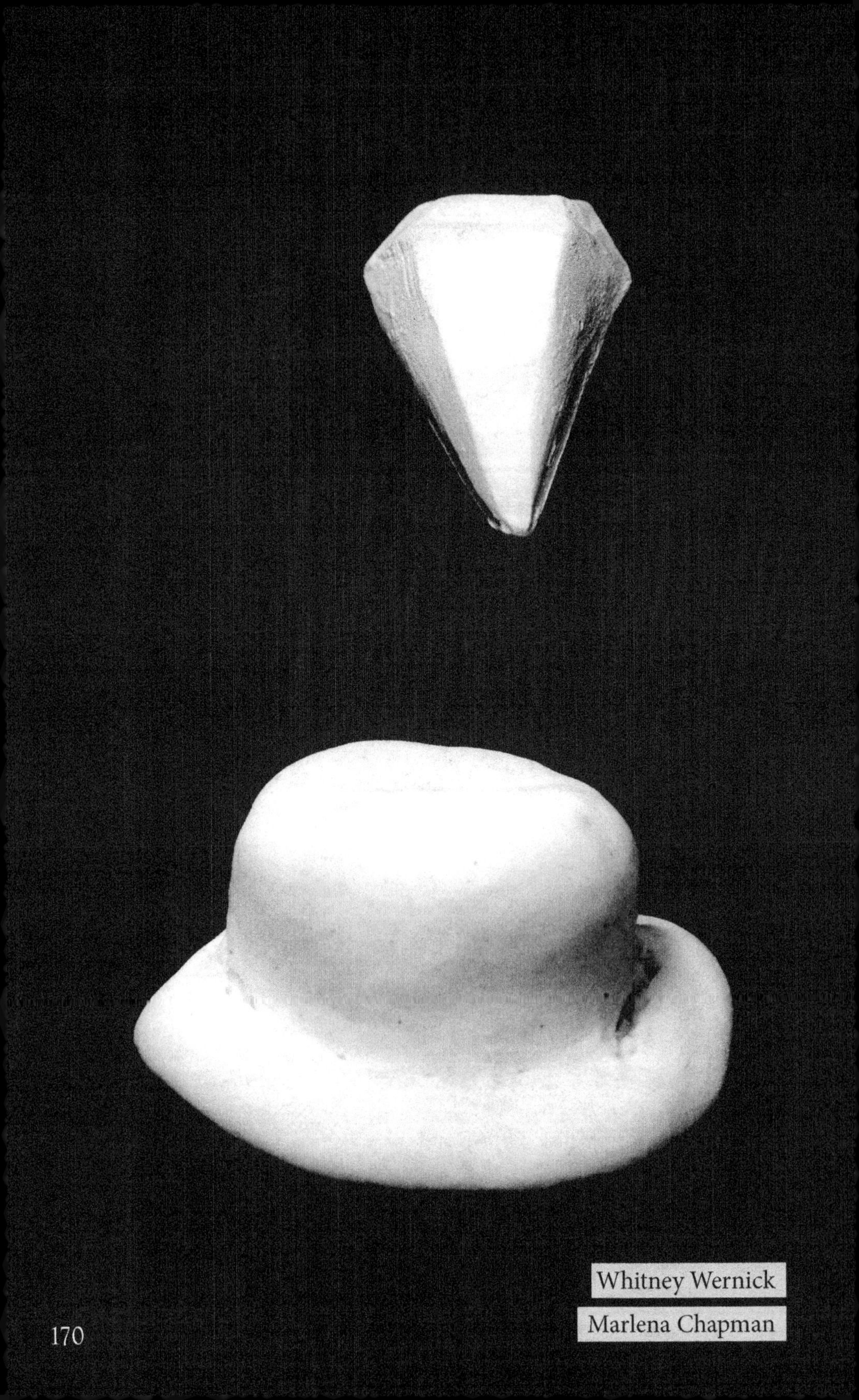

Whitney Wernick

Marlena Chapman

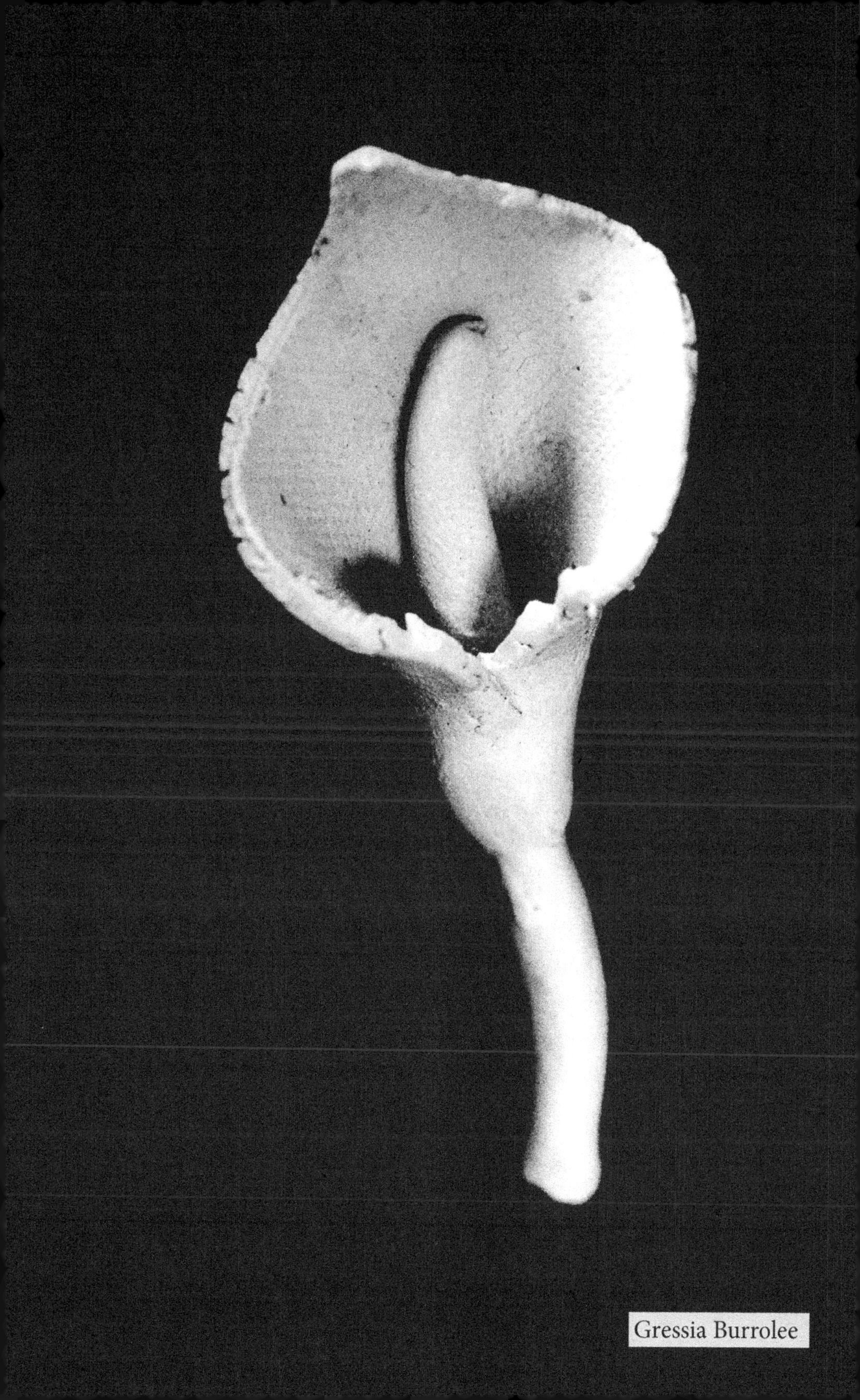

Gressia Burrolee

Jorge yawned in his warm bed. As he did so, he winced with pain. He was sent to bed last night without supper. Something to do with a missing piglet sent Jorge first to the wood shed and later to bed. It was up to the dour Grandfather; Jorge's fate was in his hands. Would there be another beating? Perhaps the wonderful smell of baking bread would bring forgiveness. At least we had the promise of a new day.

Jorge loved his grandmother's bread. He sprang from his bed, dressed and ran down to the kitchen. He did not give his stern Grandfather one single thought. He was purely motivated by the heavenly aroma coming from the kitchen. He ran through the house. The cat followed with haste. Whatever fell on the floor went to the cat. It could be a marvelous lump of butter or even just a lovely piece of bread crust. Jorge and the cat joined his Grandmother in the kitchen. There was no sign of the Grandfather. Was the punishment over for little Jorge?

The winter light now filled the entire kitchen. The mirror over the hutch sparkled. Dishes for the breakfast sat on the hutch. The bread in the oven, the bacon on the stove along with the fried eggs, everything was ready. The chili sauce had already been put on the table. The chili is always the first thing to go on the table and it's there every meal. Jorge was in his seat ready for a meal for his growling stomach.

Suddenly, like a gun shot, a loud clack broke the mood. Clack, clack that is the sound of Grandpa's boots on the wooden floor, he's up for the day and coming to breakfast. Jorge sank into to his seat. The hunger was unbearable. How could this little boy be so full of the devil? He tortured a piglet. Never mind, he was focused on the food. Grandpa's beatings had just become common place. He did not fear the old man. The hunger pains were all his young mind could hold. Jorge and his Grandfather would share a moment of peace, while the warm bread sat on their table.

- David Mario Trujillo

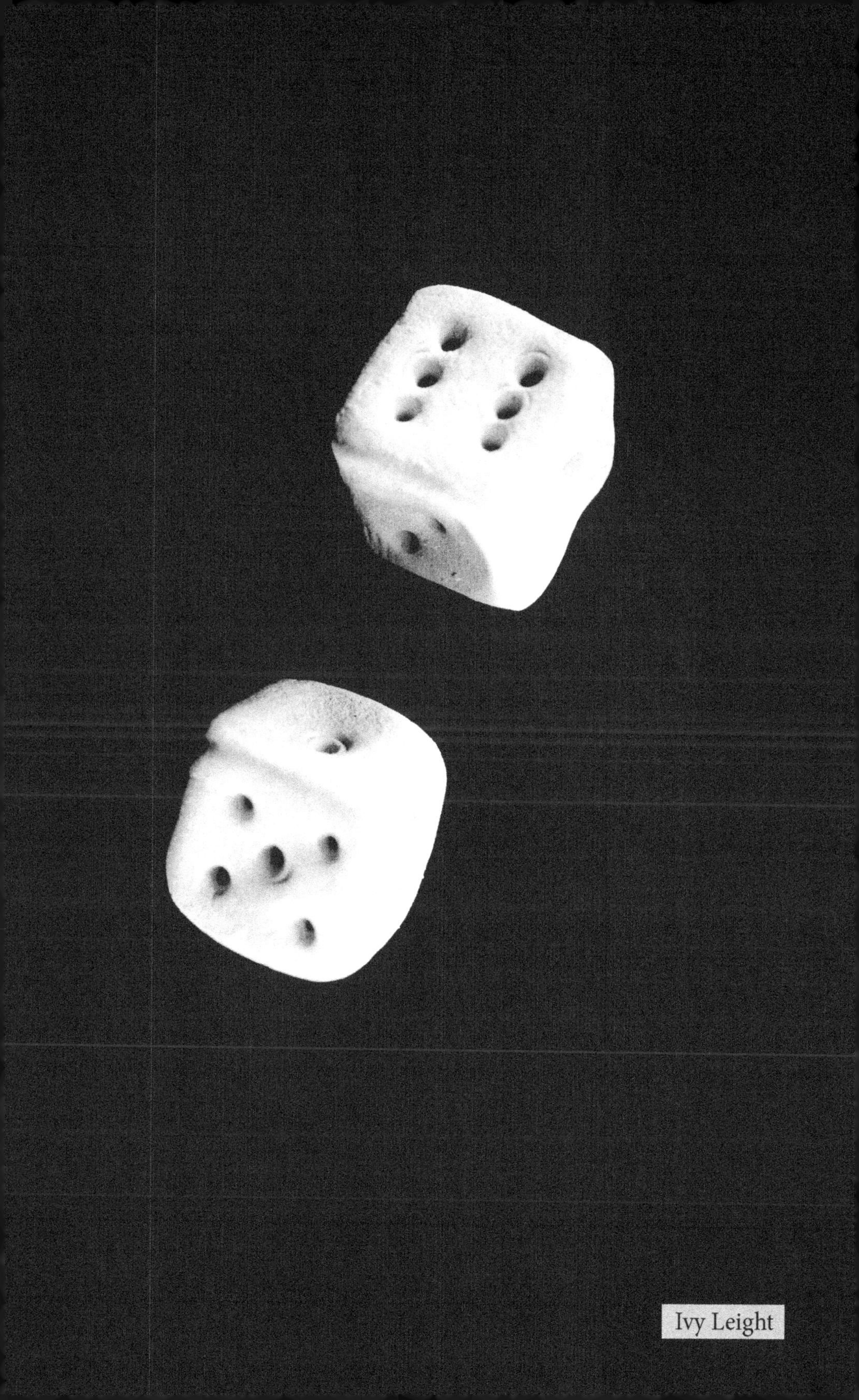
Ivy Leight

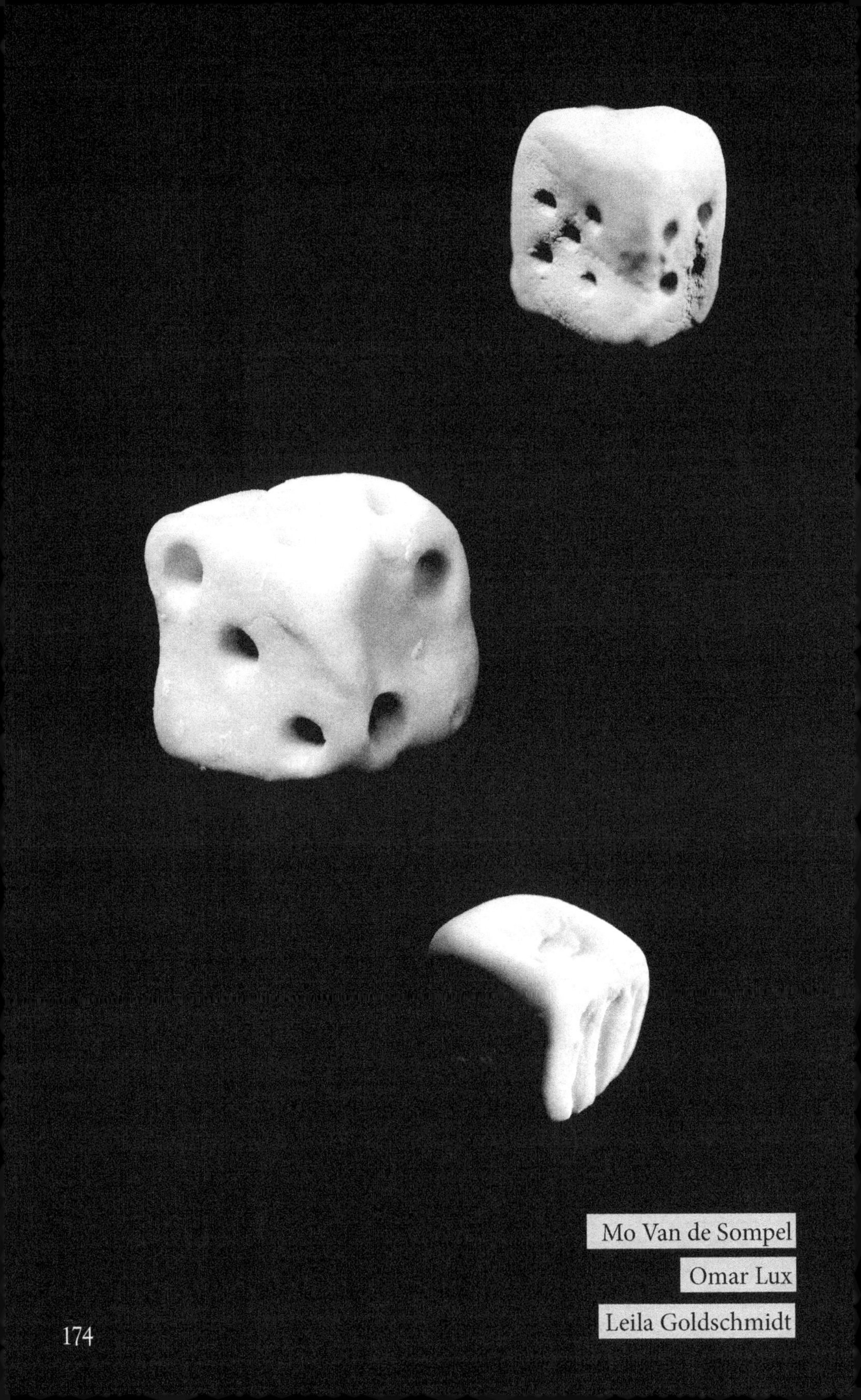

Mo Van de Sompel
Omar Lux
Leila Goldschmidt

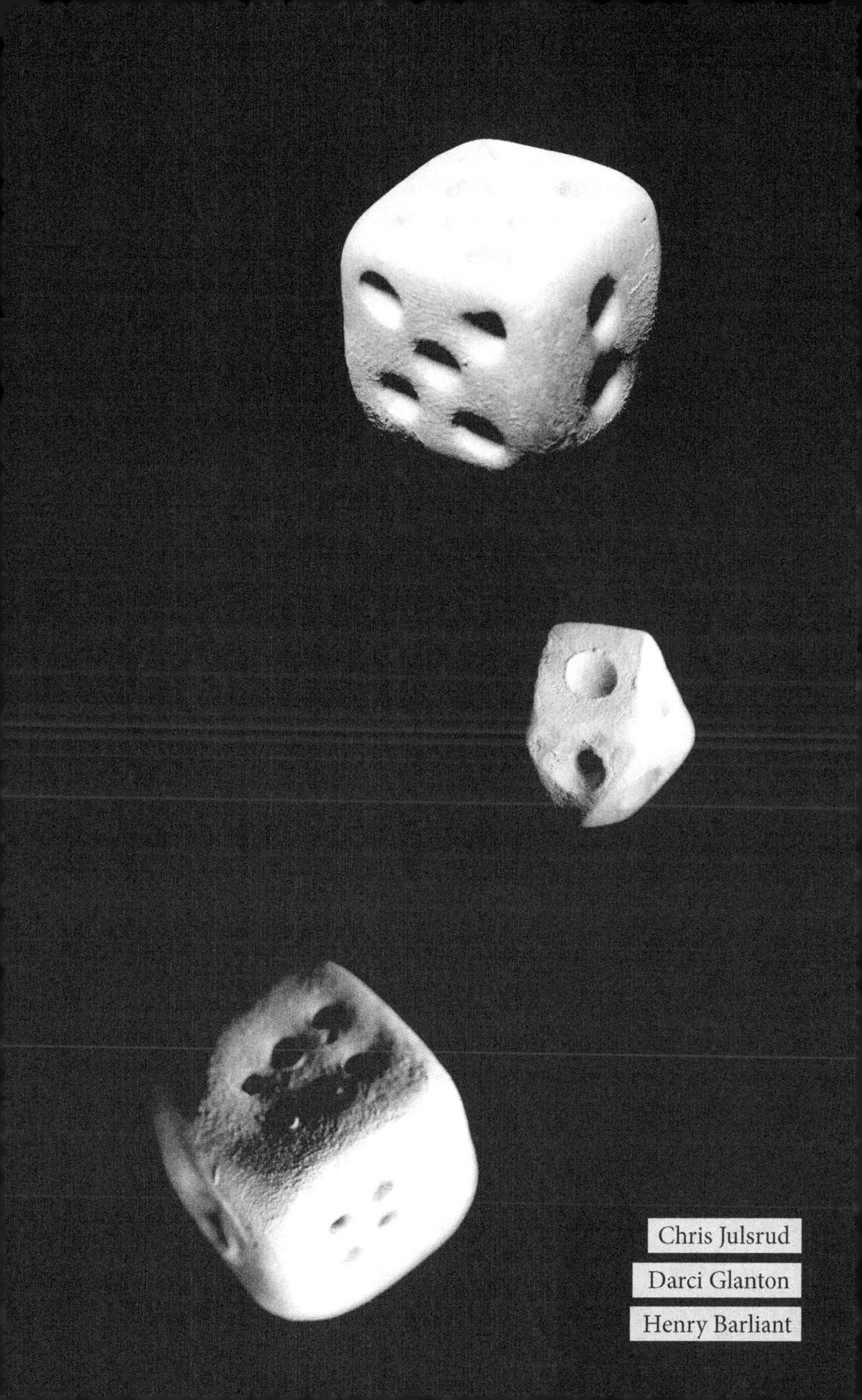

Chris Julsrud
Darci Glanton
Henry Barliant

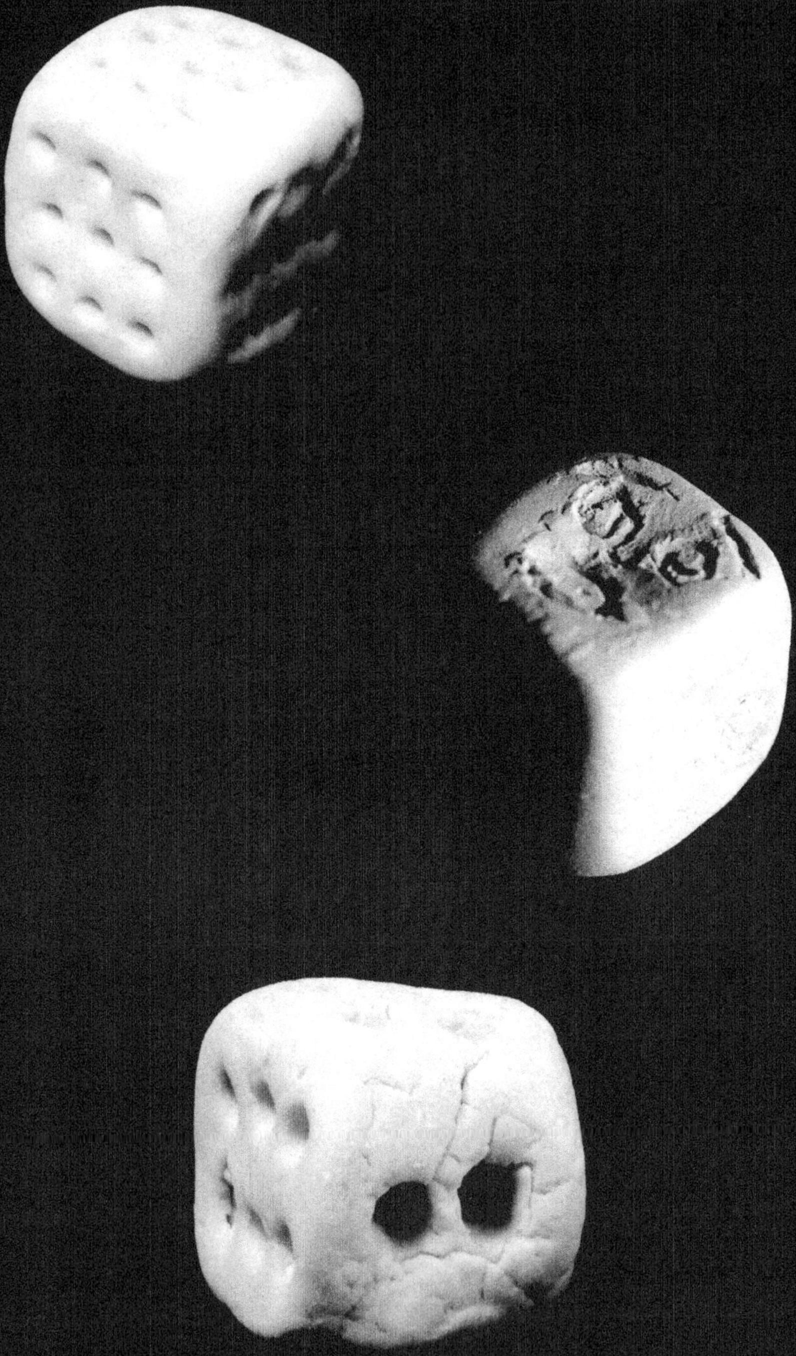

Lisel Faust

Pete Goldschmidt

Vaclav Roderick

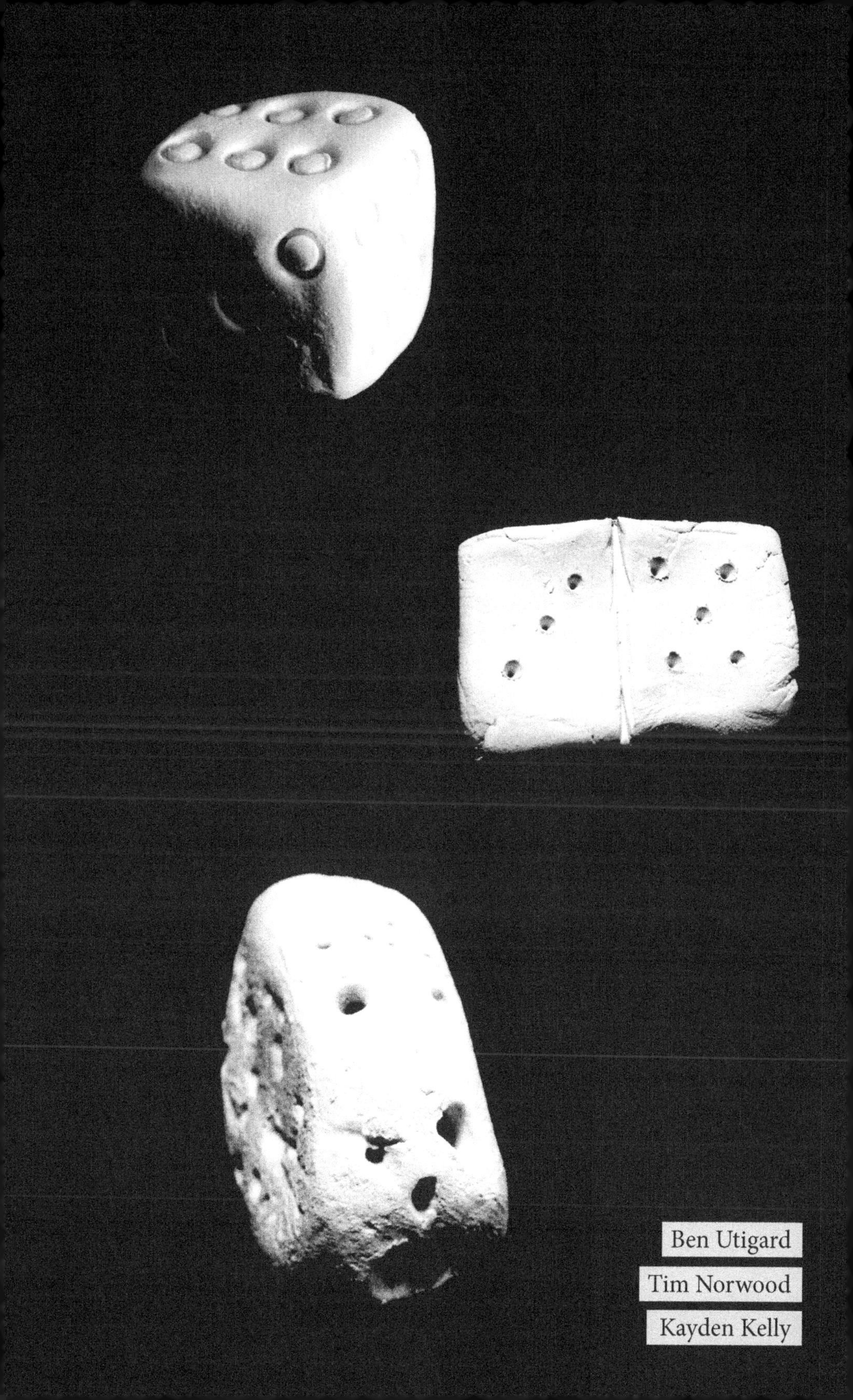

Ben Utigard

Tim Norwood

Kayden Kelly

Axle Contemporary is a collaborative project by artists Matthew Chase-Daniel and Jerry Wellman. The mobile gallery is an innovative vehicle for arts distribution. Since 2010, it has grown beyond the confines of the van/gallery, and now includes book publishing, performance art and alternative projects for socially engaged art creation and dissemination in the public sphere.

Matthew Chase-Daniel is a Santa Fe based artist working in photography, sculpture and video. His artwork has been exhibited across the U.S. and in Europe, and he has created numerous public art projects.

Jerry Wellman's paintings and drawings have been exhibited at various museums and galleries across the country, and his video animation work has been presented at national and international video festivals.

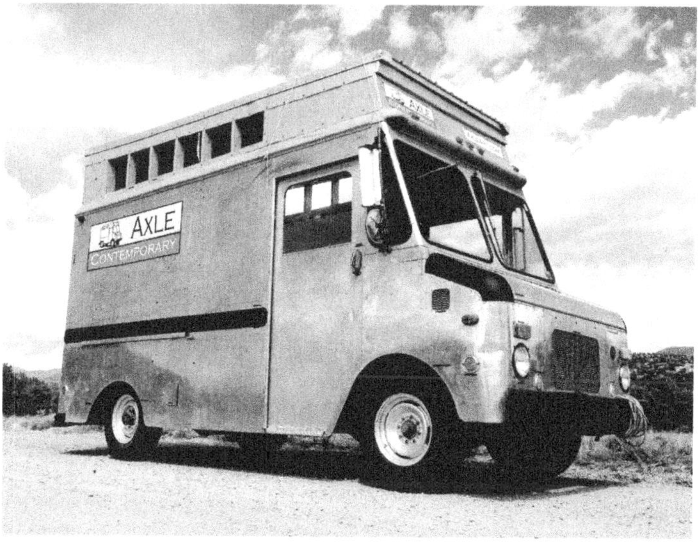

www.axleart.com

Made in the USA
Monee, IL
20 October 2026

66035306R00105